MW00490176

Basically Bipolar

Laughing Maniacally through the
Dark Delirium of a Polar Winter
...or two

REX NELSON

A production of

BASICALLY BIPOLAR

First Edition, 2018

Published by The Anglers Unwilling, White Salmon, WA, USA

Cover photo and "Ping-Pong Ball" photo by Neal Scheibe
Snowflake photos by Lance Roth
"Snowkite Sundog" photo by Jessica Cortright
All other photos and illustrations by Rex Nelson

Library of Congress Control Number: 2018911396

ISBN: 978-1-7328272-0-2
eISBN: 978-1-7328272-1-9

basicallybipolar.com

To my nieces and nephews. I hope one day this tale inspires in you a sense of wonder about the world you live in. I hope to bestow upon you a spark of curiosity. For curiosity leads to adventure, and I have found adventure to be one of life's tastiest spices. I wish for you not to miss that experience.
May the path lead you where it will, and where you will it.

"The purpose of life, after all, is to live it, to taste experience to the utmost, to reach out eagerly and without fear for newer and richer experience."
—Eleanor Roosevelt

Author's Note

There are many photographs in this book, and though they showcase a part of the world that is primarily white, many of them contain surprising colors. If you are holding a printed copy of this book, or a black-and-white e-reader, these photos will fall short of their potential. For that reason, these photos—and many others—are on display at basicallybipolar.com.

Contents

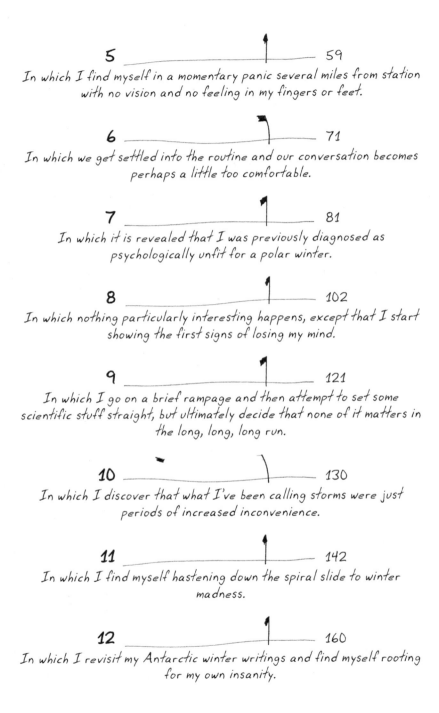

THE NORTH

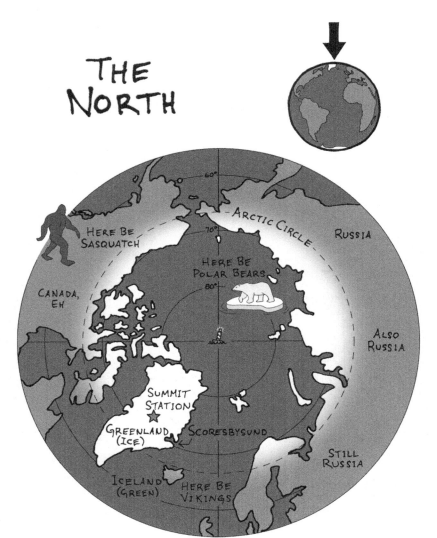

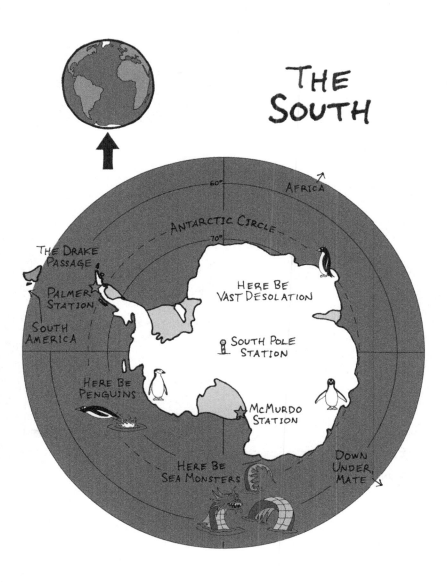

THE SOUTH

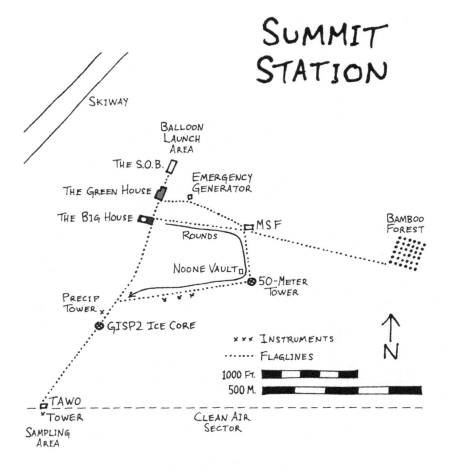

SUMMIT STATION

SKIWAY

BALLOON LAUNCH AREA

THE S.O.B.

THE GREEN HOUSE

EMERGENCY GENERATOR

THE BIG HOUSE

MSF

BAMBOO FOREST

ROUNDS

NOONE VAULT

50-METER TOWER

PRECIP TOWER

GISP2 ICE CORE

× × × INSTRUMENTS

······· FLAGLINES

N

1000 FT.

500 M.

TAWO TOWER

SAMPLING AREA

CLEAN AIR SECTOR

Foreword

This is a true story. However, it is not the author's purpose to report the events as an exact history, but rather to entertain. Also, the author's memory is not very good and will grow incrementally worse as the story goes on. Several bits are reconstructed from illegible notes and broken recollection. Therefore, the reader can assume that the following events more or less occurred, in a chronological order more or less like the one presented, and any deviations from the actual exact truth appear either accidentally or in the interests of flow, humor, or just 'cuz. The author does assure you that all the events described herein are described *exactly* as they are described.

1

In which I find myself overwhelmed and
under-oxygenated in a place that a saner person
would not consider visiting.

Day 7
Saturday, November 10

"Do you hear that?" I asked as I scanned the small, hallway-like room that is our shared office.

"Hear what?" Neal asked.

"That clicking noise."

"Um . . ." He looked at me with concern.

"It sounds like someone is typing right next to me."

Neal grinned. "It is *far* too early for you to be hearing things."

He was right. We've only been at Summit for a week. The winter hasn't even begun; we still have the sun for three more days. Hell, the turnover crew is still here. There's plenty of time for me to lose my mind, and it will be better for everyone if I don't get a running start.

But already I'm exhausted. The first week at camp was a full assault on both body and mind. Last Sunday, when we arrived at this desolation of ice and snow, the temperature was ten below zero. Overnight it plunged to negative fifty like a sucker punch from Old Man Frost. Right out of the gate we had to cover every inch of skin just to go outside. I shivered through our outdoor tasking while willing my body to work furiously toward altitude acclimatization. Surprisingly, it wasn't the cold but the drop in pressure that was doing me in. For the first several days, I suffered the effects of a rapid ascent from sea level to 10,500 feet. I've experienced altitude sickness before, and perhaps I'm even prone to it, but it took a much larger toll on me than I was expecting—like having a debilitating hangover while trying to breathe through a straw. The shortest of walks—let alone the climb into the Big House—left me gasping and breathless. Every time I stood up I got a dizzying head rush.

During that time, along with the other fresh arrivals, I took my turn clipping a pulse oximeter onto my index finger to check the oxygen saturation of my blood. Most of the others were in the mid- to upper 80s. I was in the low 80s, occasionally dipping into the upper 70s. By scoring the lowest percentage, I felt that I had won—until I investigated pulse oximetry. I read that 95 to 100 percent is considered healthy, lower than 90 is defined as acute respiratory failure, and below 80 simply said: *Contact your physician immediately.* My "win" was shattered.

I was suffering from acute mountain sickness, that much was clear, but the awareness that I was affected more than anyone else made me feel like a featherweight. It's not even that high, 10,500 feet. They told me it's closer to 12,000 feet if you account for the physiological altitude. The centrifugal force of the earth spinning causes it—and its atmosphere—to swell at the equator. So the earth is not round, it's oblong. The poles are each about thirteen miles closer to the center of the earth than the equator is. In fact, the farthest peak from the earth's center is not Mount Everest but Chimborazo in Ecuador, which is 8,464 feet *shorter* than Everest when measured from sea level. This oblong shape applies to the atmosphere as well; it bulges out near the equator and is squished toward the surface near the poles, making our 10,500-foot perch *feel* like 12,000 feet.

Thinking about all of that did nothing to assuage my feeling of inferiority, nor my constant headache.

My body's attempts to cope with this frigid high-altitude environment were thwarted by a rigorous work agenda. For the first half of the week, Neal and I worked twelve hours a day, waging a futile battle to learn all the details of the job we will be performing for the next three months. We were exempt from cooking and cleaning duties during turnover because our schedule was so full. Ridiculously full. Due to our delayed arrival, we had essentially three days—or so we thought—to learn what would normally take a week and could easily be spread to two.

Between us we will maintain over fifteen scientific instruments, provide various samples of air and snow, launch weather balloons, perform snow accumulation surveys, maintain meteorological suites, and troubleshoot any problems. That's the core of our responsibility as science technicians, anyway. We'll also have plenty of typical work tasks—reporting, inventorying, attending meetings—as well as some strikingly atypical ones, like digging out our living quarters.

Neal and I are both engineers by training and have done this type of work before at similar research stations in Antarctica— including, between us, McMurdo, South Pole, and Palmer stations. We're familiar with some of the instruments at Summit, but much of our tasking is new to us. So for the first three long and painful days we followed our predecessors, Lance and Jenny, who sprayed a continuous stream of technical mumbo jumbo toward overwhelmed ears. Much of it was lost. I kept finding myself snapping to and wondering what I had just missed. I was tired and out of breath and my throbbing mind was far more interested in ingesting oxygen than information. I'm sure Neal felt the same. Hopefully we've absorbed enough to get started, though I expect we'll be neck-deep in the operating procedures for a month. Fortunately, everything is well documented.

EACH DAY OF turnover, Jenny would bounce along an invisible white path while I struggled head-down to put one foot in front of the other. Neal had the advantage of stride with height, but still he lagged well behind Jenny. Mine could not be called a stride as my footprints had no gap between them: heel and toe practically overlapped, snuffing any notion of forward progress.

We trudged an impossibly long route—a hundred miles, I'm sure of it[1]—to visit scientific contraptions located sporadically around the station. Most are so caked in frost they seem an ancient part of the landscape yet stand out in alien contrast, like tangled framework derelicts that froze in their final act of clawing up through the timeless white crust.

Beyond station, that crust stretches to the horizon, featureless in every direction. Stripped of human influence, this environment is a flat expanse of wind-furrowed snow under a wide sky that boasts the only opportunity for variation. Without the flap of flags and the occasional building or scientific contraption, this place would be a sterile purgatory whose immaculacy is a vacuum meant to draw out impurity. But as we walked, it drew out only oxygen.

Jenny and Lance had their own system worked out. Jenny preferred doing "rounds" over checking the instruments at TAWO, and Lance was happy to avoid the long walk around the perimeter of the station. Neal and I needed to learn both, so we followed Jenny along a flagged path compacted from years of pacing yet almost indiscernible from the snow around it.

No—it's not exactly snow; it's something between snow and ice that doesn't fit either category. It's the upper layer of a glacier that mountaineers call *firn*: granular snow that has frozen into a consolidated mass. It acts remarkably like Styrofoam. At times it feels like walking on a solid Styrofoam block that supports your weight well. But much of the time, it feels like walking on a thick layer of

---

1   If you read the foreword, which is more of a disclaimer, you'll know that I cannot always be trusted. Trust me, our walk was only about a mile, maybe not even.

Styrofoam peanuts that collapses underfoot.

I would have expected a trough where the path is, but continually drifting snow must erase the distinction. Instead, there is a narrow hardened strip that shows occasional signs of footprints but looks otherwise identical to the surrounding firn. As I trudged forward, my feet kept sliding off the side of the path or missing it altogether, sinking into the peanuts and crushing my gumption.

We stopped occasionally to brush frost from cup anemometers, hygrometers, solar-tracking pyrheliometers, and precipitation accumulators—devices I didn't know yet, but would know soon and well—eventually arriving exhausted at the Temporary Atmospheric Watch Observatory.

To call it an observatory is extravagant and to call it temporary is wishful—things do not change rapidly at the extreme and therefore expensive ends of the earth. TAWO is a room, a very small room, scarcely bigger than a mudroom, with a vestibule scarcely bigger than a closet. It hums, whirs, and clicks: the incessant sounds of science, Simon & Garfunkel be damned. The minuscule space is packed with instruments: spectrometer, seismometer, aethalometer, nephelometer, photometer—basically all the *ometers*, plus a handful of other devices that don't fit the *ometer* mantra in name, but in function are essentially *ometers*.

For the first few days of training, three to five people were crammed into the slit of space available between racks of electronics, wires, and hoses. From above we surely resembled that old handheld picture puzzle with the sliding tiles and the missing square as we strategized our way around each other. Lance walked us through daily maintenance checks of all the instruments, calibration procedures for those that require it, and current issues with the few that are being fussy. Katrine, the full-time station science manager and our fun and spunky leader, bounced around doing uncommon tasks and semiannual checks. Jenny helped when needed or stood by when about to be needed or marched happily back to the Big House when not needed. Neal and I took notes, pored over documentation, and tried to wrap our heads around all these gizmos and their different needs.

Though it was overcrowded, the periods of warming inside cozy TAWO were welcome. We had plenty of chilling outdoor work to do as we learned the regular weekly tasks we would be performing for the next few months:

With climbing harnesses stretched around overalls and down parkas, we ascended the tower behind TAWO to clean the frost from several more *ometers*, as well as air intake hoses for much of the instrumentation inside the building.

In the Clean Air Sector beyond TAWO, wrapped in white anti-contamination suits, we watched as Lance raced to fill plastic bags with snow samples. Wearing only thin glove liners under thinner anti-contamination gloves, he moved his cold fingers with surprising deftness and speed. Jenny cursed all the while, her frozen digits only able to fill three small bottles to Lance's ten bags.

When the wind was favorable, we collected air in glass flasks while holding our breath to prevent contamination. While the flasks filled we would run to a distance deemed innocuous and keel over to draw long lungfuls of inadequate air back into our systems.

Neal cleaning frost off the TAWO tower instruments

Much of the training we received in the first several days was for tasks that would occur only occasionally but that we needed to know. In some cases, that just meant learning where to find an instrument and how to access it:

We followed another flagged path—this one seldom-used and consisting of gumption-sucking peanuts only—and it seemed to lead us nowhere. The flag line ended abruptly at a mound of snow like any other—except that Lance declared it the location of the seismic vault. We took turns digging for the entrance. I could only take five or six shovelfuls before collapsing like an asthmatic fish. Neal managed seven or eight shovelfuls, but they were Neal-sized. I felt pathetic and not at all helpful. It was primarily Lance and Jenny's effort that revealed a plywood sheet protecting a small tunnel. "I'm not going in there," Neal informed us bluntly. I'm a touch claustrophobic too, but it's more a fear of immobility. Call it immobiphobia; as long as I can still move my arms, I'm good. So I went in there, down a snow tube where I could barely move my arms to a snow tunnel where I crawled to an underground— undersnow?—cavern large enough to crouch in. At the opposite end of the cavern was a box with a bell-shaped glass dome perched atop it like some idol at the end of a crypt in an Indiana Jones movie, provoking in me an asinine impulse to check the walls for blow-dart holes and the floor for false panels. There was no need, for this was no idle idol; it already knew we were there. Our presence was betrayed even before we started digging. It was sensitive enough to detect our every move. It seemed to glow, until I redirected my headlamp.

Similar to the seismic vault but on a larger scale is the Noone vault, so named for the Principle Investigator[2] of that particular project. The Noone vault is next to the 50-meter tower, which we pass during rounds but fortunately do not climb in the winter months. The vault houses much of the electronics that drive the tower's sensors. We took turns digging up the entrance, this time

2   Or "PI" as we typically call them, humorously lending the mystique of private investigation to a far more dry and scholarly occupation.

with a lot more effort and some much-appreciated help from a few volunteers, as there were many cubic yards of snow to remove. Under a sealed hatch, a ladder dropped down into another snow cavern, this one the size of a small garage. It had more room than TAWO but much less equipment. I felt an urge to stretch. Neal seemed ill at ease.

Fortunately the vaults rarely require entrance. We hoped the need to dig them up again would not arise on our watch, especially for the Noone vault. Though our visits were purely instructional, they were time consuming, and the cramming of these events on top of our regular tasking was punishing. It wasn't long into our training that I began looking forward to days that were merely full, not bloated to excess. Even dinner afforded only a brief respite before continuing to overload our brains with more strangely named devices. As I drifted to sleep each night, I envisioned a worthless tangle of mathematical symbols tumbling from my ears.

The rest of the station did not share our unfortunate schedule. Regularly after dinner seven or eight people would pack into the small Green House lounge, relaxing and watching movies while we went step by step through a weather balloon launch, which has to occur in the evening—I don't remember why. All told, we paraded across the projector six times per night: on our way to the lab, on our way to launch the balloon, on our way back to the lab to input the launch data, and again leaving the lab until it was time to close out the radio connection, at which point we returned to the lab and then crossed the projector's path a final time on the way to fucking bed.

ON THURSDAY, THE Phase 1 contractors, except Lance, and the full-time Polar Field Services employees were scheduled to fly out, leaving only five of us to maintain the station through Phase 2—what I like to call the Dark Phase.[3] That morning, Lance and Jenny officially passed the torch to Neal and me. That afternoon, we had our first instrument failure: a computer contracted a virus and its owner needed us to reboot it. No problem, except that the computer was in the Noone vault—of course—buried under yard after cubic yard of snow, and it was still minus fifty degrees out there.

"Great first day!" was all the help we got from Lance and Jenny, not that I blamed them. Jenny seemed burnt out and ready to go home. And Lance, in addition to instructing our turnover, had to complete another turnover of his own, as he will be staying with us through Phase 2 in a role that is new to him. This is fortunate for Neal and me because if we have trouble with anything, Lance will still be around to help.

So instead of a great first day where the excess people fly away and leave us in peace to hunker down for the winter, the flight was canceled for weather and Neal and I dug up the Noone vault—again. That was two days ago. The weather continues to misbehave, as is the norm, and flights have been canceled again today, making it three days in a row. The Phase 1 crew is happily taking it easy while still getting paid, the full-timers continue to work hunched over their laptops in every public space, and the Phase 2 crew just wants everyone to go away so we can get settled in and have some room to breathe. With only a dozen people, this station feels cramped; I can't imagine it in the summer when there can be over forty. As it is, there is nowhere to be alone except your own room. The most frustrating part, though, is that we crammed a week of training into a horrendous few days on account of our delayed arrival, but we could have gone at a much

---

3   At Summit, what could be called summer, fall, winter, and spring are called summer, Phase 1, Phase 2, and Phase 3. My thinking is it facilitates the hiring process—who would winter at such a place when they could Phase 2 instead?

more manageable pace if only we had known their departure would be equally delayed.

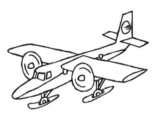

"SERIOUSLY, WHAT THE hell is that clicking noise?" I asked again, growing more perturbed.

A warm smirk appeared on Neal's face. "You've got your own personal stenographer, watching your every move."

At that point I was laser-beam focused on pointing out this errant vexation. After a pause, I exploded. "There! Did you hear that? What the hell *is* that?"

"You mean that clicking noise?"

2

In which I step back in time and recount the journey to my new "home," which seems much, much better than the journey to my old "home."

Day . . . um . . . T-minus 7 Days
Sunday, October 28

Mandatory evacuations have been ordered in coastal areas of Delaware, New Jersey, and New York in anticipation of the storm of the century. Hurricane Sandy is headed shoreward on a collision course with an Arctic front that will create what the news is calling a superstorm. No one seems to know what's going to happen but everyone expects it to be bad. Hundreds of flights have already been canceled. Public transportation is being halted in New York City, DC, Philadelphia, and New Jersey. Emergency shelters are going up across a dozen states. At about the same time the hurricane will make landfall on the Eastern Seaboard—tomorrow—I'm supposed to be flying from Denver to Reykjavik, which seems at first to mean flying right through a hurricane, but the straight-line flight path will actually proceed north out of Colorado and then across Hudson Bay and the southern flank of Greenland before arriving in Iceland, always safely out of harm's way—I assume.

Monday, October 29

I'm on an airplane. Everything seems normal. Going to knock myself out now and sleep through the apocalypse. Hello, Ambien.

Tuesday, October 30

I'm still on an airplane. I think. I don't feel dead, anyway. Though I have nothing to compare against, having never been dead—to my knowledge.

Saturday, November 3

I arrived with the rest of the Phase 2 contract crew and three full-time Polar Field Services employees to an icy, wintry Akureyri. That was on Tuesday evening. We were scheduled to continue our journey north on Thursday, but the final vestiges of hurricane Sandy reached Iceland right on our heels. The single day we had set aside here gave her a solid opportunity to catch us up, which she's done, pummeling us with blizzard conditions and canceling our flights *and* any other means of escape: all the roads out of town are closed. We're stuck.

This, apparently, is the norm. The full-timers tell us they get held up in Akureyri regularly, though it's not usually for the foul weather here in Iceland but for the fouler weather at our final destination farther north.

Now it's Saturday, and our flight has been canceled again. In the meantime, we've been preparing for the job that awaits us by poring over AHAs and SOPs.[4] Much of it is completely out of context when not on-site, so we get a lot of "don't worry, you'll see when we get there" from Katrine. It's boring, the paperwork. I'm a hands-on learner. Fortunately it hasn't monopolized our time and there has been ample opportunity for exploration, within the confines of town, anyway.

Outside, if you can manage to raise your eyes from a protective

---

4   Maybe I should explain these TLAs, but the Arctic and Antarctic Programs are so inundated with them that, in the spirit of conveying a feeling of bewildered disorientation, leaving them a mystery seems more appropriate.

stoop, it's a winter wonderland. Heavy blowing snow has caked itself to every surface. Buildings are a patchwork of colorful siding and snow white. Roofs overflow with reaching cornices. Windowsills drip icicles. Trees masquerade as snow cones. On the ground, all is hidden. But the colorful Scandinavian facade still manages to burst through in spots, providing a beautiful canvas for the blizzard's brush. Though, its brushstrokes being erasures, the painting appears to have traveled in the wrong direction through time.

Just down the street from our hotel is a lovely blue edifice. Its rows of white-framed windows wrap around protruding octagonal corners that reach up beyond the roof with tall red spires like gnome hats. At street level its windows are floor to ceiling and look in on blond wood tables, each with a candle glowing invitingly. Candelabras hang overhead. This is the coffee shop full of cockle-warming cakes and sweets where we spend much of our time. As the snow falls outside in thick flakes, the warm-hued interior remains thawing and comfortable. Each day we huddle around steaming mugs while baked goods digest in our bellies and our training regimen dissolves to oblivion in our minds.

Around the corner and up a slippery hill is an indoor/outdoor pool facility with loads of geothermally heated soaking options. Of course, swimming trunks were the last article of clothing I expected to have any use for on this venture—we're not going on a Caribbean cruise; we're on our way to Hoth.[5] But the man behind the glass told me that yes, they rent swimwear. And towels. I had a towel. That's rule number one; all hitchhikers[6] know that. In this instance, however, I wished I could trade my towel for a pair of my own swimming trunks, not because I was disgusted by the idea of wearing previously worn, at-many-times-in-the-past-rubbed-against-strange-men's-private-parts swimming trunks, but because they were not swimming *trunks*, they were swimming *briefs*. *Brief* as in not enough, too little, barely covering the,

---

5   *One*...

6   *Two*...

uh, topic. These were Bond-James-Bond[7]–style hug-the-uglies budgie smugglers. You know, like in *Thunderball*. At least, that's what I kept telling myself while I wore them.

The man behind the glass asked what size I would like and I answered proudly, "Large," though I am a small to medium sized man. The man behind the glass held up a pair of large briefs with a questioning look that read, "Are you sure? I think these are too big for you," which precisely contradicted the message I was getting from the briefs. "Extra large," I said, adding a skyward-pointing gesture because, despite his excellent command of the English language and his shrugging compliance, I was convinced this man did not understand me at all.

My rental briefs fit with a suitable looseness in some areas but insisted on being true-to-style in others. They clearly didn't fit me properly, which compounded what had started out as only mild embarrassment. But it wasn't the tightness of them that bothered me, it was their total lack of cool. These are what old European men wear, and they look so silly among the boardshorts of my generation. But rather than just owning it, wearing my size, fitting in with the locals, and not drawing attention—you know, when in Rome and all—I was wearing rental briefs that were two sizes too big, and it was apparent. My attempt to avoid looking silly had backfired. Now I looked like I was either too stupid to know my size or too embarrassed to wear briefs, neither of which was strictly true, and I found that blow to my ego far more embarrassing than the idea of looking uncool in briefs. The irony gave me a good laugh at myself, and then I was over it—not that I went back to get a smaller pair.

I exited the changing room into a glassed-in atrium with a large wading pool. A narrow waterway branched off and punched through the wall, connecting the indoor pool to one of the outdoor pools via a swimmable corridor. Preferring the full effect, I bypassed the wading pool and entered the blizzard on foot. Fat

---

7   *Three* pop culture references in one paragraph is excessive, don't you think?

snowflakes fell exhilaratingly onto my bare skin. Expecting something resembling the small sulfury hot springs I'm familiar with, I was surprised to discover two Olympic-length swimming pools complete with diving platforms and swimming lanes. They were flanked by several smaller, hotter sitting pools. Steam rose in varying thicknesses through the falling snow. I dove in and nearly lost my swimming briefs, which loosened considerably once wet. *Make that* three *sizes too big,* I thought. I swam around for an hour or more sampling the different pools and trying to get some exercise. I expect to get very little once we're on station. I'm not even sure there's any equipment there, and I doubt I'll be going out for a jog.

I found Phil and Don in the sauna and felt my embarrassment returning. I barely know these men with whom I'm about to spend a secluded and intimate three months, and though I hide it well, I am sometimes reserved or even sheepish with new people. So far, they seem great: easygoing and broad-smiled. But so am I, and yet I can be damned grumpy sometimes, though it takes a lot to get a rise out of me. I know that the slightest of personality quirks can send the dynamic of five isolated people into spiraling decline. But I'm not worried. My experience so far with ice folk is predominantly positive, and both Phil and Don have been contracting the bitter regions of the earth long enough to have passed the threshold of weeding out. I like them. Besides, it's hard to imagine the phase going bad with Neal on board.

I suppose I don't know Neal well yet, but I know him well enough. We've turned over the science technician position at Palmer Station six times now—him bookending all three of my contracts there—plus we did some training together in Denver for this gig. Neal is tall and slim with dark hair that has a mind of its own, sometimes standing, sometimes sitting, sometimes throwing a wild party. When I first met him his skin was pale from too many winters, most of his whiskers were formed into thick unkempt mutton chops, and his hair was six inches long and throwing a scandalous, gravity-defying rave. But his bright eyes and smile told his true demeanor. Now he has a full but modest beard, and his hair is a tame length, though still a bit unkempt. I expect he'll return to what I think of as his natural state by the end of the winter. He's goofy, but not awkward, and his quick wit and unique sense of humor can be crude, sophisticated, or both. I find him funny as hell, and we get along well. I even stayed at his apartment in Crested Butte once for a week while he was wintering at Palmer. I still owe him a bottle of wine for that, plus the vig.

The fifth member of our merry band, Lance, isn't with us here and I haven't met him yet. He's already been at the station for several months, and doing two phases back-to-back means there's a decent chance we'll catch him having already begun the winter decline.

I guess ultimately, it will be what it will be. If for some unlikely reason the dynamic goes sour, I have some personal projects to work on, and I know Neal will still be good company. You never know, though. I've heard rumors about a winter crew that consisted of two couples who were all great friends and had worked together at other stations previously, but by the end of the phase they weren't even speaking to each other. Perhaps their friendship became punctuated by annoyance in tight quarters; perhaps a love triangle, or square, began to form; perhaps the lack of buffering normally provided by extra people allowed true colors to fly.

Anything can happen.

Day 1
Sunday, November 4

This morning we gathered in the small Akureyri airport. The weather was immensely improved and this was the closest we'd been to leaving yet. Previously our flights were canceled before we even got out of bed. I was still skeptical that we would depart, though I had no reason to feel so. We whisked informally through security and sat looking out into the predawn light at two Twin Otter aircraft waiting on the snow-swept tarmac. Each was equipped with retractable skis, drawn up at the moment but necessary for the glacial landing we would soon encounter. To my surprise, we boarded the small planes and set off.

Our northward journey began between the long arms of the Eyjafjörður, a crazy Middle Earth name for a pretty but not spectacular fjord, at least not compared to what was coming. Wrinkled fingers of snow-blanketed mountains filled my portside view. It was ten in the morning and the low sun only glanced the peaks. Beneath us the waters of the wide fjord were inky blue and surprisingly calm. I leaned back and plugged in my earbuds to drown out the loud whine of the propellers, inwardly rejoicing in the smooth ride, which sharply contrasted with the journey to my former home away from home at Palmer Station.

Palmer, on the Antarctic Peninsula, is accessible only by sea. To reach it means to spend several days crossing one of the world's most notoriously rough stretches of ocean—the Drake Passage— on a research icebreaker—the *ARSV Laurence M. Gould*—whose motion I can only describe as wonky. She tends to rock to one side, and rather than roll back rhythmically, she lingers there, wreaking havoc on your inner ear balance and forcing you to wonder if she's taking on water. After a long awkward pause, she'll roll partway back, lurch in another random direction, and come back to rest on the same absurd lean before continuing her bizarre bobbing. When walking about, I learned to always keep a hand free and ready to grab, and to expect my path to be curved, spiraled, or even reversed in its forward motion. I would pause at stairwells, waiting for the moment when I could fall up them or control the stumble down.

As the story goes, the *Gould* came out of dry dock a brand-new ship with an angle of list that was a degree or two beyond acceptability. One side of her hull was filled with concrete to straighten her, but this caused her to sit too low in the water, so "stabilizers"—protruding from the hull like oblong water wings— were added at the waterline to increase buoyancy. It's this combination of ballast and flotation that causes her to gyrate erratically in the slightest of seas like a child's Weebles wobble. I suspect this tale is equal parts truth and myth, but for me the nausea-inducing capacity of the *Gould* is nonetheless exceptional, and is made insufferable when the Drake is misbehaving, which is its usual state.

The Drake Passage: the choke point for the Antarctic Circumpolar Current between Tierra del Fuego, at the southern tip of South America, and the Antarctic Peninsula, reaching northward from Earth's southernmost continent. This five-hundred-mile stretch of ocean is known for being unpredictable and nasty as it traverses latitudes referred to as the "furious fifties" and "screaming sixties." In only five crossings—my sixth was in the comfort of a rare and coveted flight—I experienced both the calm and elusive "Drake lake" and also saw twenty-foot waves crashing over the ship's rear deck. I spent those days primarily horizontal, with a blanket stuffed under one side of my mattress to minimize the chances of being flung from my bunk while the Drake rocked me cruelly not to sleep.

Pancake ice sweeping toward the Antarctic Peninsula cordillera

But if your stomach can manage the Drake, what comes next is magical. First, the ocean surface begins to take on a fine film of slush, which dulls the waves to a pudding consistency with an oily, slurpy sheen: *grease ice*. Then, little frozen discs begin to form, with snow in the middle and slurpy edges, bouncing gently against each other in wide swaths: *pancake ice*. Further south the pancakes grow bigger and fill in the gaps of open water until a magic carpet of white stepping-stones undulates to all horizons: *pack ice*. Seals sunbathe in the cold dry air atop the larger pancakes, and uneven ice chunks of various sizes and translucencies become interspersed: *brash ice*.[8] Next are small slabs, protruding a foot above the water's surface, then two feet, three: *multiyear ice*, and soon after, oddly carved shapes the size of a large vehicle or small dwelling: *bergy bits*. The sheer mountains of the Antarctic Peninsula cordillera emerge through distant mist. As they approach, the presence of massive glaciers is foreshadowed by building-sized formations of ice, sometimes as big as a city block—jagged, misshapen, and in the right light, aqua blue: *icebergs*. The mountain peaks are black-walled and white-capped, foreboding and desolate, but alive with majesty. The slow marching glacial ice forms a crumbling, unending wall at their feet. This is the backdrop for the remaining day of sailing to Palmer, few experiences its rival.

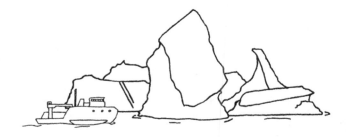

WHEN I FINALLY leaned forward and looked out the window of the small plane, I saw familiar swirls of sea ice swooping outward from the unfamiliar coastline of Greenland. A spiraling current shaped the pattern of ice below—an interesting view from my aerial perspective but without the intimacy or romance of a slow passage by boat. Palmer has that. The four-day ocean voyage, despite its long dismal moments, breathes life into a feeling of

8   Which may contain sought-after *bar ice*: crystal clear, salt- and bubble-free, haul it to the bar and chip it into a cocktail!

veritable remoteness.

The aircraft turned sharply and began an acrobatic funneling descent. Below lay Constable Pynt, astride a long finger-shaped inlet on the east coast of Greenland. Its short gravel runway was surrounded by dirty snow and bleak talus-laden ridges, void of vegetation. This remote airstrip serves the nearby town of Ittoqqortoormiit,[9] population 450. It is about forty kilometers away and accessible only by helicopter, boat, or snow machine.[10] The small airfield functions primarily as a jumping point for tourism in the nearby fjord system, or expeditions into northeastern Greenland—for the few who think that sounds like a good idea. For us it was neither, our destination being far less hospitable. For us it served only as a refueling station.

We lifted off shortly after noon for the final leg of the journey. The sun remained in a dawn state, low in the southern sky. We had outpaced its ability to rise as we traveled north from Iceland, across the Arctic Circle. But now our path turned westward and

The sun struggling to rise over Scoresbysund

9   Can I have a "q," please? Hell, make it two—in a row. Eat your heart out, Mississippi.

10   Better known in lower latitudes as a snowmobile. It's like pop and soda. Or my favorite: topper, shell, cap, camper, canopy.

inland toward the heart of Greenland. Scoresbysund, the longest fjord on Earth, stretched out beneath us like an immense bay, twenty miles wide. Its docile waters were inky black between broken swaths of newly formed, translucent sea ice. Icebergs, ant-sized from this viewpoint, speckled the entire body of water. In the northwest corner of the sound was an archipelago of dark, rough islands, their crevices packed with contrastingly soft snow. Across this scene swept the sun's orange rays. They reflected off the icy landscape after struggling to clear the mountainous horizon, and gelded a black-and-white world.

As we continued, Scoresbysund narrowed between steep and rugged mountains and forked into several branches. Long fingers of twilight water receded up sheer fjords in every direction. The distant peaks, capped with ice and snow, were rent by glaciers. I hopped from one side of the small aircraft to the other, peering out the tiny windows in awe. I had no idea this was coming.

We traced our way up one of these waterways, rock walls standing to port and starboard. The sun illuminated only the summits and south-facing clifftops. Fjords continued to branch off, many no longer dipping their toes in water, but tucking them

A glacier flowing into the narrowing sound

under long rivers of ice instead. The slow movement of these glaciers was evident in their flowing shape as they curved down from the serrated mountaintops. They ended abruptly at the water's edge below us, breaking off in iceberg slabs to float away. Soon we left the sound behind, so that only ice and rock remained. We passed over immense glaciers—*miles* wide—forming broadly carved valleys between the peaks.

The ice rose, filling all gaps in the harsh terrain, running together in smooth waves through the geological labyrinth. Jumbled earth was being slowly swallowed, overrun by a thick batter. The valleys became shallower as the glaciers grew deep. The mountains became engulfed and isolated, the ice parting and rejoining around them like honey filling the uneven landscape of an English muffin. Ridges disappeared as the ice spilled over, leaving only islands of rock in a silent white sea. Glaciers became glacier.

Soon ice blanketed the mountains completely, leaving immense undulating crevasse fields as the only indication of solid ground beneath. And then nothing. A vast white plane from horizon to horizon. Ice so thick and featureless that it pays the deeply

Fields of snow-bridged crevasses at the edge of Greenland's ice cap

buried mountains no mind. Greenland's interior is smothered under two vertical miles of ice.

After an hour of flying low over that unchanging expanse, I realized that Summit Station, like Palmer, also has its sense of remoteness.

We began our descent in low visibility. The sky had become a solid haze of foggy cloud, blotting out the setting sun and blending seamlessly with the ice below. I couldn't tell the ground from the sky, and I wondered if our pilot's senses were any sharper. But we touched down reasonably, the Twin Otter's skis no longer retracted, and slid clunkily down a runway of uneven ice.

I crawled out of the aircraft into another world. It wasn't a world of harsh and blizzard-like winter conditions. It wasn't terribly windy or even terribly cold. It was a world without features, without horizons, without orientation. It was a floating world wrapped seamlessly in a uniform white veil.

Before I had a chance to discern up from down, we were whisked from the skiway, up a flight of stairs and into a building on stilts, where we were greeted with warm soup and a pulse oximeter.

"Seventy-nine percent!" I boasted. "Beat that!"

3

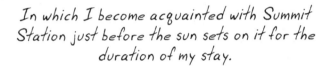

In which I become acquainted with Summit Station just before the sun sets on it for the duration of my stay.

Day 8
Sunday, November 11

Silence.

At midday two Twin Otters came to remove the Phase 1 crew, excepting Lance, and the full-timers here for turnover. The skiway was groomed, bags were loaded, freshies unloaded, fueling sorted, goodbyes spoken, and then, blissful silence. A communal sigh of relief filled the station, followed by a gasping for oxygen. We gathered in the galley and Phil promptly announced that after a week of debilitating work pace, we should take a well-deserved and much-needed afternoon off. Never have I been more burnt out from a week of work. After lunch I went straight to my room for a nap, then spent some time in the office writing to my blog. It was a marvel not to see anyone for several hours.

~

A Quick Tour

Summit Station, Greenland
Sunday, November 11, 2012

So here I am on the apex of the Greenland ice cap, at the aptly named Summit Station. A few small buildings and four companions will make up my home for the next three months. I suppose a quick tour of the station is in order.

Summit consists primarily of three buildings: the Big House, the Green House, and the Science and Operations Barn, whimsically referred to as "the S.O.B."

The Big House is perched fifteen feet above the ice atop two rows of stilts. You must climb a long flight of stairs and pass through two doors to enter. It contains the galley and is thus, of course, our usual gathering area—even at the far corners of the earth, the kitchen is where we hang out.

Half the building is an open area for dining, currently consisting of a single table. Some of the empty space is taken up by a sitting area with futons and a coffee table. The Big House also contains the manager's office, scullery, and food storage pantries. The rest

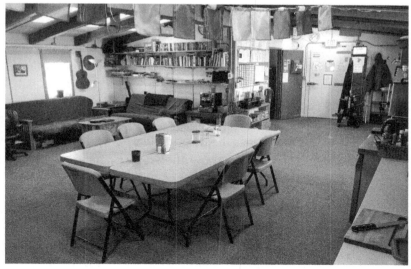

The Big House dining area, lounge, and office

of our food is frozen and lives in what I'll call a "developed ice cave" under the Big House. Atop the Big House sits a gigantic golf ball that shelters an equally gigantic satellite dish that connects us to the outside world.

The Green House is a short walk from the Big House, along a flagged path. It bears no resemblance to a greenhouse; it only happens to be painted green. Walking through it you get the feeling that from an aerial perspective it would look like the Chinese character for "I didn't think you could get lost in a building this small." Inside are two tiny laboratories, the science technicians' office, a small lounge, the clinic, a small kitchen, an equipment storage area, several utility closets, two bathrooms, and eight bunk rooms. Of course, there are only five of us here now, but in the summer the support staff are doubled up in these rooms and scientists live outside in a tented camp. (This is because a scientist's tenancy is usually on the order of weeks, whereas support staff stay for months).

Coming from the Big House you could walk around the Green House to get to the S.O.B., but it's cold out there so I walk through it. The S.O.B. is two stories tall and somewhat barn-shaped. Unlike the Green House—ironically—it looks much like a large greenhouse: long, with a gabled roof that rounds off smoothly to become the exterior walls. The S.O.B. houses the generator and snowmelter at its near end and a large garage complete with strange tracked vehicles and the occasional balloon-bound pseudoscientist (that's me) at its far end. Between is an office for the mechanic, and above that is essentially a hardware store. Despite "science" being part of its name, very little science is done in the S.O.B.—only the weather balloons. It's a garage; a nuts, bolts, and grease kind of place.

Tying everything together, all the outside thoroughfares are marked with flags every ten or so yards so you can still find your way in a whiteout (probably). For the winter we've even strung rope between the bamboo flagpoles in high-use areas. It may seem excessive, but in a bad storm you may not be able to see the next flag until it hits you in the goggles, which would be both frightening and relieving at the same time. Among all these colorful wind-tattered flags, I sometimes imagine I'm on vacation in the Himalayas, a fantasy that doesn't alleviate the chill.

Oh yes, and then there's science—the reason we're here. Science has a home too.

A kilometer away from the Big House, in the opposite direction, across a white expanse, down a long row of flags, at the edge of the Clean Air Sector, sits a tiny building on stilts that is stuffed to the gills with scientific equipment: TAWO. Every day, Neal and I trek out to TAWO to push buttons, flip switches, turn dials, check gauges, and knock off frost. In other words, we kick the tires. Our job is shared, so we take turns on the one-man jobs and tag-team the rest.

There's also the Mobile Science Facility, which is Lance's domain. It's much larger than TAWO and looks like a shipping container with windows, though it doesn't look very mobile. It sits sort of off to one side of station, has some gizmos on the roof that Lance regularly checks, and, having only walked past it, that's all I know.

So that's it, aside from a few small utility shacks. Five buildings. Five tenants.

The Phase 2 crew:

Neal – Science Tech, fellow Palmerite, flippin' tall (seriously, he hits his head on things I don't even notice)

Lance – Science Tech, fellow kitesurfer (albeit snow), surprisingly energetic (he's been here three months already and should start getting tired soon)

Phil – Camp Manager, fellow Mactowner (I knew he looked familiar; we figured out that we had adjoining offices in McMurdo, but somehow we rarely crossed paths)

Don – Mechanic, fellow Washingtonian (he lives just down the river from my stomping grounds; what are the odds?)

Rex – Science Tech, remember me? (the fellow whose blog you're reading)

~

Near dinnertime, I returned to the Big House. Phil was the only one there. "Well, did you have a nice nap?"

"I did. Man, I needed it. It's so nice and quiet here now."

"Finally!"

"It's almost too quiet." I chuckled at the contradiction. "I mean, I haven't seen anyone since lunch and it's just weird."

"Neither have I. They must still be resting, but I'll bet their stomachs will bring them around."

"Hmm, no doubt. Look at all these freshies." I stood over the piles of Styrofoam crates we had unloaded from the Twin Otters and replaced with passengers. Within those containers was our precious stock of fresh fruits and vegetables—a cornucopia start that will wither to freshie famine as the winter progresses.

"I don't even want to deal with it. We've done enough work for one week, and we need a break. But it'll be fine in the Styrofoam, so we can put it away tomorrow." I admire Phil. He seems easygoing and fun with a well-balanced sense of what is important and what isn't. He's wise and mature in his role as station manager but has a healthy childlike spirit that shines through and keeps him young and amused. His wide smile pushes aside his sandy blond beard and crinkles the crow's-feet tucked behind his glasses.

"I just wish I knew which of these crates has the avocados in it," I said offhandedly, and that was all it took. It was like Christmas: the excitement of what awaited us in the next box drove us forward long after the avocados were uncovered. Before long, containers spread to fill the room as we took stock of fruits and vegetables, fresh herbs, milk, and eggs. Lance, Neal, and Don trickled in as Phil predicted, and soon I was chopping a garden salad for dinner while the rest was being put away. We have to enjoy our limited supply of freshies while it lasts. We've all wintered before, so we know how important it is.

We sat down to our first dinner as just the five of us and began getting to know each other.

Neal: "So, everyone here is from Washington or Colorado?"

Lance: "Idaho."

Don: "Oh, that's just over the border."

Me: "I'm only technically from Washington. Never actually lived there, just crashed a lot of couches. Oregon is really home, I guess." I added the Antarctic definition of home: "That's where my storage unit is."

Lance: "Yeah, I technically don't have a home. I've been here more than I've been anywhere in the last two years." He thought for a second. "I've spent thirteen months here and five in Samoa. Does that add up? No, not quite. I was traveling back and forth, I guess."

Lance has done several contracts at the South Pole, winter included, and recently did a contract in Samoa maintaining equipment for NOAA. He's enthusiastic and adventurous, with a thin frame that he's trying to put some mass on while he's here. Shaggy bits of dark hair crawl from under his ever-present and ever-changing hat. I've never seen Lance without a hat—usually a winter beanie—and I'm certain it's never been the same hat twice. He seems to have an endless supply. As he likes to say, "It's crazy!"

Neal: "Well, since I bought my place, I've spent more time away from it than at it. I've spent more time in the Antarctic than anywhere in the past seven years."

Me: "Likewise. Not seven, though. Five?"

Phil: "What year were you at McMurdo?"

Me: "Mmm . . ." I thought for a moment. "That would have been oh seven oh eight." This is standard speak for a contract that begins during one year and ends the next, typical of an austral[11] summer season, though in my case it was a full year.

Phil: "And that was your first deployment?"

Me: "Yep. And you said you were with LDB that year, right?"

---

11   *Austral*: southern. As opposed to *boreal*, which is northern. Try to keep in mind that the seasons are swapped. It doesn't make things any less confusing, but at least you'll know *why* they're confusing.

Phil: "Yes."

Me: "I can't believe that our offices were right next to each other, but I'm not even sure that we actually met."

Phil: "Well, I spent a lot of time out of the office."

Me: "Way out at LDB, I imagine." The Long Duration Balloon facility is located on the permanent sea-ice shelf southeast of McMurdo, seven or eight miles away from town—a distance worthy of *way out* in Antarctic terms.

Don: "Hey, we should be having a beer!" He was right; this was the first significant night of our season together, and I was finally feeling up to it, my weeklong altitude headache having graciously abated.

Lance: "Oh, yeah, there's some left over from last phase. You want one?"

Don: "Well, yeah!"

I think Don may be one of the sweetest men I've ever met. I don't mean to detract from his manliness—he *is* the mechanic, after all—but he is genuine and warm with a huge grin that spreads across his whole face and is rarely missing from his expression, and never missing from his demeanor. He's got rosy cheeks and a shiny forehead that reaches up to short, sandy white hair. If he grew a beard, he'd make an excellent Santa Claus, and I bet he'd enjoy every jolly minute of it. I wonder if the winter will even affect him.

Lance brought out several beers and we continued to acquaint ourselves. Already the dynamic is great. It's encouraging that everyone is fun and personable. I have a solid feeling that the winter will be a good one.

Day 9
Monday, November 12

It's Monday, the first day of what I'm sure will become an institutionalized routine. But it's an odd-feeling Monday because despite yesterday's afternoon off, I still feel like I'm in desperate need of recuperation. Although today was no respite, it being the busiest day of our week, the lack of constant bustle allowed me to begin collecting myself again. I even found some time to take pictures of the frost that collected on the station overnight. The bamboo flags have nearly two inches of ice buildup on their windward side and one inch on the leeward. A uniform coating mutes the Big House's deep blue siding to a frosty gray. The wooden stairs on either side of the building appear to have a thickly textured coat of white paint.

Until now the sun has been up for a couple of hours each day, but only scrapes the edge of the sky. At this latitude, the sun doesn't rise in the east, climb overhead, and set in the west. It circles. If this were summertime the sun would be up all day, marching slowly around the compass, a little lower in the northern sky, a little higher in the south. Right now, as we approach winter, the sun skims just below the horizon from east to south, where it peeks partially over the edge before slinking down again to continue its clockwise rotation. What this means is the entire day is a long, slow sunrise followed by a lingering sunset. When the skies are clear, the days are beautiful, and with a few clouds thrown in near the horizon, they're incredible.

Alas, the sun will set tomorrow and then remain below the horizon for seventy-six days. Tomorrow the arctic winter will truly begin. To my amazement, the temperature has already dipped below -70°F, though only briefly. That's almost twenty degrees colder than I experienced during my winter in Antarctica. I expected it to be cold here, but I didn't expect it to be *that* cold. Clearly the altitude plays a significant role. Today wasn't as bad, bouncing around in the forties. That's *negative* forties, of course. We don't bother to say "negative" or "minus." It's implied, always. Rarely does the temperature climb above zero in the winter, and if it does, we'll be sure to add a "plus" and a surprised expression.

At the end of our workday, Neal and I began looking at recipes and the food inventory, since we'll have to start cooking this week. Neal's day is Tuesday: tomorrow. During our training back in Colorado, he admitted that the thing he was most nervous about was having to cook. "I mean, I can cook, but I've only ever cooked for myself. So, you know, I'm really good at ramen noodles and hot dogs and bachelor crap like that. I don't think they're gonna want ramen every week."

"You'll be fine. I'm sure you can cook just fine. I mean, I'm sure you can at least cook simple stuff like spaghetti."

"True."

"Everyone likes spaghetti, dude."[12]

I'm actually excited to start cooking. I want to make that delicious lemon sole dish that Kira's mom made while I was staying with Kira's family in South Africa this summer. No, winter. Their winter, our summer. It's bewildering sometimes, bouncing back and forth between the northern and southern hemispheres. Anyway, I used to dislike cooking, but as my mediocre skills have improved, I find myself almost enjoying it. Almost. It's certainly satisfying when a meal turns out well. Kira is an incredible cook and I've learned a few tricks from her in the couple of years we've been together. I'm always impressed by people who can take whatever odd combination of ingredients is available and turn it into something delicious. Kira can do that. Me, not so much. But we've got an industrial kitchen here and an entire stock of foodstuffs. It'll be like having a twenty-four-hour supermarket in the basement. All I need is the foresight to pull my ingredients from the freezer ahead of time.

Day 10
Tuesday, November 13

The plastic bindings on our skis are too narrow for the massive expedition boots we normally wear around, so I put on a smaller boot with less insulation and expect my feet to get cold. We're heading to the bamboo forest, a grid of 121 bamboo poles in the snow about a mile from station. On a weekly basis we measure

---

12   I say dude sometimes. I hate it when I say dude, but there I am, saying dude. I'm not sure why I dislike it. It's an interesting word, having evolved from describing a top-hat-wearing, waxed-mustache, freshly-shined-pocket-watch-on-a-chain dandy to describing a board-shorts-wearing, mop-haired, freshly-waxed-surfboard-on-a-leash . . . um, . . . well, *dude.*

every pole as part of a snow surface survey. I think. I don't actually know. It's a study of some sort anyway, and it's our job to collect the data. I'll look it up later. I know we're supposed to ski instead of walk so we don't create any artificial drifting.

Already I've discovered that on long outdoor excursions, maintaining the ability to see without inducing frostbite is a near-futile effort. At these temperatures, the moisture in my breath doesn't have a chance to escape my vicinity before freezing onto something. Local favorites are my eyebrows, eyelashes, and—believe it or not—nose hairs, but the vapor also enjoys adhering to my hat, neck gaiter, fuzzy parka hood, and, most frustratingly, my goggles.

So like any self-respecting pseudoscientist, I've begun to experiment. On this trip through the bamboo forest, I try a thin gaiter over my nose and a thicker one over my mouth. I'm hoping that the thin gaiter will allow my moist exhalation to pass through more easily instead of funneling up into my goggles, where it condensates quickly into a translucent film of ice. This transforms my vision into a white haze, which is actually not much different from what I can see without the goggles except that the reference points have been removed: i.e., the poles we're supposed to be measuring. The thin gaiter works for a while, but eventually it saturates, and like a wet T-shirt in a breeze, it transfers the cold directly through. My nose stays reasonably warm for reasons beyond my understanding yet not beyond my appreciation—perhaps the warmth of my breath—but the skin on my cheeks starts to get extremely cold. That's okay for a while because if I can feel that they're cold, then I know that they're alive and not frozen solid. But soon, when I poke my cheeks with my pencil, I don't feel a damn thing, which is bad. I ask Neal to look at them and he says they're just starting to lose color. So I pull a pair of hand warmers from my pocket and place them over my cheeks. I would like them directly on my skin but that would be too much direct heat, so I put them between the inner and outer gaiters. I suppose this makes me look like a chipmunk, but I'm so bundled up no one can tell, and anyway, I don't care as long as it's working, which it is, for now.

So from head to toe I'm wearing a big fuzzy hood, wool hat, goggles, two neck gaiters, "cheek" warmers, wool baselayer top, fleece pullover, down parka, thick gloves over glove liners and hand warmers, wool boxer briefs, thick long underwear, insulated overalls, thick wool socks, and boots with so much insulation I'm actually two inches taller. All of which makes it cumbersome to ski, difficult to breathe, nearly impossible to write down data . . . and my damn goggles frosted over anyway.

On the up side, all these layers of clothing make for the most exciting wads of bellybutton lint.

~

Sunset

Summit Station, Greenland
Tuesday, November 13, 2012

Today the sun sets with finality. It won't rise tomorrow, or for the next two and a half months. From this point forward I suggest that you read this blog in the dark. The pictures will look better, yes, but mostly it's to get you into the proper mindset.

~

My first polar winter was in the Antarctic, at McMurdo Station. The setting of the sun was significant. That I could glean from the people around me, yet I didn't appreciate the full gravity of the event at the time. I didn't know that the sun's absence was going to drive me mad.

Through the summer I caught glimpses of what the winter might be like. I heard weird stories about winter-overs. I was warned about the "Antarctic stare." I got the feeling that my new-found friends were all impressed—and some concerned—when they learned that I would be wintering. It's too bad that many summer contractors would never consider a winter—basing the decision on hearsay alone. It was my first deployment so I didn't know any better, which was great: I had no preconceived notions. I entered the winter with a healthy mindset, thinking it would be an interesting experience. And that it was. Had I entered it fearfully though, it would have been a long and challenging wait for the reappearance of that great orb, that precious source of light, of warmth, of life. That's not to say that the winter wasn't challenging. It was. But an unjustified fear at the onset of four months without the sun would have made it much, much worse.

The weather observation that Neal logged this morning reported the visibility as infinite. A nice clear day to soak up the last rays of solar stimulus. But throughout the morning a slow, thick mist coalesced upon station, and by midday I could barely see TAWO from the Big House. Sunset was a bust.

At dinner Don casually informed us with a smile, "Well, the Tucker's broke." So our emergency vehicle is a bust too.

These are bad omens.

Day 11
Wednesday, November 14

We had our first go at collecting the surface snow samples today. Neal struggled to get into his clean suit, which has to be stretched—to the limit in his tall case—over many thick layers of insulation. On its first outing last week, Neal's suit earned a huge tear in the crotch. One size does not fit all.

To protect the samples from contamination, we're also required to wear a double layer of fresh plastic gloves that won't fit over our winter gloves, so we can only wear glove liners under them. Before sampling, we "wash" our hands in the snow to cleanse the gloves, which means our inadequately insulated fingers start cold and only get colder. Manipulating the sampling bags and bottles with stiff fingers wrapped in flapping layers of slippery plastic is a real son of a bitch. Now I fully understand Jenny's cursing.

As we crouched on all fours behind TAWO to collect the samples, I suddenly heard Neal yell, "Shit!" When I looked up he was in midair, stretched out superman style, diving for a sample bag that had escaped his precarious grasp and was taken by the wind. From my perspective I saw two huge expedition boot soles and a

Carhartt crotch loosely surrounded by torn clean suit. I laughed heartily.

He recovered the bag quickly, which was paramount to ever seeing it again. The visibility was horrendous. Much worse than yesterday. The air was evenly opaque, a gray-white in all directions, like the day we arrived. No, worse. The ground was indiscernible from the sky. Only when I looked straight down could I see muted rivulets in the terrain that proved I was not walking on clouds but indeed standing on something tangible. While we collected snow in our white clean suits, Neal said, "It's like working in a giant Ping-Pong ball. Even you are invisible except for your head and feet."

Blending in with the Ping-Pong ball

It was true. Neal looked like a pair of floating boots beneath a disembodied head, with an occasional crotch.

Later in the day, Neal wrote in his blog that this was the last day we had any chance of seeing the sun. I'm not sure which of us got the date wrong, but it doesn't matter. There are only two dates we need to remember: the winter solstice and the sunrise. These are the landmarks of our crossing.

4

In which I wish I wasn't so isolated from my loved ones but change my mind when something shiny is dangled in front of me.

Day 13
Friday, November 16

The past two weeks have gone by in such a daze that I forgot the twins were due yesterday. When I called, my brother seemed in a daze too, unsure whether he or anyone else had told me the news. "I guess I haven't called you yet," Ethan said. "We have twins." Later I got a slew of pictures from Mom. In them Ethan is smiling, but he definitely has *oh, shit* in his expression. I wish I was there.

I lived across the country from my family for several years before I started remote contract work, but I often wonder if these distant jobs cause me to be even more disconnected. I sometimes feel forgotten, or maybe just off the radar. I think these feelings are primarily due to my isolation. Distance is one thing, but inescapability is another altogether. I *can't* go see my family. None of us can. No one's going to risk landing an aircraft here in the middle of winter if one of us has a family emergency. We know that. That's what we've signed up for. I missed Brett's wedding while I was in Antarctica. I wasn't sure my new sister-in-law would ever forgive me.

It's difficult, the inability to be with my family during times like that—times like this. This is an absorbing lifestyle full of wonderful people, travel opportunities, and long adventures between contracts, but it certainly has its drawbacks. If a family member were to slide into poor health, I would have no choice but to ride out the emotional isolation here.

I need a change of subject; it's time to escape into a book and fall asleep.

Day 14
Saturday, November 17

It's useless. I'm just not tired at bedtime, which keeps me up late and makes getting up in the morning slothful. It's happening much faster than I expected: these are winter's tendrils beginning to take hold. I'm particularly tired today for no apparent reason, especially since yesterday's weather was so lousy it kept us from doing much outside work, so the day should have been restful. The overcast sky, fog, and blustering snow that began just before the sunset have steadily built over the course of the week. It's awful out there. Is that what's getting to me: the dreary weather? No, it must be the light. This happened in the Antarctic too; the fall season—if it can be called that—harassed me with bouts of insomnia as the duration of daylight changed. It took some time to adjust. A few weeks after it was fully dark, I stopped having as much trouble sleeping, but the juxtaposition of fatigue and wakefulness returned with the sun.

Adding emotion to a weary day, Kira called upset, claiming she didn't know what was going on with me. I had no idea what she was talking about. She said I'm being distant and I'm not responding to her emails. But I *am* distant—I'm across the globe. And of the two emails I've sent in the past two days, she was copied on one and the sole recipient of the other. Specifically, she was hurt that I hadn't responded to a particular email about a friend of her family: a *sangoma*, a traditional African healer and fortune-teller of sorts. He told her my fortune, or rather he somehow knew my past. It was bizarre.

When I was in South Africa I never got the chance to meet this man, though Kira wanted me to. He is Kira's mother's mentor, having helped her attain a PhD in anthropology studying indigenous South African healers. Actually, it would be more accurate to say that Kira's mom *became* a healer, or at least damn nearly. Perhaps if she wasn't both female and white she would have been allowed to cross the final rite.

Kira was initially afraid to tell me this for fear that I would find it crazy. I guess I don't blame her; the almost otherworldly nature of such traditional medicines is often misconstrued as primitive and silly among the so-called civilized. This may be especially true for the work of a *sangoma*, divining among ancestors, good and evil spirits, and the world of dreams to relieve affliction. To be a *sangoma* is to be a soothsayer, and I admit that I have a hard time buying into much of it, though I do find it fascinating, especially the dream aspect. Kira's mom has personal spiritual locations in the wilds of South Africa that she was guided to by her dreams. She dreamed the details of these places, though she had never seen them, and located them afterward.

I'm much more open to this kind of thing than Kira seems to realize, especially having once had a foretelling dream of my own that later caused me to shudder in disbelief when the odd events in the dream actually occurred. I wish Kira's fear hadn't caused me to think it taboo to ask her mom about her experiences. I believe there is much more to this world than what our senses alone can discern. There is an occasional element of something intangible, something supernatural, that we just cannot understand, and I find that intriguing.

And so I found the words of Kira's *sangoma* intriguing. He told her, "Your boyfriend, he likes to drink, hey? Not too much, but he really likes beer! He loves music and he plays the guitar. And he has a very strange background that he should write a book about." Kira swears neither she nor her mom have ever discussed any of this with him. And so my palm has been read, my sooth said. It's creepy, but interesting. How could he possibly know that I've been wanting to write a book? I guess I should get cracking on that.

Kira leaves South Africa tomorrow. She has a long journey ahead of her: first to Virginia, where her postdoctorate work is based, and then through Chile on her way back to Palmer Station. I'm sure it's hard for her to leave; she's attached to her home and to her family. Maybe that's partly why she's upset. Her friend the *sangoma* is a symbol of home, and what he says is important to her. But just because I didn't respond to her message immediately doesn't mean I'm being distant, does it? I've barely had a chance to digest it. And it's interesting, so I prefer to discuss it live. Did I do something wrong?

I talked her down over the phone, but I still don't understand and it's frustrating. Ugh, I can't even think, I really need to get some sleep. At least tomorrow is our "day off" and I can sleep in. Maybe that will help, even though I'll still have some work to do.

Day 15
Sunday, November 18

What an incredible day! And just when I needed one.

After a week of dreary fog and blowing snow, the skies awoke clear and crisp this morning. In the afternoon a yellow-orange crescent moon, its golden hue all the more prominent in a darkening world, rose in the southeast and clung to the southern horizon for several hours. It crossed behind the silhouettes of frozen flagpoles as it passed. That was the cosmic teaser, the prelude. It wasn't until the moon set around dinnertime and plunged us back into inky night that the lights began.

A nascent glimmer in the southern sky slowly stretched into a green band above the Big House. This is what I've been waiting for, and no small part of why I came to the Arctic this winter. Not just any winter—the solar maximum. The sun's eleven-year activity cycle will be at its peak this year, which means plenty of sun spots and solar flares and other events that send showers of cosmic rays across the magnetosphere. It should be a very good year for aurora, as the earth's magnetic field funnels these particles toward the poles to crash into the atmosphere in lustrous array. My Antarctic winter was during a solar minimum; I saw some mild aurora but only heard stories of glorious displays.

Neal and I froze outside taking pictures. The emerald band expanded overhead and reached down in vibrant curtains, their motion a shimmering vinyasa. Directly above, long green lines narrowed into the starry distance, an interstellar runway to the Milky Way.

Celebrating the aurora

The poles, bleak and desolate though they may be, offer an unrivaled beauty. Most people know of aurora, even if they haven't seen it, and associate it with the far north as the northern lights, the aurora borealis. Some are even aware of the aurora australis, the northern lights' southern sister, but who knows of diamond dust, of blue ice, of moondogs, ice fumaroles, or, by far the most amazing thing I've ever seen, polar nacreous clouds.

It was mid-August, near the end of the Antarctic winter. I hadn't seen the sun for over three months. This was the coldest part of the year. I was standing on the roof of the Arrival Heights lab—McMurdo's equivalent to TAWO—watching strangely flowing clouds blanket the northern horizon like smooth, wavy brushstrokes of gently rolling seas. Too smooth, too flowing, as though they had been polished to perfection. But it wasn't the unique shape of these clouds that had me glued in place, awestruck, despite the bitter cold. They were iridescent neon, gleaming opaline, radiant pastel, mother-of-pearl; a million words couldn't describe their million hues. They were a fine sheen of oil on a calm puddle, rainbow-swirling a slow and seductive hula dance on their own private island of sunlight, a sunlight far too skyward for surface-fettered eyes to see, and they wildly illuminated the polar night.

The smooth brushstrokes and intense coloration of nacreous clouds

I didn't notice the cold. I didn't notice the wind. I didn't notice that I was no longer standing but kneeling. I don't even know how long I was out there. To this day I've seen nothing so spectacular.[13]

Nacreous clouds brightening an Antarctic winter

~

Joyously Breathtaking, Sadly Destructive

McMurdo Station, Antarctica
Sunday, August 17, 2008

Over the past week, Mother Nature has repeatedly showcased one of her most resplendent offerings. A cloud. Not a common cloud; a high-altitude cloud of pure ice crystals. A stratospheric cloud.

The earth's atmosphere is classified into regions according to temperature. Going up from the surface, the temperature drops through the first region—the troposphere. This is where the vast majority of clouds reside. Above the troposphere is the strato-

---

13 Years later I was hit with a powerful nostalgia for this moment while watching *Antarctica: A Year on Ice*, a film created by Antz Powell, a fellow McMurdo winter-over. Antz captured the same day in beautiful time-lapse photography. The film does an incredible job conveying the feeling of extended living in Antarctica. If you come across it, keep an eye out for yours truly: I'm the one in the red parka.

sphere, which starts as a cold layer. Continuing up, the temperature increases through the stratosphere, decreases again in the mesosphere, and then increases dramatically in the thermosphere and on into space.

What? you say. *Space is hot?* Well, not exactly. Space itself is very cold; it's a void, nearly, and heat will rapidly radiate away from any unfortunate particles that find themselves there. However, unlike Earth, those particles have no atmosphere or magnetosphere to protect them from solar radiation, which can heat them to thousands of degrees. So, space is ridiculously cold in the shade and ludicrously hot in the sun. It's a summer day that you just can't win.

But I don't want to talk about space, I want to talk about the ozone layer, so I'm going to talk about clouds. Trust me, it will all come together.

There are clouds that sometimes form above the troposphere, in the cold layer of the lower stratosphere. They are called nacreous clouds, and they require particularly frigid conditions. For that reason, they occur only near the poles, and only in the winter. They are much more common in the Antarctic than the Arctic, but I'll get to that later.

Nacreous clouds are spectacular to behold. Their rainbow appearance is a result of sunlight diffracting through ice crystals. Because nacreous clouds occur at a higher altitude than most clouds, they reflect that sunlight down to areas where the sun is still well below the horizon, making the clouds appear extremely bright—especially if you've just endured a polar winter. This intense luminance, combined with their full-spectrum coloration, makes them unique and stunning.

But, as every silver lining has its touch of grey, the gloomy side to these fascinating clouds is that they play a large role in ozone depletion. Yet the clouds are not to blame. In fact, nacreous clouds are documented in the diaries of early Antarctic winter-over groups over one hundred years ago, long before the onset of ozone depletion.

First of all, what is ozone? Ozone is just oxygen, in a less common (and less stable, and not breathable) form: O_3 instead of O_2. It resides primarily in the stratosphere and does a fantastic job of absorbing ultraviolet radiation from the sun, preventing us—and all the other plants and critters—from adverse effects like skin cancer or death. (No joke! If you're just a little phytoplankton floating on the vast sea, a little too much ultraviolet light and *pfft*, you're dead!)

What's happening to ozone? It boils down to airborne chemicals that act as ozone depletion catalysts, which means they are able to break down ozone without being altered themselves. Chlorofluorocarbons (CFCs) are a great example. A single CFC molecule can degrade hundreds of thousands of ozone molecules before it is itself removed from the atmosphere.

So, how do nacreous clouds fit in? Well, complex chemicals like CFCs have to be broken down before they can react with ozone. On the surface of nacreous cloud particles, this happens much faster than it would normally. So the clouds aren't actually depleting ozone themselves, they're just speeding up the breakdown of chemicals that subsequently deplete ozone. One of the resultant gases of CFC breakdown is chlorine monoxide (ClO), which builds up in the stratosphere during the Antarctic winter. When the sun returns to the Antarctic, the ultraviolet light breaks ClO apart into Cl and O. Then the loose chlorine atom reacts with ozone like this:

$$Cl + O_3 \rightarrow ClO + O_2$$

Ozone gets turned into ClO and oxygen. Sunlight breaks apart the ClO—again—and with the same chlorine atom, the process repeats, and repeats, and repeats, and repeats, and repeats.

But why doesn't this happen in the Arctic, too? It does, but to a lesser degree. This is because nacreous clouds are more common in the Antarctic. There is a clear circumnavigation of open ocean around Antarctica, where an unbroken wall of wind wraps around the continent. This wall forms an atmospheric barrier called the polar vortex. It separates the air over Antarctica from the air swirling around the rest of the planet, and it allows the Antarctic to become considerably colder than the Arctic. In the Arctic, landmasses contribute to atmospheric mixing, bringing in warmer air from lower latitudes, so nacreous clouds are less likely to form.

Can we just have the short version, please? Yes. During the Antarctic winter, when the polar vortex is strongest, nacreous clouds form. They break down airborne chemicals into little ozone-depletion machines. When the sun returns to the region, the machines turn on and chomp a big hole in the ozone layer within the vortex. Then the warmth of the sun breaks down the vortex, the barrier dissolves, the nacreous clouds disappear, and the ozone hole mixes with the rest of the earth's atmosphere, thinning the ozone layer everywhere.

But hey, at least there are pretty clouds to look at.

～

What will this polar ice cap present next to dazzle me? Maybe there are better auroras to come, or perhaps a multifaceted moondog? I'd love to see one of those. Either way, I'm content to ride the high from today's light show for a while. It's energizing.

Day 16
Monday, November 19

To my pleasant surprise, the beauty continues. Overnight, an incredible layer of crystalline hoarfrost descended on everything. Under the waxing moonlight of day, every surface reflected a million pinpricks of light back to the eye. The flagpoles all had a thick new coat of sparkling white feathers, layered upon layers. Up close, the ice took on the unlikely form of a moth's soft antennae, and even fluttered to life under my breath. It only took a moderate touch to dislodge these delicate fractals. And though they were beautiful, the compelling childlike joy of dispersing dandelion seeds with a kick was also in the freeing of frost's grip.

The small guylines holding the TAWO tower were so thickly frosted that they were as big around as a softball in spots. That is, until Neal reached them—the same childlike joy also compelled him, it seems. While he clung to the top of the tower with one hand, cleaning a solid white mass of instruments and air intakes with a long-handled brush in the other, I snapped photos of an intensely pastel sky.

Our home on the ice can be astonishingly colorful. Perhaps the monochromaticity of a frosty-white world lends extra brilliance to what color there is. Or maybe it's the pureness of the air, or a combination of the cold and the altitude, or the result of my eyes growing accustomed to the dark. Whatever it is, the way the midday northern sky blends upward in solid bands from deep baby blue to soft pink to pale and pure white is an expecting mother's dream.

This earth is an amazing place. These polar wonders have brought me solidly and thankfully back to the here and now after a couple of emotional days. It's good to be reminded of why I'm

The pastels of dusk over Summit Station

here, why I come to these places that keep me apart from friends and family, why I go on these crazy adventures: to encounter the world and all its gifts. I get to see marvels that many people don't even know exist, and I wouldn't trade what I've experienced for anything.

Introduction

In which I address you, the reader, directly, thus stepping briefly out of the narrative and forever outside the box of literary norms.

Hola! Mucho gusto.[14] Call me Rex. No, it's not my real name, but it's the name most people call me these days. It's a nickname pinned to an ice person by ice people. In some ways, it's the person I became while living in Antarctica. But none of that matters. I'm introducing myself now—and probably breaking several important rules of authorship, damn them all—so I can clarify a few things and paint this picture more fully. There is a colorful fringe to this white backdrop that will help you understand just how the hell these five muppets[15] came to be sitting intentionally

---

14   This is how you say "pleased to meet you" when in Mexico.

15   This is how you say "moron" or "idiot" when in Britain or a Commonwealth nation. I once knew a Kiwi[15a] who had earned the nickname "Muppet" for crashing an ambulance.

15a This is how you say "New Zealander" when just about anywhere, except maybe in the produce aisle.[15b]

15b This is how you nest a footnote inside a footnote that's already nested inside another footnote, thus confusing the shit out of your word-processing software, and possibly your readers. Sorry about that.

on top of the Greenland ice cap, knowing that a long, dark, frigid winter was on its way.

I guess I need to start with the white backdrop, the big picture, which actually means I need to start on the other side of the planet, because for many, if not most, the road to Summit Station begins in Antarctica. Not to worry, it will all make a strange sort of sense in the end.

Antarctica. No one nation owns or controls it. It's shared. Everyone plays nice. The continent is governed by the Antarctic Treaty, signed initially in 1959 to protect Antarctica as a "natural reserve, devoted to peace and science." Mining of mineral resources is expressly prohibited, as is any military presence—unless in direct support of science—creating a cooperative haven for peace, the environment, and scientific research. In a way, it is an international utopia.

Currently the treaty has over fifty signatory nations, but in order to have a say in the governance of the continent, a country must be "conducting substantial research activity there." This limits the field to about thirty countries that maintain approximately ninety research stations among them. Of these about forty stations are year-round, the remaining being manned only in the austral summer. All these stations are spread throughout the continent, though most are on or near the coast. They come in all sizes, ranging from six to two hundred people in the summer—McMurdo Station being the exceptional outlier at over one thousand—and they thin to a skeleton crew or no one at all during the winter.

One of the common misconceptions is that these temporary Antarctic residents are all scientists, but the majority are not; they're mechanics and cooks and managers and carpenters and logistics personnel of all sorts. I would guess that only a quarter of Antarcticans are actual scientists, even fewer if you don't count their students and lackeys.

My job is closer to the science end of the spectrum than most nonscientists. I'm a science liaison. I directly support many science projects, but I have no direct organizational association with any of the scientists. My position is an option on a proposal to do research in Antarctica. A scientist may request a field camp, or helicopter support, or lab equipment, or a technician to monitor and occasionally calibrate their *ometer*—that's me.

In the case of the United States Antarctic Program, here's how it works: The National Science Foundation runs the show. They hire a logistics company to perform the show, often some big military contractor, and this company provides all the necessary support so the scientific research can happen. It's a huge undertaking. It means air and sea support, utilities, communications, food and housing, transportation, medical services, construction, waste removal, field support—everything you would need to run a small town, and more. My job falls under this umbrella.

The workers performing these roles are typically contracted for a single season, meaning a summer or a winter. Thus, in Antarctic parlance, "contract" and "season" are interchangeable. In the US Program, no one stays "on the ice" longer than about a year. There are requirements that you take a break.

On the scientific side, the National Science Foundation is also running the show, essentially deciding what research will be conducted and awarding grants to those who will conduct it. Areas of study run the gamut: biology, astronomy, geology, oceanography, meteorology, volcanology, paleoclimatology, glaciology—basically, all the *ologies*.

The story in the Arctic is logistically the same, but the lands there are all part of one nation or another, so politically, it's different. The US has its own stations in Alaska and works with other nations—including Greenland, Canada, and Russia—to do research on foreign Arctic soil. The National Science Foundation still heads the monster, pulling the strings behind another contracted logistics company, and the same substantial infrastructure is necessary to support the research. Again, most of the station residents are worker bees like me, and a smaller percentage are scientists. Really, the major difference between the Arctic and Antarctic Programs is scale, which is why the more expansive Antarctic Program is a typical gateway to working in the Arctic.

So that's the backdrop; the easy, factual bit. The colorful fringe won't be so straightforward. Explaining it would be impossible so I can only dance around it, suggesting its vague outline through my own experience. Perhaps you'll get a glimpse of what it's all about, if it's about anything.

To work at the ends of the earth requires an adventurous spirit, and the people you meet there generally share this trait, plus a pinch of crazy and a sprinkle of quirky. They are a random group who don't fit the standard mold, but they are also part of a club, of sorts. They've all wandered down the same peculiar side alley, driven by curiosity. Down that alley they found an eccentric door that said, to their surprise, "Come on in." Those with the requisite minimum of adventurousness entered, without knowing that stepping through that door would permanently enroll them in the club.

Through the door is a subculture at the least, and a foreign culture in some ways. In general, the patrons of this club are talented and outgoing, curious and witty, lively and open-minded. Above all, they are simply outside the box of societal norms, and damned comfortable there. It's this combination of ingenuity and oddity that makes the people of Antarctica shine.

Many people ask me how I found my way into that atypical club: "How did you end up *there*?" they say. The simple answer is by word of mouth. Metaphorically speaking, I was handed a flyer with directions to the door. This seems to be the case for most: you meet someone who has been, the idea intrigues you, and off you go. But the simplicity of that reasoning falls short of satisfaction. The true answer lies behind the intrigue, and to get to the bottom of that is a challenge. It requires the question to morph— it must become the question that I sometimes ask myself: " *Why* did I go to Antarctica?"

I've spent some time considering this, and I'm still not able to pin down any defining moment or specific juncture in my life that incubated me to become Antarctic bound. When asked why he should want to climb Mount Everest, George Mallory is famously quoted as answering, "Because it's there." His answer suggests that there is no reason, or at least no logical one. The reason is emotional. The reason is *desire*, a feeling whose motivation wears a multitude of guises: glory, achievement, fortune, enjoyment, or simple curiosity. So I must regress, subtly adjusting the question again, this time to ask: "Why did I *desire* to go to Antarctica?"

For me, the answer falls somewhere between enjoyment and curiosity. The enjoyment is rooted in adventure, and curiosity is what plucked me from the main road. *Antarctica*, the flyer said, *wildly different and interesting . . . an ambiance unlike any other . . . exotic vehicles! . . . warm beverages!* The idea piqued my desire to explore and experience a new and unique environment. It's only a partial answer though, only a shedding down to the next layer, begging yet another question: "Where did my adventurous curiosity come from?"

My first thought is that it developed over time, encouraged by experiences that each grew grander in scope than the last. Those little adventures groomed me, yet none of them were uncommon. They explored side alleys, yes, but well-trod side alleys, and surely many people have walked some combination of those side alleys without ending up in the Antarctic. But maybe they would have, given the opportunity and the right timing—and the flyer. I admit, Antarctica wasn't even a blip on my radar until it was revealed as a possibility. So maybe the answer really is as simple as *by word of mouth*, given that those words land in the right ears at the right time.

Concerning Everest, Mallory also said, "If you cannot understand that there is something in man which responds to the challenge of this mountain and goes out to meet it, that the struggle is the struggle of life itself, upward and forever upward, then you won't see why we go. What we get from this adventure is just sheer joy. And joy is, after all, the end of life. We do not live to eat and make money. We eat and make money to be able to live. That is what life means and what life is for." Mallory explains that his desire to engage Everest is "above all for the spirit of adventure to keep alive the soul of man."

For some, that "something in man," that livelihood of the soul, at some point comes alive kicking and screaming and demanding to be fed. But for others, it may slumber contently, never waking, and those folks may not see why we go.

In the end, I don't know that the reason can be truly understood. I don't know where that slice of spirited soul comes from or how it chooses who to bite and how hard. I must be satisfied that for me, the reason is simply that I am adventurous—whether that characteristic was developed or innate—and the desire to go to Antarctica was simply there when the opportunity arose. It just sounded like my kind of club.

And so I went. But what I experienced was beyond anything I could have anticipated. Unknowingly, I had been enrolled in this bizarre club where much of what I thought I knew about people no longer applied. I was suddenly surrounded by travelers and adventurers who didn't operate on the prescribed plane and who weren't afraid to be themselves. It took some time before I felt like I fit in, but eventually I realized that *everyone* fits in, or rather, "fitting in" is an element of "normal" society that is largely removed. It's a culture of inclusion. In this way, the untarnished beauty of this pristine continent is elegantly mirrored in the genuineness of its people.

But it's also more than that. Antarctica is a little like Stephen King's Overlook Hotel: it *shines*. It wills itself to become a part of anyone who goes there, and it keeps a part of them when they leave. This is the best I can describe the lasting feeling I have from my tenure there. I will always be an Antarctican, even if I never return, for Antarctica has captured a small slice of my soul—just for safe keeping—and replaced it with a connection. I feel an instant camaraderie with anyone who has spent some time on the ice. Realistically, it's a small thing to have in common, especially since Antarcticans are so diverse, but on some deeper level we share a strange and wonderful world that is known to few. I'm not sure how much of this feeling is from the location itself, or how much is from the immersion into a *ras el hanout*—a blend of the tastiest spices in the market—of free-spirited people. Antarctica is a charming, wondrous desolation peopled with colorful lively characters. It's the Muppet Show on Ice.

With that free-spirited nature comes a willingness to not only accept the pinches of crazy and sprinkles of quirky, but to encourage them, and that encouragement helps define the culture. Antarctica fosters an attitude where individuality is applauded and conformity is quietly shunned. Costumes are acceptable anytime and anywhere.[16] Facial hair can take any shape.[17] Parties have themes like crossdressing or sadomasochism or Jell-O wrestling.[18] My favorite party evolved—or devolved, depending on your perspective—into an underwear warm-water fight.[19] Despite any innuendo, these gatherings may be purely platonic, or they may not.

McMurdo Station, being exceptional in its size, presents an exaggeration of the Antarctic culture, which becomes a paradox. When the shunning of conformity is taken to an extreme, nonconformity becomes the norm, the expected. Nonconformity becomes conformity. I once entered a music festival behind a young man who complained when he was required to wear a wristband. "What's next? Are they going to make us wear uniforms?" he cried. "You already are," I told him, surveying his patchwork pants, tie-dyed Rastafarian shirt, hemp necklace, patchouli reek, and blank, realizationless stare. McMurdo can be like that, sans the stare—unless it's winter, when blank staring is

---

16 During my summer at McMurdo, the janitorial staff often had themes like *Superhero Saturday* or *Wear a Wig Wednesday*.

17 I've worn lightning bolts for sideburns and once sported a trucker's 'stache that extended below my chin, where it crossed itself and made a turn back up to become my sideburns. And if you think that's weird, then you've never seen neck beards on a crew of firemen.

18 The organization of such events at a government-owned facility—even in your private dormitory room—is a good way to get yourself fired, so some of these parties are not commonplace, and awareness of them is often not widely distributed.

19 There is no way to properly describe this without digressing down a long tangent. Maybe in *Basically Bipolar 2: The Palmer Years.*

ubiquitous. It's a campus-like town whose antics breed a college-binge feel, with a thick coat of weird.

In my experience, the smaller stations share the adventurous spirit, the acceptance, and the encouragement, but they're not so outrageous, and I like them better for it. They have a much more tightly knit feel; a cozy, warm-drinks-around-the-woodstove kind of feel, with the occasional outrageous party thrown in. Even then, nearly every face in the room belongs to someone you know intimately, keeping that family vibe.

It's a matter of opinion, really. I like the smaller stations better, but some people prefer the larger population, where there's a lot more going on. What remains consistent are those traits that have everyone there thinking that going to Antarctica is a fun idea. Through those similarities, large station or small, ultimately everyone tends to get along. There are exceptions, of course, but that too is accepted. It's a good-natured culture where one thing is true: you'll be perfectly welcome to be yourself, no matter how strange you or anyone else thinks you are.

Perhaps I'm painting a magical picture of the harshest of continents, but in reality, it's not for everyone. The baggage you bring may be mitigated or intensified, and more likely the latter. A few people step off the plane, rub their eyes for a confirmatory glance, turn around, and get right back on the plane.[20] Some decide early on that Antarctica is not for them, but they manage to withstand a summer season and don't return. Everyone must draw a line in the snow. I think these are the people who find themselves straddling their own personal line, and though it may be drawn further afield than many, it does not quite reach the Antarctic. Yet like sand washing clean with the tide, snow washes clean with the wind, and lines can be redrawn.

Many who find themselves in Antarctica become attached to it —or maybe it's more fitting to say that Antarctica becomes attached to them. Like I said, it gets in your soul, man. These folks will return for a number of seasons and eventually move on. I

---

20   That's the rumor anyway, but I'll get to rumors later . . .

tried to fit into this category. At the end of six years doing polar contracts, I decided it just wasn't sustainable for me. I grew tired of the repetition and the limitations. I began to crave something new. I got island fever. But I found it isn't long before the white continent is tugging at your coattails, like a stray puppy that, try as you might, you just can't seem to abandon.

Perhaps I'll find myself in the final category of Antarctican. These are people going for the lifetime achievement award. Some are happy returning year after year to the same job. Some take a full-time position at the headquarters in Denver and only deploy occasionally. Others change it up by taking different positions or applying to different Antarctic stations or field camps, or by mixing in contract work at other research locations like Toolik Lake in Alaska, Palmyra Atoll in Hawaii, or Summit Station. This is how Summit comes to be filled with Antarctic contractors. It is a colony, or territory, if you will, of the Antarctic worker's nation. It's a hot spot for a change of scenery despite the ironic fact that the scenery is the same.

So, I hope I've parted the drapes enough to provide a glimpse of why we go. As this polar tale unfolds, I hope you get a not-*too*-frightful view into the mind of someone who is intrigued by places like Antarctica or the Greenland ice cap. I encourage you to imagine a slew of like-minded intrepids all gathered together and isolated from the arguably saner part of the world. We are that little group of kids on the fringe. We are the goths, the burnouts, the vocationals, the scouts, the art club, the cycling team. We are the anglers unwilling to cast our line in the main stream. I hope you're imagining mayhem, but I hope you're also imagining creativity and vivacity and unconventionality. That's Antarctica. And by proxy, Summit Station as well.

SO THERE WE were, five muppets sitting intentionally on top of the Greenland ice cap, knowing that a long, dark, frigid winter was on its way.

5

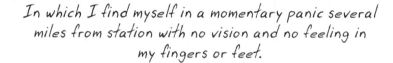

In which I find myself in a momentary panic several miles from station with no vision and no feeling in my fingers or feet.

Day 17
Tuesday, November 20

I have a sporadic twitch in my left eyelid. It's been coming and going for several days. The internet says: malnutrition, fatigue, stress, or nervous system disease. I'm banking on fatigue, or maybe some lingering turnover stress—anything but nervous system disease. Turnover wrecked me, and I'm still waiting for a recovery that doesn't seem to be coming. Instead I've grown more tired.

Adding to my malaise, the arctic air is incredibly dry and sucks the moisture right from my skin. My lips have dried out, as have my airway and nasal passage. I wake up in the night to the sound of whistling, which turns out to be my own breathing through drywalled supersnot. I found a humidifier in the linen closet and set it up in my room. I'm not sure if it's helping. In fact, I'm pretty sure it's not helping because last night the water drained out inexplicably and drenched the only clean socks I have left, forcing me to reuse dirty socks, which, in addition to being icky, for some reason just aren't as warm. There's a saying in the polar regions: change your socks, change your attitude. And it's true. So true.

So after a long day of recycled socks, I shifted my attention to the runner-up means of attitude adjustment: alcohol. The Phase 1 beer didn't last long, leaving us dry, which contrary to the socks, is not a good thing. The boys have pushed to brew our own as quickly as possible, so we already have two five-gallon batches in the works. It will take several weeks from brewing to drinking, so if we want to be the ones imbibing the reward it only makes sense to front-load this cheerful chore. Unlike the Antarctic Program, where alcohol is frowned upon yet copious, and brewing is now strictly forbidden, at Summit we're allowed to brew. Polar Field Services encourages us to use brewing equipment and a stash of brew kits left behind by a previous contractor. It's a refreshing change, though I don't understand the discrepancy since it all falls under the same government agency, ultimately. Perhaps drinking is just less problematic here than it has been at the Antarctic research stations.

I've become the station brewmaster, having the most experience with homebrewing. Don is eager to help and I'm glad to have it, even though I've found that I can be lazy in my technique. One of the nice things about brewing in a frozen wasteland is that contamination is of little concern. After boiling, when the beer is at its most vulnerable, I can just set it outside with the lid off to cool down so I can pitch in the yeast. Anywhere else that would earn you a sour beer fermented by wild yeast—that is, if something worse doesn't take hold first and ruin it altogether. I've figured out that cooling the beer outside at -40°F takes exactly an hour and a half.

Today I was checking on our second batch as it bubbled away in the fermenter and for no reason I can come up with, the gurgling heartbeat was making me giggle. Neal caught me and said, "That's right up there with the stenographer you keep hearing. How's that eye twitch?"

It's a lighthearted and mutual friendship of heckling, so I get to laugh blatantly at Neal too. I smile whenever he hits his head on the cooking pots that hang from the wood beams above the galley. "At least they give," he says.

Neal's total lack of grace on skis is even more comical. "I'm a snowboarder," is his excuse. There are no "light" boots his size in gear issue, so he has to ski the bamboo forest in his expedition boots, which don't fit in the chintzy one-size-doesn't-fit-all ski bindings. The plastic side tabs meant to contain his overwide boot toes have broken off in the cold, and his skis flop about willy-nilly. It's a solid excuse for his clumsiness on them, but I still laugh when he falls over.

We skied the bamboo forest today and by the time we finished it, neither of us was laughing; we were simply cold. This is true every time we tackle the grid of bamboo poles, and we're always in a hurry to return. We finish skiing the forest opposite the corner we start it, opposite the packed path that leads back to the MSF. On our return, rather than ski around the forest to the path, it's quicker to ski straight back toward the Green House, across a wide-open stretch of unmarked, seldom-trod snow. After two hours of trying to write down numbers with increasingly cold fingers, I'll take the shortcut every time. So far, on every return voyage there comes a point when the snow beneath my feet says *wop!* as though the Masters of Krikkit[21] have arrived. A tiny yet horrifying drop causes me to jump and shudder as a subsurface layer of snow collapses. I imagine it's a miniature version of what it feels like to be in an earthquake, unable to trust the ground beneath your feet. It may happen several times on the way back to the Green House, but even when I'm expecting it, it still scares the shit out of me. Sometimes the *wop!* is followed by the sound of snow collapsing away from my feet and into the distance, much like a soft tearing of paper.

I finally looked it up, the bamboo forest. Our operating procedure—which we continue to kludge our way through, learning

---

21   Just another *Hitchhiker's* reference. If it doesn't make sense to you, don't worry about it. In fact, you might as well get settled into the nonsense now because it's only likely to get worse as the winter befuddles my mind.

still-unfamiliar monthly tasks—says:

> *An important issue for all the investigations regarding*
> *the relationship between the composition of atmosphere*
> *and snow here at Summit is the timing of snowfall, and*
> *how much it is redistributed by wind or lost by sublima-*
> *tion. The bamboo forest was established so that accumu-*
> *lation could be measured frequently. We request weekly,*
> *but use common sense and wait for decent weather.*

Today's weather was indeed decent. Another gorgeous day for
outside work, and perfectly calm, which was good because the
temperature dropped back into the fifties and the slightest puff of
wind would have been miserable. While we skied the forest the
temperature continued to drop, but it was still enjoyable, despite
the inevitable cold fingers. We were graced by a soft predawn
light illuminating the low southern clouds in a road-cone orange.
Though the sun no longer breaches the horizon, the midday
almost-sunrise is still long and lingering.

Already our "day" is surprisingly short and dim; we only get a
handful of hours that fade from dark to dusk and back. Full night
dominates from 2 p.m. to 9 a.m. Even at midday, when this icy
world is at its struggling brightest, the night will not be driven out
completely. That deep blue band settles low in the northern sky
like a shifted horizon: the earth's shadow on its own atmosphere.
Above that, the soft rosy layer wants not for rays from the golden
orb. Those shimmering ambassadors of day are zipping by still,
above our heads and just out of reach.

Day 18
Wednesday, November 21

We've become very comfortable with each other in a short
period of time. It's clear that none of us is easily offended and
political correctness is unnecessary, which leaves no joke off the
table. We're all at ease knowing that we can spout off whatever
nonsense comes to our lips and are likely to be met with encouraging laughter, if not further nonsense. Perhaps this is aided by

the fact that we're all guys.

Neal: "So when was the last time they had an all-male phase here?"

Phil: "Well, somebody posed that question at the start of the season, but I never heard an answer. It's been a long while."

Neal: "We should tell them it's a bad idea."

Phil: "But what if there was one girl, and two people really liked her but only one got to sleep with her?"

Neal: "That'd be one happy guy." Neal is always the optimist. "Or girl. Actually, that would be the worst: two girls and they're both lesbians!"

Don: "And then we couldn't make gay jokes."

Phil: "Oh, that would depend on how radical they are. I've heard more filthy gay jokes from gays."

Lance: "That's where I get all my good gay jokes!"

Neal: "You know, my first winter at Pole, there were no available women. But there *were* women, and it made it better. It was nice because it was a balance."

Don: "Are you saying you wish one of us was a woman?"

Neal: "Absolutely."

Lance: "Neal wishes all of us were women!"

Me: "Sounds like a good balance."

Lance: "Yeah, for Neal!"

Me: "Unless we were all lesbians. How much would *that* suck!"

Neal: "In that case I don't think there would be any sucking at all."

WE'VE BEEN WAITING for an appropriate day to do the ICESat transect. That means following a long zigzagging route on snow machines while recording GPS points and stopping to measure bamboo poles. The data we collect provide ground truthing for a NASA satellite that is meant to measure ice-sheet elevation changes.

We need particularly good weather to do ICESat because it's time consuming—in other words, bone-chilling—and it requires us to travel several miles away from station—in other words, it's sketchy in the wintertime. The weather has not cooperated until now. Last week visibility hampered us; this week, calm northerly winds, which at first seems like an odd restriction. We're given a range of wind directions and a minimum air speed that define when we can collect air and snow samples and when we can operate vehicles. Outside those criteria, the samples are likely to be contaminated by exhaust from the station. I'm not sure I agree with the vehicle restriction, since we don't also turn off the generators, but those are the guidelines. So, ICESat has been on hold.

The delay has given Don time to fix the Tucker, or at least get it into a state that it can pass as our emergency vehicle. We don't have the parts to repair it—a common problem for a remote station; there can be no visits to the local parts store—so Don just disconnected the broken bit: the front differential. The Tucker will work, but now it's only two-wheel drive, or rather, two-track drive. It's an interesting vehicle, looking like a giant mechanized bug: two large windows facing forward, surrounded by an excessive number of headlights, and a box-shaped cabin sitting atop a framework of appendages that end in four triangular tracks and a serrated plow.

The Tucker is our rescue vehicle should we become stranded during the ICESat transect. A few miles from station may not seem far, but in a place like this it's a potentially dangerous distance, especially in the winter. We bring a slew of safety equipment: two personal locator beacons, two satellite phones, a handheld GPS, a transponder that regularly transmits our location back to station, and two survival bags, all packed into a safety-orange "polypod" trailer that doubles as an emergency shelter. All this considerably outnumbers the equipment required for the scientific aspect of the transect, which basically boils down to a yardstick, some snow sampling bags, and a fancy GPS receiver.

Neal and I headed out immediately after breakfast to capitalize on what little light is available. We were each on our own snow machine. Neal wielded the yardstick. I towed the polypod. We followed the skiway to its south end, then made a right into unmaintained territory where the terrain is bumpy and cumbersome. Though our world appears flat and smooth in all directions, the surface is wind-carved into jagged yet strangely flowing furrows called sastrugi: snowy corrugations frozen in place and defying the laws of gravity by overhanging themselves while appearing soft and dispersible. They're not, which isn't much fun, but the extremely cold, hardened snow squeaks as you walk—again, remarkably like Styrofoam—which *is* fun.

We followed a sparse flag line about a mile out to a seemingly forsaken weather station where we took snow samples, an excellent way to pre-chill the extremities before a long day outside. It was cold. Extremely cold. Sixty degrees.[22] At temperatures like that it's easy to get frostnip, and you have to pay close attention to any exposed skin. Even skin that is covered can nip, especially if it's touching a wet gaiter that's freezing through. The warnings are not obvious. At first your skin feels very cold and uncomfortable, but you've gotten used to that so it's easy to ignore. Next it gets tingly and even a tiny bit painful. This moment is key; the sensation is subtle but extremely important to notice because the next step is numbness, and if your skin is numb, you'll have no idea that it's freezing solid. I like to touch questionable areas with something icy. If I can feel the cold, it's fine; if not, it's time for a buddy check.

Neal, his rig much snappier without the polypod in tow, raced ahead to the next flag and measured its height. I followed, pulling as close to the bamboo as possible to get an accurate GPS reading

---

22   I didn't know it, but I was about to endure the most miserably uncomfortable three hours of my life.

while writing Neal's measurement on a form. The ICESat flags are spaced just distant enough that they're difficult to see in low light, so the form also served as a map, telling me which flags to turn at, and in what direction.

Our forward motion, though slow, transformed a calm, bitter day into an absolutely frigid one. As my breath collected in frozen form over my general head-and-shoulders area, I began playing the unconquerable goggle game. I discovered that stuffing my goggles inside my parka caused a worrisome chill to my core without actually defrosting the goggles. Eventually I gave up, parking the goggles high on my forehead and peering through the narrowest slit between my hat and neck gaiter. I decided that if the exposed skin around my eyes could feel the freezing airflow across it, then it was okay. I risked it to alleviate the frustration, which was mounting on top of an increasing discomfort. I was getting miserably cold already, and we were only halfway through.

Neal kept his goggles on, though they were thoroughly frosted over by the midway point, and I could see by his erratic path to the next flag that he was almost blind. When I crashed into him, the absurdity of our situation hit home. A difficult bit of sastrugi near a flag caused my machine to swerve and tilt so badly that I instinctively bailed, leapt right off. It wasn't a choice but a reaction, probably deeply ingrained from years of mountain biking: if you're going down, get the hell away from the bike. My machine righted itself right into the right of Neal's machine while I rolled alongside him to his left. I would say he looked surprised, but who could tell?

My machine was left straddling the flag and needed to reverse, but with the weight of the polypod behind it the treads just dug a hole. We had to lift the front end and drag it straight with the skis angled to clear the flag. It was tough work and actually warmed us up a bit. That's when Neal admitted that he had been relying entirely on me for navigation up to that point, and we both had a solid, much-needed laugh.

Since we were stopped, it was a good time to test the satellite phones, which Phil had requested we do. I was oddly excited about this, having never used a satellite phone before. But that first-time use would have to wait. One of our two phones was inaccessible inside its case, which was frozen shut. The other phone turned on but didn't have the will to make a call and promptly turned itself back off. It didn't like the cold either. If I could, I would have done the same.

Before heading off again, while my mood was still light, I took a moment to absorb a panoramic view of the infinite white desolation. It was a perfectly clear day with endless visibility. Overhead, the brighter stars were just visible in the twilight. To the south, a long flat white blended into a horizontal band of gold. To the north, a long flat white was capped by blue and pink pastels. To the east and west, a long flat white only. In every direction, nothing. Absolutely nothing. Not a hill or even a rise, simply snow and sky. It is a surreal and surprisingly harmonious sensation to be engulfed in emptiness. It's a reminder that we're only little things in this big world, yet in a strange way I also felt more connected. *It's just you and me, buddy*, I thought to the world.

The warmth of physical work wore off quickly, and as we continued the transect I became colder and colder. I was wearing four thick layers of clothing, expedition boots, and large fuzzy mittens with two hand warmers in each. The warmers are only helpful for about twenty minutes, and despite replacing them my hands were uncomfortably cold. I could barely feel my fingers, cheeks, and feet. I continually wiggled my toes, hoping to increase blood flow. I had to put my goggles back on simply for the small warmth they provided my face. By the end of the transect my feet were frighteningly numb and my goggles, needless to say, were frosted over.

At that point we were about four miles from station. The twilight was darkening rapidly but for the fortune of a half-moon. We struggled to see through the goggle haze as we turned toward station, and after only a short time we lost the flag line.

I felt suddenly desolate, as though stranded on a featureless and inhospitable planet. Not just inhospitable, but hostile. We were surrounded by nothingness with no flags to orient us while light and warmth were being expeditiously squeezed out. I pushed back against a brief panic. We stopped to assess the situation and clear our vision.

"We should probably radio station and tell them we're lost," Neal said with a touch of sarcasm that belied our circumstances.

"Yeah," I agreed as he pulled his radio from his hip.

"Shit. It's dead. I should've had it inside my jacket." The cold kills batteries, no matter their charge level.

"Hang on, let me try mine." I didn't want to dig out my radio. It meant removing a mitten to unzip my parka—two entrances for the cold. And it was fruitless; I couldn't raise station from that distance anyway. We were on our own.

"Well, this is why we carry a GPS." Neal was levelheaded, and that was a comfort. But the handheld GPS was of no use to us. It appeared to turn on, but the screen only displayed gibberish. It was too cold.

That was it; we had no other means of knowing where station was. We would have to keep going in a straight line and hope we got into radio range without missing station altogether. It was a risky prospect.

Then, much to my relief, Neal noticed the red blinking light atop the 50-meter tower, now distant and low on the horizon. He suggested that we didn't need the flag line or the GPS. Thank God it was such a clear day.

We continued in that general direction, unable to see the red light with our goggles back on. Nor could we see the striation of the surface, which forced a slow pace and provided occasionally unpleasant jolts and drops. I could barely see Neal in my periphery, a dark blur between a fuzzy headlight and taillight. We kept our distance from each other, knowing that we wouldn't see a collision coming.

As the freeze penetrated deeper, I continued to become more uncomfortable. At first, we stopped every few minutes to scrape the frost from our goggles and check our heading, but that was chilling and time consuming and I was growing more and more concerned about my numb feet. We both wanted to be indoors by the quickest method possible, so we discontinued our frequent stops, choosing instead to let our goggles freeze entirely and drive blindly on. For the remaining miles I could see nothing but a fuzzy-bright nimbus where the moon should be. This became my lighthouse beacon in the blind night: by holding it at eleven o'clock was I able to maintain my heading. I only stopped at long intervals to quickly check for the little red light and that Neal was reasonably nearby. At least there was nothing to run into out there.

When we finally reached station, Don and Lance commandeered our snow machines, saying simply, "We'll take it from here. Get inside." It was -65°F. There were hot drinks waiting, and I sat wrapped around mine like a prisoner over his meal until the feeling returned to my fingers. Then I changed my socks. My feet were bright pink—alive, though I still couldn't feel them. I took off my balaclava and innermost neck gaiter, but my thin outer gaiter had frozen into a solid ring that I couldn't fit over my head and had to knead before I could remove it. Neal's gaiter had frozen against his skin, leaving him with a stripe of frostnip from the tip of his nose to his left eye. My feet remained numb for an hour.

Most of our electronic safety measures failed: the satellite phones, Neal's radio, the handheld GPS. Phil stopped receiving breadcrumbs from our transponder about midway through the transect. It's possible that our personal locator beacons were still operational, but I doubt it, given the sad state of the rest of our electronics. Besides, *if* one were to power up, and *if* it were to get a GPS signal *and* a satellite connection to the outside world, our location would be transmitted back to station via our spotty internet uplink. In fact, I'm going to go ahead and say that the personal locator beacons didn't work either. Hell, my goggles didn't even work. The only thing that did work was the fancy GPS receiver in the polypod, which is stored in an insulated case with several bottles of hot water and powered by a hefty marine battery. Unfortunately, it's useless as a safety measure because we have no way to access the data in the field. But if it came to it, I guarantee you I'd be trying to rewire that marine battery to anything and everything. Even if I only succeeded in lighting something on fire it would be a win.

That was the most miserably uncomfortable three hours of my life.

The kicker, the *real* kicker, is that the satellite we're supposed to be ground truthing for was deorbited two years ago. It no longer exists. The damn thing has crashed into the ocean.

6

In which we get settled into the routine and our conversation becomes a little too comfortable.

Day 19
Thursday, November 22

It's thirty degrees warmer today, which is irksome after yesterday's ridiculous escapade. Not that I'd want to do ICESat in twenty-knot winds, freezing fog, blowing snow, and practically no visibility at all, but still, it's thirty degrees warmer. The temperature swings here are wild, and there's a direct correlation with storms. We'd love to do our outside chores on warmer days but those days are exclusively shitty with intolerably high winds and penetrating snow. The calmest, clearest, and deceivingly most pleasant days are by far the coldest.

Today was a nice warm maelstrom, so, like the century of Antarctic explorers before me, I put on my cold weather gear and bravely forged through the desolate and unforgiving wasteland. Sheets of snow whipped across my vision in thick pours, giving only an occasional view of the flag line I was attempting to follow. I stumbled over drifts and fell into furrows that weren't there ten minutes ago. The windward side of my clothing developed rigor mortis while the deathly cold probed every weakness. I fought the harshly blowing haze of suspended ice all the way to a warm kitchen where a home-cooked meal awaited me.

It's Thanksgiving, a good day for a storm. Lance and Don prepped the bird, stuffing it to overflow with our dwindling freshie supply, which is going bad quicker than we can prepare it. We suspect much of it froze on the tarmac back in Iceland while the flights were delayed; it likely sat in the plane for three days. The green beans arrived looking deadish and covered in brown spots. The carrots turned black on the outside and soft in the middle. Most of the milk was separated.

A week ago Don "salvaged" the wilting—and by then lightly moldy—green beans, but none of the rest of us would touch them. "They're okay!" he claimed jovially, but we weren't convinced. In an effort to save the remaining carrots of probable edibility, Neal made an orange meal of carrot soup and sweet potato burritos. That was when Don's nonfascination with excrement became known.

"Our poo will all be colorful!" he exclaimed broad-smiled as we dished up. This coming after a couple of similar comments earlier in the day, he made it a point later to assure me that he's not obsessed.

I wouldn't say that poo conversations are the norm at these stations, but I wouldn't say that they're discouraged either. Like much else, they are accepted. These are uninhibited folks. In fact, just before my first trip to Antarctica, while having my last meal in New Zealand, a total stranger—but fellow Antarctican, and that goes a long way—told the whole table all about her polyps. It was odd, to say the least. So Don's poo comments hadn't even fazed me, and his guilt emerged not in his quips but in his concern that we might think them strange. I didn't know it was possible to be both bashful and unabashed about the same topic.

It occurs to me that I haven't had a Thanksgiving or Christmas in the "real world" for many years. I suppose they're not too different here except that we don't have television for the sports fans, which doesn't bother me in the least. The meal is still emphasized, as is lounging around and enjoying the company of family, which is definitely what we have become in a short period of time. Living and working together, sharing every meal, every evening and weekend, has that effect. Contrary to becoming sick of one another, I think we're all enjoying the group dynamic. I wonder if my deployments have been lucky in this way. They've all been a little different, but the feeling of belonging to a family has been consistent, especially among the smaller populations.

While the Thanksgiving bird cooked, our temporary little family lounged patiently, drinking wine and chatting. Phil was happily making pies and whipping cream. He asked us, "How do you blokes like your cream: light and fluffy, or a little thicker and more liquid?" followed a little too closely by, "Wait a minute. Fuck you guys, I'm the one making it!"

Lance agreed. "If you don't make it, I won't have any at all!"

The feast was big and fantastic. One of the perks of wintering is that your metabolism is amped to counteract the cold, so you can gorge yourself guilt-free; it's just more fuel for the much-needed fire.

After dinner we all sat down to a movie together for the first time, our bellies too full for anything else. Don picked it from a long list on a community hard drive, surely collected over many seasons, and later decided it was awful. In a dream, the boy and girl ride a stuffed toy pony onto a boat overflowing with forest and sail off. The curtain falls.

"What the hell was that?" I said to a room with no answer.

Day 20
Friday, November 23

Next to the coffee machine in the Big House is a window through which daylight could pass, if there was any. Under the window are a few planter boxes in which small scattered sprouts reach up toward the grow light that hangs above them.

"Whatcha got growing there?" I asked as I arrived to dinner and found Phil watering.

"They're marigolds."

"Oh, that'll be nice." Having marigolds near the dinner table will be very nice. They'll be the only other living thing on this frozen rock, not to mention the welcome color and aroma they'll provide. "That's a full spectrum light, then?"

"It sure is."

"It's probably not going to be enough to stop the raging hordes of melatonin!"

"Well, it can't hurt," he said.

"True."

McMurdo had an entire room dedicated to full spectrum lights during the winter. We called it the "happy room." The idea was that the lights encourage your body into believing it's daytime, so your body slows its melatonin production. There were people who used the happy room regularly, claiming it helped elevate their mood or combat their insomnia. I found it was a nice place to sit and read now and then, but I didn't notice any changes in myself on account of it. Maybe I needed to use it more often to benefit from it. My mood remained positive enough, and my insomnia was manageable, unlike some who really struggled with it. I also had the advantage of having sole access to a remote lab facility that contained a small sitting room with a comfy bed, should I become stuck there for weather. I took more than a few afternoon naps. My circadian rhythm seemed to gravitate toward that sleep schedule, and I believe those naps helped me a lot. It became clear to me that the winter affects everyone differently, and you just have to figure out what works best for you.

More than once the subject of marijuana as a sleep aid came up. In a world where that would earn you a one-way ticket to unemployment, but also where a lot of people sorely missed their intoxicant of choice, it was no surprise. I prefer a few nice hoppy beers myself, but in hindsight it was still strange not to see the green stuff around now and then. In the cumulative three years I spent in Antarctica, I only saw weed once, and in a strange parallel with college life it was also exhaled out of a dorm-room window through a cardboard tube stuffed with dryer sheets.

The topic of marigolds and grow lights and melatonin led our current conversation to marijuana as well, and the unfortunate fact that much of the time it is considered too recreational and taboo to be taken seriously as a medicine.

Me: "I'd be surprised if we had medical marijuana in the clinic. Do we?"

Phil: "Wouldn't that be nice. I think they should issue an ounce to everybody. I'd okay watchdogging an ounce."

Neal: "That's just gonna create a black market if you stop at an ounce."

Lance: "Yeah, it'll be just like the yogurt: 'Stop using it, we have to save some for next phase.'"

Our supply of yogurt is low. At turnover, Tracy, the station operations manager, asked us to use it sparingly since there won't be any more until after Phase 3, when the summer begins. I'm not sure why yogurt isn't included with each phase's freshies, but there must be some reason. Neal has actually started making his own, since we do have our own supply of milk. I get the impression it isn't going so well though. The milk isn't behaving.

Me: "We just need a greenhouse to grow our own ganja."

Neal: "Yeah, why the hell don't we . . . we're misusing our grow light over there!"

Phil: "Well, you bring the seeds and I'll grow it, but unfortunately, that would not benefit us."

Me: "Hmm, right, wouldn't be ready in time."

Lance: "What we need is a drug dog to carry it for us. They never suspect the drug dog!"

For getting through the winter, what they should issue us are supplements for vitamin D and thyroid hormones. Still, I would settle for some pot, and I would even use it medically: to help me sleep. But with any luck, I'll have less insomnia than I did my previous winter.

Day 21
Saturday, November 24

It's hard to believe that only three weeks have elapsed since I arrived here. It seems like yesterday, but also like I've been here forever.[23] The work pace has certainly slackened since that first hellish week—though that hasn't alleviated my gasping for air every time I climb the stairs to the Big House. Some days are fuller than others, and though Sunday is our "day off," a true day off is rare. We all have duties that need to be performed daily, even if the bare minimum only takes a short time. With rounds, TAWO checks, weather observations, and the evening balloon launch, I'd say our absolute minimum workday is a little over two hours. But Neal and I have the advantage of a shared job, so we're able to trade every other Sunday off, which will be nice if I can figure out what to do with myself for a full day in the dark. I guess I'll figure that out tomorrow.

Today I seem to have spent a lot of time watching a large gravity-defying corniced drift grow outside my rapidly diminishing window. Already it's about one-third buried, helped along by the

The Big House with a mottled winter coating

23 Just like the Overlook Hotel, ominously.

storm that's been raging the past few days. The Green House has been buried in the winter before and actually has an egress hatch in the roof should the doors become barricaded. The Big House has taken on a stylish camouflage look from the recent blowing snow. The storm has been intermittent and not severe enough to halt operations, but on my walk to TAWO yesterday I could only see about six flags in either direction. Beyond that was simply blind white. Well, in the dark it's more of a blind deep blue. Despite the foul weather, it's actually kind of fun out there; the sense of where you are and the potential danger is exhilarating. Plus, at -20°F my goggles freeze more slowly.

Day 22
Sunday, November 25

~

All in the Name of Science

Summit Station, Greenland
Sunday, November 25, 2012

Welcome to TAWO, where the shroud of mystery surrounding science is pulled back to reveal a myriad of scientific instruments. Some are new and shiny, some are cobbled and clunky, some look like they belong in a B-rated 1970s sci-fi flick. Most of the equipment is atmospheric, meaning it takes samples of the clean Greenland air and examines it for particulates, trace gases, radionuclides, and other scientific stuff. It's not our job to understand the science per se but to keep the instruments running and recognize when something is amiss. Rather than bore you with the details, I'll just mention a few gizmos with fun names: the nephelometer. And that's about it.

We also take care of the meteorological instrumentation suite, which basically runs itself as long as it's free of frost, which is never. So, if kicking the tower doesn't dislodge the frost, then up we go. Well, up Neal goes, usually. I'm not fond of heights, nor do I enjoy climbing an icy tower in massive expedition boots and trying to work locking carabiners with thick gloves. A helmet is a requirement but goggles are a necessity, unless you want all that frost falling on your face and down your neck gaiter. Brr.

After we've checked that the tower is clear and all the TAWO gizmos' numbers are rightish and the proper lights are flashing, then the fun can begin. That's different from day to day . . .

We take air samples that get shipped back to NOAA and are examined for greenhouse gases and other airborne chemicals. To avoid contamination, we have to hold our breath when we're near the sampler. If you haven't tried it, you should cover yourself in thirty extra pounds of extreme cold weather gear, go to the top of your nearest 12,000-foot mountain, and hold your breath while you run ten meters, fiddle with some knobs, and run back. It's exhilarating, honest! I'm intoxicated just thinking about it.

We collect surface samples of snow and dig meter-deep pits to sample the layers accumulated over time. For this we wear clean suits and double layers of plastic lunch-lady gloves to avoid contamination. Never mind that our faces and fuzzy hoods are sticking out, and there are no clean booties big enough for these kicks.

We collect precipitation samples (if it ever precipitates, which it hasn't, at least not from overhead—only sideways).

We launch a weather balloon every evening.

We measure over a hundred bamboo poles every week.

We clean, label, and weigh a seemingly endless supply of sampling bottles.

We brush frost off optics, air intakes, wind cups, cables, gas cylinders, eyelashes.

And that's not all. We cook, we clean, we shovel snow, we shovel more snow, we "perform other duties as required . . ."

~

Day 23
Monday, November 26

I haven't heard a peep from Kira in several days. I was thinking she should have arrived in Chile by now, but I don't know. It has me frustrated after she called near tears a week ago because I wasn't being responsive enough. She seemed to think I had lost interest in her, and I still haven't figured out why. I even reread our correspondence: perfectly normal, reasonably spaced, certainly not unhappy. I still don't get it. And now I don't hear from her for days. I know she's busy, and normally it wouldn't bother me, but under the circumstances it's hypocritical. Really, I guess I just miss her, but it's still frustrating.

We're two weeks into the night now and already it's getting harder to get up in the morning. Melatonin is at large. I have to turn on my lamp and stare blankly for a minute or two before I can function. At least we don't have any super morning people; no chipper, bouncy bullshit in the early hours. Neal is alive in the morning but not bubbly. He gets up early and I often hear him on the roof while I'm still in bed. He's already dressed and clearing frost from the vents with the new broom Tracy bought in Akureyri and that he broke the next week, leaving a perfectly vent-sized handle. Lance is wide awake in the morning too, but he's already had to launch a weather balloon by the time I see him at breakfast. Don seems to start the day with an even keel, but Phil is as useless as I am. He's always trying to finish the morning meeting in under three minutes. I'm on board.

At this point we're clearly becoming well settled into the routine. Neal and I are finally comfortable with the majority of our tasking. The day-to-day stuff is simple now, and though we still have to read up on less common tasking, most of our days are much shorter. The familiar tasks take half the time they once did. This means our workday is no longer full much of the time, and I think the same is true of the rest of the gang. Our mealtimes have lengthened, and we're settling into a routine that is fairly relaxed. It's nice.

Now we can sit back and wait for our minds to settle into the winter groove, which is more of a canyon.

7

In which it is revealed that I was previously diagnosed as psychologically unfit for a polar winter.

Day 24
Tuesday, November 27

"Where are we digging this hole?" Neal asked.

"Oh, hell, I don't know. Out there somewhere." I gestured vaguely toward the TAWO door.

"You know, it's not my lack of knowledge that's holding me back, it's my ambition."

"We're agreed then. Out there somewhere, don't really care where."

We've been dreading the one-meter pit ever since finishing ICESat, when Lance said, "Wait till you do the meter pit with no gloves!" I wondered how anything could be worse than ICESat.

The meter pit is part of a snow accumulation study that relates back to the ice core drilled here at Summit in the early 1990s. That ice core, named GISP2, was the finale of the Greenland Ice Sheet Project, which began in the 1970s as an effort to understand climate history. Most of the scientific data we collect ties in with GISP2 in some way. At the time it was the deepest ice core ever recovered, providing a history of over 100,000 years. Since then, cores drilled in Antarctica have pushed the clock back as far as 800,000 years.

This historical information is available because a glacial ice cap is like a slow-moving river. The ice at the bottom started as snow at the top, thousands of years ago. That snow accumulated at the start of the river and was continually buried as fresher snow fell. As a layer of snow becomes more deeply buried, the increasing weight of snow above it eventually compresses it into ice. Under all that pressure, the ice continues to "flow" slowly and doggedly downward toward bedrock and also outward toward the edges of the ice cap, where the glacial river ends.[24]

Summit Station accumulates about a meter of snow each year, but its elevation doesn't change because that snow is sinking into the glacial river. This is why the Big House and TAWO are raised above ground level. Their stilts are being continually buried in the river, but the buildings are designed to be raised anew.[25] The ice cap is always in motion, and that imperceptible yet determined flow is what allows us to retrieve history from an ice core. Every inch of depth is a window looking further back through time.

From these simple cylinders of buried ice, scientists are able to infer an incredible amount of information about the state of our planet at any given period of time. Bubbles in the ice provide naturally collected samples of the atmosphere and its composition. Inclusions in the ice—dust, pollen, ash, radioactive particles—give information on volcanic eruptions, forest fires, desert extent, and variations in solar activity. Even the water that forms the ice itself contains a wealth of knowledge; it can be analyzed to determine regional temperature, ice extent, ocean volume, precipitation, sea surface biological productivity, and even how widespread the

---

24 These days, the glacial "down and out" is truer than ever. For instance, when Glacier National Park was established in 1910, it had about 150 glaciers. Now it has under thirty. Before long we'll have to start calling it Climate Change Was Not a Hoax National Park.

25 In the case of TAWO, this ability flatly contradicts its "temporary" designation.

earth's wetlands were, among other things I'm sure.

Much of this is done by looking at isotopes—that is, atoms of the same element but with different numbers of neutrons. I never quite grasped the usefulness of isotopes until now.[26] It's simple, really: one isotope may be more or less likely to do something than another. For example, oxygen has three stable isotopes: ^{16}O, ^{17}O, and ^{18}O.[27] The oxygen atom in a water molecule can be any one of these isotopes. Research has taught us that water with ^{16}O evaporates more readily, while water with the heavier ^{18}O condenses more readily. So the percentage of ^{18}O in an ice core tells us much. Water that evaporates from the ocean's surface contains both isotopes. As that water vapor moves into colder air near the poles, the ^{18}O water is first to condense out as precipitation. So the less ^{18}O there is in an ice core layer, the further that location was from open water—and therefore, from warmer temperatures —at that time. This information allows us to determine the past climate of a region as well as the extent of the ice cap.

Of course, the information is regional so it takes an entire network of ice cores and sediment cores and ancient rocks and other paleoclimatology tricks to develop the big global picture. Also, to understand the information in an ice core, it's necessary to understand how the ice cap and the atmosphere interact with each other, which is no small part of the science done here. Many of the samples we collect are used to determine how surface snow relates to the air that it falls from and how that snow changes as it flows into the glacial river. In the case of the meter pit, which occurs monthly, each layer of fallen snow is sampled many times as it slowly becomes buried. By the time a layer becomes one meter buried, thus reaching the bottom of the pit, it has been sampled multiple times at shallower depths in previous pits, and

---

26   Actually, I never quite cared.

27   If you're not familiar with isotopes, the nucleus of an oxygen atom always has eight protons, and usually has eight neutrons, for a total of sixteen: ^{16}O. In the case of ^{17}O, there is an extra neutron, and ^{18}O has two extra neutrons. If you're not familiar with neutrons, they're just dead weight, so don't worry about it.

also at the surface. Actually, as a case in point, there was a distinct layer of solid ice apparent in the meter pit today, between the usual layers of foam-like snowpack. This icy layer was from a rare event that occurred in the summer, when the Greenland ice cap achieved record levels of surface melt during a warm spell. That layer was formed several months ago and it's not yet half a meter buried, so it will be sampled many more times in meter pits to come. This method of repeated sampling provides a record of how the snow has changed since it was deposited and in turn, a better understanding of the information in the ice core.

Unlike the relatively easy weekly samples of surface snow, the meter pit consists of thirty-three carefully collected samples from the carefully measured wall of a carefully shoveled hole. It takes a hell of a lot longer, so the penetration of cold into poorly insulated hands has agonizing depth.

After digging the pit, it seemed necessary to have a long warm-up break inside TAWO before sampling. Even though it was warm out—ten degrees—and only a little windy, Lance's words had us concerned. If the pit was going to be colder than ICESat, we were going to get as warm as possible beforehand.

Neal was putting on his clean suit when I stepped out to grab the new box of plastic gloves we'd left outside with the other equipment. When I returned, he had made no progress. He was at the exact same point in putting his suit on, but the floor was littered with shredded white remains.

"I had a Hulk moment," was all he said. I laughed, but I get it. Those suits are a pain in the ass for me, and I'm only a quarter of Neal's height, give or take. At least we have plenty of spares for future Hulk moments. I might indulge in one just for fun.

Finally dressed, we emerged from TAWO to find the weather changed. The wind had picked up considerably and the light was quickly turning flat. We were entering the Ping-Pong ball again.

It's incredible sometimes, that uniformity of light. Shadows and distinctions can disappear entirely. You can have full knowledge that there is a drift in your path that could trip you up. You can be searching for it with all your concentration and still fall flat on your face without seeing it. The light wasn't that bad yet, but it looked like it might get there. Over the course of sampling, the visibility dropped to a few hundred meters in blowing snow; I could no longer see the Big House.

Still, the pit wasn't nearly as bad as ICESat. The temperature held. My hands were surprisingly comfortable, but for some reason my toes were cold.

"Rex, there's something wrong with you," Neal said. His extremities were the opposite, which does seem right.

After another warm-up break, we went back out to collect the surface samples. So far, I've been filling the bottles that Jenny cursed over during turnover and Neal has been doing the ten "Whirl-Pak" bags that Lance made look so much easier. But I've been finishing well ahead of Neal. It's almost painful to watch him desperately trying to tear off the narrow perforated strip and then grab the tiny tabs to open the bag. I can't help him because the samples have different purposes and therefore different methods of processing, and the metal scoop I've been using is okay for my samples but will contaminate his. Near the end Neal has to curl his fingers into a fisted ball to rewarm them—or at least halt the chill—after every bag. Otherwise he can't get the tabs at all. We'll trade next time and see how that goes.

Day 25
Wednesday, November 28

The inside of the Big House's back door has a coat of sparkling frost so thick that the window looks no different from the rest of the door. That's the *inside* of the door. The hinges, the handle, even the jamb is smothered. The icing on the icing is a handwritten message on a piece of paper taped at eye level that should say, "Do not touch with bare skin or tongue" but instead says in big block letters: ICY. Judging by the layer of frost over the tape I'd say the sign must have been there all along, but I hadn't noticed it consciously until today. That's because safety warnings are deft at pointing out the obvious, and therefore suggest subliminally that I'm a complete imbecile. If all were heeded, their ubiquity would surely cause the shriveling of my self-worth to a deprecated pudding.[28] So my mind ignored the ICY warning intrinsically—out of self-preservation—and only revealed the message to my consciousness when it became amusing. Icy. No shit. I assume the warning originally referred to what was beyond the door, but since it now refers to the door itself, the jester in me wants to add another sign that says simply DOOR. I'm sure I could do better if I cared to put some thought into it; it's not nearly as witty as some of the signs I've seen in the Antarctic:

On a bicycle: PLEASE DO NOT RIDE ME, I AM UNDERAGE.

On the charred skeletal remains of a vehicle fire: NO SMOKING, FOR SALE, and RETRO—Antarctic cargo shorthand for *retrograde*, or in other words, *return*.

Next to a field camp outhouse: a speed limit sign with the *S* and the *D* removed and a small "oz" added so it read PEE LIMIT 25OZ.

My favorite sign was on the road to that field camp. We were driving a PistenBully from flag to flag on a foggy day. No—my recruited helper was driving; I was holding on and trying to anticipate her mistakes to avoid whiplash. A PistenBully is hard to drive. It's a big box on two clunky tracks and it steers like a big box on two clunky tracks. My helper shouldn't have been driving; she hadn't gone through the training, which, as I recall, focused more on checking the oil levels before going through the convoluted starting process and may not have involved any actual driving at all. So I figured, why not let her drive? As a dining attendant —i.e., pot scrubber—she was so excited to be leaving station that I couldn't help myself.

"Do you want to drive?" I asked, once we were several miles down the sea ice road to the camp, and well beyond the watchful eye. She lit up.

As she was getting accustomed to the touchy steering and I was failing to get used to the choppy ride, a signpost appeared

---

28 Just like most exit signs—the ones located above an obvious exterior door—are attempting to beat me into a pudding.

suddenly and surprisingly out of the haze. Miles from station, miles from the field camp, in the middle of nowhere on a continent free of road signs, it read: OBEY THIS SIGN.

I PUT THE guacamole with the dirty dishes because it had a brownish top layer and smelled a little funny to me. When I finished cooking the fajitas, Lance asked if there was guac. I told him I'd tossed it and that sour cream would have to do. I cooked the steak medium rare and nailed it, so I was proud of myself until Don pulled a piece out of his bowl and said it was a little underdone for him—not unfriendly or disappointed, just matter of fact. Lance and Neal both gobbled it up, which is saying something, especially considering that Neal claims to be a vegetarian.

We know each other's dietary scruples intimately now. Phil will eat just about anything. He wrestles with Don over the Marmite and with Neal over the Cholula. Don loves to sprinkle "fairy dust" on everything. I need to ask him what the hell that stuff is. Lance isn't picky, but he's trying to keep a high-protein diet to gain weight, so he prefers some form of meat at every meal, which makes the menu difficult only because Neal is a vegetarian—that is, unless you put a bleeding rare steak in front of him. Me, I prefer solid food to soup, raw vegetables to cooked, homemade to prepackaged, but I'll happily eat anything—as long as it hasn't turned.

While we were cleaning up after dinner, Don noticed it. "Is this the old guac?"

"Yeah, it's gone a bit brown and it smells funny," I told him.

"Oh, it's still good!" he said excitedly, and he put it back in the fridge.

Neal immediately quipped, "Don will eat anything rotten, but nothing spicy or undercooked!"

I really made the boys wait for dinner today because the black beans refused to cook. I presoaked them and they simmered for nearly three hours but still weren't done. I was feeling strangely guilty about it and I apologized profusely for the delay. It really doesn't matter—we have nowhere to be in the evenings—except that we've become so accustomed to dinner at five o'clock sharp that our bellies begin complaining shortly thereafter.

Eventually I resigned. "Sorry, guys, maybe we should just eat. I don't think the beans are getting any better."

Don showed me his empty glass of suds. "Oh, I don't mind. I'm happily having this beer!" Ever since we bottled it, he's been asking constantly, "Why would it matter if we try it early?"

"It'll be flat," I'd tell him. "It needs a couple weeks to mature too, or it just won't be very good."

When he asked again yesterday, Lance stuck on my side. "Patrick could never wait either," he explained. "The day after he had a beer that wasn't ready, he'd have another and claim it still wasn't good!"

But tonight, Don swore it was good.

"You didn't even save me a sip!" I complained.

"Well, I'll just open another, if that's okay."

"You'd open it if I thought it was okay or not," I said with a smile.

"True!"

He poured another room-temperature beer and gave me a sip. He was right: it's ready to drink after only six days in the bottle. Into the cold storage it went: fifty bottles of beer on the wall.

Day 26
Thursday, November 29

Kira finally emailed this afternoon. The poor girl has been in transit and she realized how hard it is to be in contact. I know. Even when there is opportunity, you are surrounded by new friends and reuniting with old ones. Things are happening and it's easy and fun to get swept up in it. She said she felt stupid and guilty for her previous outburst, and it was easy to forgive her. She's on the final leg of her journey to Palmer now, aboard the *Gould* and about to cross the Drake. I don't envy her. I hate that wobbly damn boat. Hopefully her crossing won't be too bad. I mean, it'll be bad, it's almost always bad, I just hope it isn't *too* bad. She handles it better than I do, at least.

We had a lazy day today, having managed to get almost everything finished early in the week, despite relatively crappy weather. It's a shame in a way because it was downright balmy out there today, the warmest we've seen yet: just a few degrees below for much of the day. Now I'm wondering if we're actually going to break zero. Only a few more points on the scale and we'll have to start adding a "plus" when announcing the temperature. As is usual with the warmth though, it's terribly windy, so our final weekly task—a special weather balloon specifically for measuring ozone—is still on standby.

The wind led me to thinking warm thoughts by reminding me of kitesurfing, which naturally conjures visions of sun and surf and cervezas. I spent much of the afternoon perusing beach rentals in Baja. I miss outdoor sports already, and I've only been away a month. That's the main reason I decided this would be my last polar deployment.[29] As much as it irks me to look at, I just can't bring myself to change the background on my desktop, which was recently Lance's. It's a great picture of him snowkiting here in broad daylight, only a handful of weeks ago. We've talked about doing it, but there's just not enough light anymore. So they may be warm thoughts, but they're dark too.

Lance brought it up again today at lunch, on account of the wind.

Lance: "Since you don't have much to do today, you wanna go kiting?"

---

29 To be fair, I actually decided my previous season at Palmer would be my last. But Greenland presented itself as a new location and a new experience, so I figured I could manage the comparatively short three-month duration. Damned adventurous spirit.

Me: "I was actually thinking about that earlier. We'd get lost quick, though, I think."

Lance: "Not me. I'll be holding the camera!"

Neal: "What you need to do is just get downwind of him and catch him when he goes flying by."

Phil: "Or put a long piece of cable wire on him."

Me: "But a tether would defeat that whole feeling of freedom you get from being naturally powered. Just like sailing." Phil has a sailboat that he spends a lot of time on between deployments, so I thought this analogy might appeal to him.

Phil: "Mmm, yes, there is an element of freedom there."

Me: "Besides, a tether would just be downright sketchy."

Lance: "Yeah, if you were tethered it would probably just pick you up and you'd be flying."

Neal: "At that point you'd *be* a kite!"

We all laughed and the conversation paused, allowing my thoughts to drift back to sailing. It's something I've only done a bit of but I'm intrigued by it. I find it shares the same feelings of freedom and presence that I get when cycle touring. You can go anywhere without being shackled by fuel, the freedom-sucking tether of most other forms of transportation. And you are kept present by the relaxed pace, reminding you that the journey itself is indeed more important, and lending you the patience to reach your destination. In that way, I've found it's a joy to tour on a bike, watching people zip by in vehicles that only allow them to view the world through a screen, traveling at such a speed that they miss all the simple things that make cycling fantastic: a butterfly in the flowers on the side of the road, a wildly patterned ladybug on the handlebars, a glimpse between trees of a sunlit meadow. At a bicycle's pace you see these things. You see the bugs coming at you in enough time to flinch, if not dodge. Sometimes that flinch is just a quick sucking in of breath, and if you're lucky you'll also suck in the breath that was just sucked in by the bug. You're *in* the environment. You are present, in the moment. You view the scenery with so much more clarity, modesty, serenity. I think of sailing in the same way, but without all the damn pedaling.

Me: "Where do you keep your boat, Phil?"

Phil: "Anacortes."

Me: "Brr, isn't the water cold up there? I think I'd rather have a boat in the Caribbean, or the Mediterranean."

Phil: "No, mate, Puget Sound and Vancouver Island are some of the best sailing in the world. There are hundreds of islands to explore and the mountains are just stunning."

Me: "But you can't really go swimming."

Phil: "Well, you *can*." He said it in such a way that acknowledged the cold water. "But there are an endless number of inlets and coves and you can just get lost out there and not see a soul for days."

Me: "Oh, nice, I hadn't thought of that. It *is* beautiful up there."

Lance: "Have you seen a lot of orcas?"

Phil: "Of course."

Lance: "I would love to have a sailboat. Nothing fancy, just a little one I could live on and sail around a bit."

Phil: "Nothing stopping you."

Lance: "I could keep it right there on the lake at Sandpoint."

Phil: "Perfect. You can get a simple cabin sailer for cheap. Maybe a twenty-seven-footer or so would be fine."

Me: "Have you done any ocean crossings?"

Phil: "Yes, I've sailed twice across the Atlantic. I haven't crossed the Pacific, but I crossed the Tasman Sea from Tasmania to New Zealand."

Me: "Wow. What's that like?"

Phil: "Well, the Tasman lived up to its reputation!"

Me: "I bet!" I laughed. "But what I meant was, what's an ocean crossing like? I mean, I think sailing around the world would be awesome, but I've always wondered about the ocean crossing part. It just doesn't seem very appealing. I expect it's pretty boring."

Phil: "It's no more boring than here. In fact, it's basically the same thing as wintering."

Lance: "Yeah, you can't go anywhere! But instead of ice in every direction, it's ocean."

Phil: "Right. Well, the details are different, but there are a lot of similarities."

Neal: "You're stuck with your companions for months on end." Everyone got a laugh out of that. I guess that means no one feels stuck—yet.

Phil: "In particular, the passage of time is the same. It's that strange way that time becomes elastic, you know? At the start, you're settling in and getting to know your role and your companions, and thinking, What did I forget? And then you get into the groove of things and time sort of stretches out so you don't know if something happened yesterday or last week. You're no longer on a trip—you're just in life mode and it's different. It's like a weird dreamland where you're absorbed in this little bubble and the rest of the world doesn't exist anymore."

Me: "Wow, that *is* just like wintering."

Phil: "Yeah. So you're in this groove, and in an ocean passage the only measure of time is moving this pencil dot across a big chart that's just a huge empty space."

I couldn't help but picture the stars dotting our winter sky, and imagine the sun plotting its long crossing below the horizon.

Phil: "But a week out from your destination, time changes—the elasticity of it. At that point you're starting to think about arriving and there's this undertone of excitement: What's the shipping going to be like in the channel? What's the weather? What are the tides gonna be? How do we want to time our arrival?"

Lance: "What restaurant do I want to eat at first?"

Phil: "Exactly!"

Neal: "Where are my pants?"

We laughed at the suggested image of Phil sailing the seven seas in his underwear. We'd probably be doing the same. But Phil was right; an ocean crossing sounded exactly like a polar winter.

We continued to talk about boats and sailing, and I could see that Lance was even more enamored by the idea than I was. Between us, we picked Phil's brain clean.

Phil: "The best way to learn is to just go for it, and I'll bet you never look back."

DON IS INSPIRED by our new homebrew. He showed up for dinner with a slew of empty bottles, gathered from somewhere—they seem to be hiding everywhere. He nodded toward the second batch of beer relaxing in its carboy. "So, Rex, when will that be ready to bottle?"

"Sometime in the next few days will do," I told him.

"Okay, I don't want it to go bad. I think it's gonna be good."

"Maybe, but right now it's still warm and flat. Don't make me hide the straws!"

"We don't have any straws."

"Oh? Have you already been looking?"

We had a lot of fun poking jabs at each other during dinner. Lance made a turkey pot pie for Neal, who had mentioned how much he likes the dish. But Neal filled a bowl with just the filling and informed us that he doesn't like crust. Lance was on him immediately.

Lance: "I could have just heated you some cream of mushroom soup! I slaved over a hot stove all afternoon to make that crust, and it turned out perfect!"

Don joined in the critique with a jab at Neal's "vegetarianism."

Don: "You ate the steak fajitas yesterday."

Neal: "Well, you shouldn't try to comprehend my eating habits. I don't comprehend them myself. Sometimes steak looks good. I almost had some of that sausage I cooked for you guys the other night because it smelled so good. But then I remembered how bad it would be to put all that grease and fat into my body."

Me: "So, you fed it to *us* instead!" I laughed, then added, ". . .

which we greatly appreciate."

Neal finished his second bowl of pot pie filling and asked if there was any dessert.

Lance: " *What?* You don't eat your crust and now you want dessert?"

Neal: "Is there any pie left from Thanksgiving?"

Lance: "Pie has crust!"

Phil: "All the pie's gone, mate."

Neal: "How about the cheesecake from turnover?" This question was meant as a joke since that cheesecake would be a month old by now. The sad thing is, I finished the last piece only a few days ago. Don would have been proud.

Phil: "Have you finished all the Snickers yet?"

Neal: "No, I've probably only had ten since we got here. That's less than one a day, *and* I've lost ten pounds!"

Phil: "Is that because you were wearing your boots when you weighed in?"

Neal: "No, it's probably because I was full of shit."

Phil: "I'm afraid you're still full of shit."

Day 27
Friday, November 30

Another quiet day, for the most part. I spent some time this morning photographing the full moon, which had a cool-looking hazy-rainbow halo caused by the freezing fog that was enveloping the station. The fog turned to blowing snow of course, in which we got some excitement attempting to launch the ozonesonde, egged on by Lance. We launch the evening weather balloon in fifteen-knot winds regularly, but they're only four or five feet in diameter, whereas the ozonesonde balloon is closer to eight.

"Oh, it'll be fine. Just go for it!" Lance teased us.

The ozonesonde itself—the part that hangs from the balloon—is a goofy little contraption. It has a tiny electric pump and a straw[30] and two little liquid vials that have to be filled to specific

---

30   Don't tell Don.

levels with chemicals and then plumbed together and the whole thing gets plugged into a radio and stuffed along with its batteries and a handful of warm rocks into a Styrofoam box that you have to tape together just so, all the while being careful about the straw and the antenna. It's a production.

The ozonesonde usually ascends well into the stratosphere, typically to about thirty-five kilometers—a height the larger balloon allows it to reach. It's a bit of a game to see how high one will go and then speculate why one went higher or lower than another. Their purpose of course is to measure ozone, which is earning greater interest in the Arctic lately.

We seem to have mitigated our impact on ozone depletion since the Montreal Protocol treaty in 1987, which has helped regulate chemicals that affect the ozone. The chemicals involved are slowly decreasing in the atmosphere and the hole over the Antarctic is no longer growing, though it is expected to take many decades to recede. Atmospheric conditions in the Arctic, however, have started to show similarities to those in the Antarctic—something predicted by climate change models—and that's priming the area for its own ozone hole. Just last year the Arctic region experienced a record loss of its ozone layer, and scientists expect that to get worse. It is not a promising sign.

Neal walked the balloon out of the S.O.B. and I connected the sonde. The balloon immediately began billowing and wildly distorting in the wind, nearly pulling Neal over like a toppling redwood.[31] It bounced off the ground several times and even off Neal's head before bursting undramatically. It just sort of flopped over dead, without the expected pop, an elastic snap, or even a puff of satisfaction. Still, the whole event was funny, except that we'll have to start the production all over again when the wind is cooperating.

"Dammit," I said, "We shouldn't listen to Lance."

---

31   I'm not even getting tired of making all these "Neal is so tall . . ." jokes.

AT DINNER WE poured the first "cold ones" of our own homebrew. Except Phil, who doesn't drink beer; he prefers wine or scotch, and not too much of those either. I think he enjoys beer, but it doesn't agree with him. He asked for a half-inch taster of the homebrew though, then kicked back on two chair legs at the dining table to enjoy it.

Don was finishing up an interview for Toolik Lake in the office, so we brought him a beer, to his appreciation. Then, just as we were turning back to join Phil at the table: *thump!* We caught just a glimpse of Phil's surprised face between his upturned legs as he went over backward. We howled with laughter.

"You're cut off!" Lance cheered, and laughter was unabated long after Phil righted himself. Eventually we calmed down and grew silent. I tried to hold back a chuckle but failed, succeeding instead in starting another row, which also made its ebb in time.

Phil was clearly okay, but Neal cleverly pointed out our neglect of his well-being. "So, Phil. Are you okay?" he asked sarcastically, and we were off again.

After we regained our composure, I looked around the table at each of them. I had the feeling we had been in the middle of a conversation before all the laughter, but I couldn't remember the subject.

Me: "Where the hell were we?"

Neal: "We were talking about the psych eval."

Me: "Oh, right."

Phil: "I've done several winters and never had to take one."

Phil has been doing polar contract work for a while, so I'm not sure how he has avoided the psychiatric evaluation, which is required to winter in Antarctica. He either wintered there before they necessitated the test, which I doubt, or he sidestepped it somehow, which I don't doubt, or his winters have all been here at Summit, where a psych eval isn't required—I'm not sure why. Lance, Neal, and I have all taken the psych eval.

Phil: "I wonder if people who work in these environments are abnormally idiosyncratic or . . ."

Me: "A lot of them kinda seem to be, don't they?"

Phil: "Or is it just that you see that part of people?"

Me: "The part you wouldn't normally see."

Lance: "Well, yeah, because you spend 24/7 with them."

Neal: "I think coming to a place like this *is* an idiosyncrasy."

Phil: "Which is why you do a psych test." He smiled before joking, "But you really should be *failing* in order to come up here!"

Me: "You have to be crazy to want to fly more missions!" I laughed.

Phil: "Exactly!"

Lance: "A guy I know has to do them regularly for his job, and he says that you fail the first time for being too honest, the second time for being too dishonest, and you finally get it on the third."

Phil: "So, what's on the test?"

Lance: "They ask the most ridiculous questions."

Neal: "Lots of them about blood. Or fire."

Lance: "And animals. Like: 'Do you enjoy teasing your pet?' But who doesn't enjoy teasing their pet?"

Neal: "Yeah, but you know it's the wrong answer. In *Big Dead Place* there's a great guide to the psych eval. It says you have to pretend you're a middle-aged white male from Minnesota in the fifties. You have to impart an old-fashioned set of values. You know: 'Of course I don't hit my wife, that's just wrong!'"

Me: "Um . . ."

Neal: "Not that I . . ." He backtracked. "Maybe that was a bad example."

Lance: "My favorite is: 'Do your eyes ever get tired from too much reading?' I mean, I can't see straight right now!"

I laughed with Lance, but then realized I didn't get it, and then realized there was probably nothing to get. Lance was just having fun.

Neal: "Or: 'Do you like to fix doorknobs?'"

Phil: "Serious?"

Lance: "It's crazy!"

Me: "They repeat questions over and over again, but they're reworded each time, like they're trying to catch you in a lie."

Neal: "The whole test is a nonfilter, really."

Me: "I could barely move my wrist after filling in all those bubbles."

Don: "Bubbles?" He had just come out of the office, grinning with beer in hand.

Neal: "We're talking about the psych eval."

Don: "Oh, that kind of bubbles. So it's a multiple choice test?"

Me: "Eight *hundred* of them."

Neal: "Well, there's an interview with the psychiatrist, too. But mostly, yeah, it's a multiple choice test."

Lance: "'Would you rather be a librarian or an architect?' What does it matter?"

Phil: "It doesn't make sense that you should have to retake it every year; either you're crazy or you're not. Have any of you ever failed it?"

What a loaded question, yet I felt my hand slowly raising. I looked around the room. Nope, just me.

Me: "I failed the first time—just like Lance's friend said: too honest."

Phil: "So you're crazy! You never should have been allowed back!" He was grinning ear to ear with delight.

Me: "I definitely shouldn't be here!" I laughed with him.

Of course I'm crazy. We're all crazy. We all know that. But it's an adventurous crazy, not a looney tunes crazy. I *should* be here. In fact, I *belong* here. Still, I felt the need to explain myself.

Me: "I told the psychiatrist that I'd smoked pot within the past year, which is an automatic fail. What sucks is I knew how stupid it was as I was saying it, but I was just following the advice of this guy I knew who had been to McMurdo. He said, 'You've already peed in the cup,' and something about not lying to a psychiatrist, which kinda made sense. And then it turns out this guy has never wintered, so he's never even taken the psych eval! What a dipshit! I mean, me too, for listening to him, but him for being a dipshit."

Don: "Have you ever told someone what you do for work and they give you that look, you know, like their face is all twisted up for a sneeze?"

A collective, resounding "Yes!"

Lance: "I always have to explain that I do it for the time off."

Phil: "A lot of people have no concept of time off."

Neal: "When I tell them I just bum around and snowboard for three or four months, they always ask, 'Don't you get bored?' and I say 'Well, if you mean bored enough to work, then no!'"

Day 28
Saturday, December 1

My eyelid still twitches. I've grown so used to it that it hardly seems worth mentioning. But now that I think about it, it's been going on for an alarming length of time. And now I'm starting to have trouble sleeping. I guess it was wishful thinking to hope that I wouldn't. I'm exhausted by the evening, but for some reason not sleepy. Last night I was cold and felt a little weird, and when I finally did fall asleep, I woke up hot, as though my body was fighting a sickness. Surely there's nothing here to catch. Still, I wonder if the ever-present smell of garlic on my fingers portends some dastardly illness? That's been going on for a week. Or has it been two? Either way, it's not normal.

"Good morning," the gang greeted me as I entered the Big House for breakfast.

"Mwrmwnn," I mumbled, then gathered myself. "I feel like . . . like there's a tight band around my head. Is that normal?"

Don watched me put jam on my first piece of toast, but didn't see me quickly eat it and switch to honey for the remaining two slices, which I brought to the table. "What happened to your jam?" he asked, confused.

"What jam?" I replied, confused myself.

"Don't fuck with him," Neal advised. "He's the mechanic; we need him. Fuck with Lance instead."

Which is exactly what I was about to do—again, unwittingly—by being in Lance's spot at the table. It's surprising how institutionalized we've already become. At every meal Phil heads the table, flanked by Lance and Don, followed by Neal and me. There's no reason for it, it's just become our routine.

"I do wish you'd stay in your assigned seat," Don said with his usual smile. It was hard to tell if he was being sarcastic or serious. I think it was both.

When Lance arrived, he took it in stride and sat on the exercise bicycle as Phil started the meeting. "The forecast is much of the same: overcast and windy. There's not a lot going on today, so I'd like to meet after lunch to discuss ICESat safety."

The *perception* of safety, he must mean.

He continued, "Let's see, what else? You guys haven't had to climb the tower in a while."

"Why do you say things like that?" Neal exclaimed with a denunciatory tone. "Now we're gonna have to climb the tower for some reason."

I laughed at Neal's superstition and then egged him on. "What was it that Phil said last time?"

"Um, 'We haven't had to dig up the Noone vault in a while.'"

"That's right. Well, we haven't," I replied, pushing him closer to the edge.

"What the—?" Now Neal's tone was incredulous.

"Do you feel the band getting tighter, Neal?" Phil asked with a grin.

"No, that's Rex with the band. And the twitch and the hearing things. I'm just superstitious."

IN THE AFTERNOON we learned that Nick Johnson, an Antarctic contractor for many years, committed suicide. It's especially strange news after Neal mentioned his book, *Big Dead Place*, just yesterday. I wintered with Nick, though I didn't know him well. McMurdo's large population naturally lends itself to cliques, even in the winter, though they are all open and nonexclusive. Nick and I crossed paths enough—everyone does—but we ran in different circles. We did have an incredibly fun New Year's Eve together the summer before, making late-night inebriated psychedelic music on the synthesizer in the chapel. I have no idea how we ended up there, but I suspect we were just following Nick's good mood on a zany impulse.

Despite not being close to Nick, the news still hits home. He's been a significant part of the Antarctic family, with a sardonic wit and a love of the continent. It's dark news for a dark place, and I haven't digested it yet.

My window is now two-thirds buried by snow.

8

*In which nothing particularly interesting happens,
except that I start showing the first signs of losing
my mind.*

Day 29
Sunday, December 2

Kira arrived at Palmer today. She's excited to be back but says she keeps expecting to see me fiddling in the weather room or entering the galley. I miss her too, and I sometimes find myself wishing away my current experience for our move to Oregon. What are the odds that she would find a position as an assistant professor in the state I call home? And what are the odds that while I was still in South Africa I would find an interesting job in the same town, at the same university, *and* in the same department? It's uncanny and exciting, and more than a little serendipitous. We'll be living in Corvallis, only a couple hours' drive from my closest friends and stomping grounds. Still, I have to remind myself to be in the moment. I'm in a new and exotic location and I want to be sure to make the most of it.

It's Sunday, so today I made the most of it by sleeping late and spending the afternoon listening to NPR—which our shotty internet managed to stream—and bottling beer with Don, who offered the knowledge that all food has traces of mouse shit in it, and ground pepper has the highest concentration. But no, really, he's not obsessed with poo.

Lance spent his Sunday setting up a toy electric racetrack in the MSF, which he redubbed the Motor Speedway Facility. I don't know where the track came from or why it's here, but it doesn't surprise me. At the beginning of my Antarctic winter, Danny—a friend from the summertime—passed to me an original Nintendo to hold for him until his return. It was new in the box, with the plastic still on it. *This is probably worth some money*, I thought as I opened it. Over the course of the winter, I became an expert at *Super Mario Brothers* and *Metroid*, though they weren't as exciting as I remembered from my youth.

With twenty-six feet of toy racetrack, Lance claims to have the longest racecourse in Greenland. It may even be true. His girlfriend, Hannah, told him he was acting like a seven-year-old, which may also be true, but we have to entertain ourselves somehow.

Day 30
Monday, December 3

A prepackaged apple pie appeared in the fridge. I guess someone didn't get their fix from Thanksgiving's pies, or they developed an addiction. I've certainly been craving sweets a lot more lately. The fire demands its fuel.

I was guiltlessly dishing up a slice this morning when Neal called me out.

Neal: "Pie for breakfast, eh?"

Me: "You know it. I mean, it's probably just as healthy as the granola and yogurt I usually have."

Neal: "Well, I don't know about that."

Me: "Sure it is, man. Granola is full of sugar and oil—"

Don: "And mouse shit."

Me: "And yogurt's probably got a fair amount of fat—"

Don: "And mouse shit."

Me: "But apple pie is full of healthy stuff. It's got fruit and flour and eggs and milk."

Don: "And mouse shit."

Me: "It's like that Cosby bit where he's supposed to make breakfast for the kids but ends up giving them—"

Neal: "Chocolate cake! Yeah!" I love it that no obscure reference is ever missed by Neal.

Don: "Look, Phil is having pie too. You've started a movement."

Neal: "I'm about to go start a movement." A mischievous smile crawled across his face.

Don: "But you haven't even finished your coffee."

Neal: "It's not coffee; it's tea."

Don: "Is it chamomile?"

I laughed at the progression from coffee to tea to chamomile, which we've already agreed is the wussiest of herbal teas.

Neal: "No, it's a very manly tea."

IT'S THE BEGINNING of another week, and our busiest day. We front-load the week as much as possible in order to catch every weather opportunity. Some tasks require precipitation, some require wind, many are reasonable only when it's calm. This week is looking like a total crapshoot; the weather forecasters have given up and lumped the next three days' forecasts into one: bad. I'm anxiously watching my window, which has about five inches remaining.

The weather seemed reasonable as we headed out, but during the walk to TAWO, Neal earned a coin-sized raised blemish on his cheek. It was a solid frostnip in a short amount of time and it came right after I had commented that it wasn't so bad out, just a bit windy but warm. I can't believe I'm calling -30°F "warm." We're becoming acclimated and maybe that's not such a good thing.

As we ran through our routine inside TAWO, Neal started hearing noises. "It's a regular pinging sound, sort of like sonar," he claimed. "Do you hear it?"

"No. It's too early for you to be hearing things," I said with a wry smirk.

"Ha, ha. Stand here."

I moved closer to Neal. "I still don't hear anything. Wait a minute, let me just . . ." As a joke, I stood on a stool to get my ears near to the level of his. It backfired. "Oh yeah, I do hear it now." It was disappointing; I wanted *not* to hear it. I know Neal hears the stenographer in our office, but he has always craftily maneuvered the conversation to never admit it explicitly. He's fucking with me.

The pinging sound was coming from the fan on the networked power strip that allows us to turn TAWO's spotlight on and off remotely. I suspect the bearings are shot but the power strip will probably survive without the fan. Even if it doesn't, I'm not sure why we need it. If it's nasty enough that we think we'll need the spotlight to find TAWO, we're sensible enough to not even try.

I had my first go at the Whirl-Pak snow sampling bags today. The fucking perf strips and tabs are impossibly small and whoever designed the damn things should, I don't know, grow some bigger hands. I mean, I've got small hands and I can't get these buggers open, so this guy must have some wee stumps. Okay, that's not fair. What he should grow is glove liners, two pairs of slippery plastic gloves, and a circulation problem. In general, my fingers don't seem to get as cold as Neal's, but it took me just as long to fill the little bastards anyway. "Why the hell do they need *ten* of these things?" I asked. Neal just laughed. I think it made him feel better that I had a hard time with them too, so that's a win at least. I don't know how the hell Lance raced through them like he did. Maybe that's just it: if you don't race, you're frozen long before you finish.

At dinner Lance admitted that he's already tired of the toy racetrack. "It's just no fun with only one person," he said. Neal told him we'd stop by tomorrow after the bamboo forest for tea and time trials.

Day 31
Tuesday, December 4

After the bamboo forest, it completely slipped our minds to stop by the MSF for tea and time trials.

Day 32
Wednesday, December 5

My eye is still twitching, but the quality has changed. It seems stronger, yet duller, or blunter. It's as though the original nerve ending has grown tired and given up the fight, but in a show of solidarity, the surrounding tissue has taken it up.

On a more positive note, I finally figured out my humidifier: if I remove the reservoir, then there's no water to run out and soak the carpet, or my socks.[32]

Day 33
Thursday, December 6

I'm left with the top two inches of my window. I guess from a practical sense it doesn't matter. It's not as though it's letting any light in; it's always dark out. There are a few hours in the middle of the day that offer just enough light to make out the horizon— on a reasonably clear day, that is. We spend that time doing the things that are nicer with some light: snow samples, bamboo forest, ozonesondes. Otherwise a headlamp is my constant and only companion. This is one of my favorite simplicities about living on remote research stations: I don't have to burden my pockets with keys or a wallet or phone. These things mean nothing here. They sit in a drawer awaiting more complicated times. I only need my headlamp. And lip balm. Oh, and my radio of course, which is actually a bigger pain in the ass than the whole keys-wallet-phone thing. Shit.

We managed to complete most of our tasking early again this week, which is surprising given the poor weather that began a

---

32   What the hell kind of logic is that? If there's no reservoir, then there's no water to humidify with!

couple days ago. I guess I should stop expecting the weather to be anything but poor. Visibility has been extremely low but at least the wind and temperature have been manageable, which is the important bit. What does visibility matter in the dark?

On days like this, when there are no extraneous tasks left to do —or if the weather won't allow them—we take turns going to TAWO. It was Neal's turn today, so I did almost no work all day. It's boring when this happens, but I can usually fill the time. I read. I write in this journal. I write to my blog if the mood strikes me. I organize and edit old photos. With the doldrums of polar winter setting in, though, sometimes these simple things that shouldn't require motivation suddenly do.

The paltry ambition I managed to gather today was put toward quality of life. I baked a loaf of bread. It's a simple act with great reward in the morale department. We have frozen loaves of sliced bread, but the only artisan bread we get is the artisan bread we bake. I added some leftover brewing barley to the recipe, which I had saved for this purpose, and the loaf came out crunchy and delicious. I think next time I'll save some hop sediment and throw that in too. Hoppy barley bread sounds delicious!

Day 34
Friday, December 7

~

Darker the Night

Summit Station, Greenland
Friday, December 7, 2012

The faint light of dawn is being squeezed out. With just two weeks to go until the winter solstice, we're left with only a thin band on the horizon—when we can see it. Lately, the wind has been relentlessly lifting fine snow and ice into the air, obscuring the horizons, the sky, and the nearest building, plus any chance of seeing aurora. I see occasional faint green bands at times when the air settles, but we don't know what aurora we may be missing in the bluster. It would be so nice to have some clear skies, even if it meant colder temperatures. Still, when the ice-filled air is just right, the hanging haze of prisms bends and breaks the moonlight into fuzzy rings of colorful halo, which is cool.

When the moon is full it stays above the horizon, spinning in circles around the sky. But now the moon is waning, which means it's rising and setting every day. It took me a while to wrap my head around this. The light came on when I learned that the moon orbits the earth on the same plane in which the earth orbits the sun. The planets are all basically on the same plane too, which surprised me; I guess I've always pictured the solar system to be more three-dimensional than that.

Here at Summit, we're standing near the earth's tilted axis of rotation, leaning toward the sun for half the year and away from it for the other half, so the sun is either up all the time or down all the time. Well, that's not entirely true: during the spring and fall when the axis leans to one side or the other, the sun rises and sets. The same thing happens with the moon, except that the moon circles the earth in a month, which means it's continually up for about a week, then rising and setting for a week, then below the horizon for a week, then rising and setting again, etc. It's interesting: during a polar winter you'll never see the new moon, and during a polar summer you'll never see the full moon.

In a few days the moon will disappear for its week below the horizon. During its passage through the new moon, it joins the absent sun. When the moon is up it is a definite source of warmth and beauty, and it provides a lot of welcome light. As we approach the solstice without it, next week will begin our darkest time.

The effects of that darkness are just starting to take hold. I haven't lost it yet (I know you're all waiting for it), but I'm feeling consistently tired and my motivation is waning. Melatonin is on a pitiless march, industriously building the cobwebs that will soon entangle my thoughts. Getting out of bed in the morning is a bloody nuisance.

～

The aurora forecast claimed "active" today, and the sky even cleared for it, but there was nothing. At least the break in weather allowed us to get the ozonesonde off successfully, which only leaves an air sample and a snow sample to finish the week.

After lunch I helped Don try to fix the Green House's washing machine, which has been on the fritz. It washes the load but often refuses to spin it dry, forcing you to haul a soggy sack of clothes to the Big House to finish the job. We bypassed a door-lock sensor to trick the spin cycle into running. Then Don tried a load of laundry and was left with the usual dripping mess, but for some inexplicable reason it's working for me this evening. Of course, I'm willing to spend an hour screwing with it until it works. That spares me from gearing up to go outside, which requires a colossal effort, especially when I'm already dressed for lounging and bed. Don had to finish his laundry at the Big House this afternoon, which I guess wasn't the end of the world since he was headed there anyway. It was his night to cook. He fried up battered fish with fries. It was great.

Lance: "Fish and chips is pub food. We need a beer!"

I agreed and went to the back to grab four bottles. As I returned through the kitchen, Neal's voice emerged, riding on a slightly agitated undertone.

Neal: "It's Friday. Ask again in five minutes and it will still be Friday."

Neal seems to be the only one who can keep track of the days. Now I'm wondering who already asked what day it is and how many times—and if it was me.

Lance: "Do we need to have a morning meeting tomorrow, on a Saturday?"

Phil: "God, I hope not."

Phil is expert at making us wonder if we're going to skip something official. He's so laid back that we expect him to do it, but we're fooled every time. We also know, though, that if Phil thinks it's important, it is: even something as seemingly casual as the morning meeting.

Phil: "Do you know what you're doing tomorrow?" He looked expectantly at Lance.

Lance: "No, and I won't know in the morning either."

This is often the nature of our jobs; we may not know what we'll be working on until we find something not working. At the morning meetings, when Phil asks Lance what he'll be doing that day, Lance often answers, "I'll find out when I get there."

Neal: "We should have the meetings at lunch, after we've done whatever we need to do for the day."

Lance: "Or, in the morning we should talk about what we did yesterday."

Phil: "Well, I'm pretty sure the idea is to discuss what we're doing for the day so we're all on the same page."

Oh, we're all on the same page all right. The page where—

I've just caught myself staring into the steam plume of my humidifier. It's mesmerizing like a fire, but a poor substitute. I am absolutely feeling the effects of the cold darkness, as evidenced by my inability to complete sentences. Perhaps it's more obvious now, this being my second polar winter, because I know what to expect and I can't just shrug off the subtle signs of ineptitude. They're becoming more frequent now. On my way to launch the weather balloon this evening, when I crossed the threshold around the side of the S.O.B. where the entrance floodlight casts only shadow, I stopped cold. I could see only black painted on black. I knew I was standing on a drift that, somewhere to my right, dropped off into a six-foot-deep moat around the building. I also knew that to my left was a swath of churned-up snow where Don drives the track loader on his way around the S.O.B. to fill the snowmelter. The tracks would trip me. The moat could break me. I could see neither. I had a knife-edge of clean snow between hazards, and I slowly, carefully began walking it. After my eyes adjusted for a few moments, I had the faintest guidance; there was a slight difference in the shade of dark at the moat's edge. Then I remembered that I *always* carry a headlamp.

Day 35
Saturday, December 8

I'm sore, my back especially. It's pathetic; it was only twenty minutes of yoga. My body was reluctant to say the least, and afterward walking felt awkward and pubescent. But my energy level jumped significantly, though not enough to even consider joining Lance for his evening spin on the stationary bike. What's the point? I'm not going to be fit when I leave here no matter what I do. The winter won't allow it, physiologically. I was resigned to that even before arriving.

During my Antarctic winter, a group of us met in the gym every week to play soccer. It was an honest effort to maintain some level of fitness, but we didn't realize how futile it was until Winfly—the initial wave of returning summer contractors. Many were friends from the previous summer and we invited them to join us. It was immediately clear that we were no longer on the same level. What felt like effort, exercise, and fitness was simply an illusion; the new arrivals ran circles around us. The pace of the game was suddenly overwhelming and it sharpened a realization that our physical abilities were as impaired as our mental faculties. Over the next several weeks most of the winter-overs stopped attending. I stuck it out until Mainbody, the true start of summer, but it was disheartening. I began to feel like I *needed* to keep going, like I was clinging to the final threads of my body's ability—a scary thought. I wanted to maintain what minuscule fitness I still had, no matter how difficult that had become, physically *and* mentally.

Yet here I am for some reason, in the dark again. Wintering the high latitudes is bizarre and mind-numbing, yet interesting and special in so many ways. I wish I could think of one right now.

The temperature dropped well into the fifties today. I suppose I've been asking for that in a way, and I can't complain because we got a clear morning to finish our sampling and watch for auroras that refuse to appear. Then, with nothing left on the weekly agenda, an after-lunch nap seemed like a brilliant idea, except for the after-lunch emergency response training that we have every Saturday. I'm the only one here who has never taken a Wilderness First Responder course, which is comforting—for me.

The Antarctic Program put me through more trainings than I can count, and though they primarily covered specific scientific equipment related to my position, they also included search and rescue, emergency dive accident management, firefighting,[33] and countless on-station trainings like glacier and sea ice travel and how to check a PistenBully's oil. Somehow I dodged the bullet on anything medical, though.

Phil asked the group who could remember what some acronym means and I shrugged my shoulders.

Phil: "Hell, I couldn't remember either. I had to look it up in my notes."

Me: "It's not a matter of memory; this stuff is pretty much all new to me."

Phil: "Oh, shit, I forgot this isn't review for everyone."

For every wintering team at Summit, PFS specifically hires at least a few people who have some medical training in addition to their primary skill set. It's a necessity; we don't have a doctor. All we have are a medical phone-in service, a stash of common supplies and medications, and each other.

Phil quickly polled the room, determining that, of our group, Neal is the most knowledgeable. He's a WFR and an EMT, though both certifications have lapsed.

Neal: "It doesn't matter what I remember. As far as I'm concerned, it's you guys who need to know this stuff, in case I fall off the tower or have a heart attack or something."

Lance: "From all the red meat you keep eating."

Don: "You know, lots of old men die of heart attacks when they're on the toilet."

---

33 It seems ironic that in order to be sent to Palmer Station in the Antarctic, I would first be wrapped in firefighting gear and placed in an 800-degree room.

Me: "The toilet?"

Don: "You know . . ." and he scrunched his face up like he was desperately trying to squeeze one out. And so our derailment goes.

I woke from my after-the-after-lunch-emergency-response-training nap to the sound of Phil and Don coming in the back door. Their conversation was easy to hear through the thin walls.

Don: "Well, what are you going to do now, take a nap like everyone else?"

Phil: "Yep, I think so."

Don: "Me, too."

So there was no point in getting up. But my institutionalized stomach had me awake for dinner, and Don greeted me as I arrived at the Big House.

Don: "Well, are you ready for a beer or what?"

Lance: "By Don's one-week rule, the next batch is ready."

Don immediately got up and grabbed one. Perhaps it was jostled in his excitement, or just a little too warm, but it foamed over aggressively into his dinner bowl, much to our amusement.[34] After the first swallow, he made a face like a kid trying brussels sprouts.

Don: "It's different." That was all he could manage as we stared at him, smiling.

Me: "You made a face."

Lance: "He made the same face when he first tried the other batch, and now he loves it!"

Don: "It grew on me."

Me: "That must have happened before you got to the bottom of the first bottle, because you were enjoying it by then."

Lance: "Well, then he doesn't have far to go before he likes this one too!"

Don made another, different face—a *you're fucking with me* face.

---

34 Several more exploded on us over the next couple weeks, so you never knew what you were going to get.

AFTER DINNER AND several pints, we gathered in the lounge to watch *180° South*, which Lance has been recommending as a great take on enjoying life and not falling into the routines prescribed by modern culture. As crazy people who aren't afraid to spend the winter on top of a polar ice cap, this isn't a problem, but the theme speaks to us.

"The best journeys answer questions that in the beginning, you didn't even think to ask," the film states. So as we watched I began to wonder: What questions are being answered by this polar journey I'm on? I wasn't immediately sure. I thought about why I came here, why I'm living this untraditional life at the ends of the earth. What dawned on me was ironic. In a way, my isolation in this unreal place is actually an attempt to be more connected with reality.

Modern culture has disconnected itself from the earth, from what is fundamental, from what is real. It fosters a coddled existence that is rendered mundane by comfort and constancy. Our idea of travel, especially as Americans, is to spend a week at an all-inclusive resort immersing ourselves in the same culture we already know. Our idea of adventure is to wander out of that resort for an afternoon, not actually mingling with the local people but watching them from a safe distance out of fear and hearsay. Our idea of intrigue is to find a marketplace where the food still has its head and feet attached. Many of us don't even appreciate where our own dinner comes from. Too many of us are appalled by the idea of slaughtering a cow. Hell, I'm appalled. We're simply disconnected, and that gap cultivates a fear of the unfamiliar.

Perhaps it's natural to fear the unknown. But that basal instinct has the cloaked fervor to captivate our senses, to perk our ears and widen our eyes. Instinctively, the fight-or-flight mechanism triggers those reactions, pumping adrenaline into the body to escape with its hide. But in this world where man is king, with truly little to fear, we can simply avoid the discomfort by avoiding the unknown, and most of us do. Yet some of us recognize that a surge of fear is also a surge of excitement, and that surge can be experienced without dire consequences because those generally don't exist.[35] Fear of the unknown can become exciting when harnessed and embraced.

I want that surge. It's a means of connecting with the real on a primal level, a way of feeling more alive. That's partly why I'm here, I realized: this is a new experience, a facing of the unknown —and I thrive on that. I'm essentially chasing a fix, a high.

But there's something else also. I can't ignore that I'm an avid outdoorsman and love experiencing any ecosystem the world has to offer. I suppose the complete lack of life atop this giant ice cube renders it not exactly an ecosystem, but it's a rare and fascinating environment nonetheless. I enjoy getting deep into a wilderness, away from the obvious touch of mankind, if not the ever-present subtle touch.[36] Wilderness is where the rest of the earth is, the larger, nonhuman aspect where property boundaries are blurry swaths drawn by evolutionary success, by the contribution of advantage to the future of a species. This is where life is wild and freedom is real, and it is a graceful and humbling tranquility to be immersed in it. Out there I get a better understanding of the world around me. In that way, too, I feel more connected to the earth, reminded that I am one with its system, and it makes me feel alive to be surrounded by it.

Kira's uncle described living on a farm in Zimbabwe as having an intense feeling of being alive. On a day-to-day basis, he said, you never knew what might happen. The wildlife is not contained in Zimbabwe like it is in South Africa's game parks. You may have hyenas in your field, an elephant in your driveway, a crocodile in

---

35   Well, unless you're BASE jumping.

36   It *is* nice to have a trail, usually.

your swimming hole, a baboon in your kitchen. He's had many encounters with dangerous wildlife and explained that experiences like those make you aware of your own mortality. They tap into your fear and therefore induce a sharp sense of your own livelihood. He had some *stories*.

I got a few slight but exhilarating tastes of that in South Africa:

At Mapungubwe National Park a herd of elephants waltzed right through a broken security fence and into our camp. Kira showed her fear of elephants, a fear solidified in her youth when she was charged by one. I approached more boldly but never closer than Kira's dad, who knew the guidelines, having spent a lot of time researching in the bush. Between them I gained a healthy respect—a blend of attentive wariness and fond admiration—for these majestic creatures.

In Mountain Zebra National Park we joined a family friend who studies cheetah. We got out of the car, normally a breach of park safety rules but allowed under our scientific circumstances, and marched into the bush. We crossed open shrublands and pushed through thickets while listening to her stories of running from herds of buffalo and standing ground when charged by her research cats. She was disappointed that we couldn't find Sarah the cheetah because Sarah the cheetah charges her every time. Though I would love to have *had* that experience in a past-tense kind of way, I didn't want to *have* it in a *holy shit that cheetah is charging me and I think I'm peeing my pants a little* present-tense kind of way. We found George the cheetah instead, and it was enough for me to simply stand exposed with a wild cheetah ten yards away.

In Addo Elephant National Park, while I was driving Kira's tiny car down a narrow dirt road, a herd of elephants suddenly emerged from the bush and surrounded me. I had no choice but to move with them, in the middle of the pack, until the road widened and I could let them by. The final two began to fight right in front of me. I hoped I wasn't next.

In the Cederberg Wilderness Area a gigantic baboon with canines the size of my forearm came charging out of the bush and right into our personal space—seriously, I'm talking inches—to swipe a bag of groceries. Kira released a primal scream I have not heard the likes of since. That shit was scary. I was definitely feeling alive for the rest of that day, and very much on my guard.

Joining the herd

Perhaps to look death in the eye is to feel the most alive. Certainly to be immersed in the wild places of the world is to be surrounded by life. Even if my current choice of wild location is a lifeless void, it still emphasizes my place in the scheme of things. Gazing up at the stars while miles away from station, with nothing in sight but a few flags, is to be an insignificant speck on a broad sheet of paper under a potentially infinite unknown. We humans are simply another species on our own little world, a part of that world's natural balance and not above it, as we like to think.

But if we continue to tip the scale to our greedy will, we will soon find that the scale has a limit, a toppling point that will dump not just the excess weight but most of the rest of humankind with it. The balance will swing back and the resources we've decimated will thrive again. The earth will rebound. Though it will be changed, it will survive. But we may not. The few who remain will be those who have lived without televisions or cell phones or cars or grocery stores. As a developed culture we may think of these survivors as simple, uncivilized, barbaric even. But where we are ignorant and dependent, they are strong. They are not appalled by the idea of gutting a carcass or eating a grub. They know where to find water and how to create shelter. They recognize the signs in nature that forecast weather, signify food, or portend danger. And that is why the meek will inherit the earth: because they are still connected to it.

Geez, what a soapbox. Maybe I've had one too many pints. At least I know our homebrew is doing its job.

Day 36
Sunday, December 9

I'm lying awake in the middle of the night and it's funny because I'm bored. Aside from the hour of instrument checks and half hour of balloon launch—it being my Sunday to work—it felt like I did nothing. All day, boredom had me searching for ways to occupy my time. I read, napped, worked on a blog post, and spoke with my brother on the phone. Now it's late and I'm in bed only to lie awake and continue to be bored. Really, it's funny.

Ethan was frantic when I talked to him. He answered the phone with "Don't have twins!"

"I'm not sure I want any kids at all," I told him. "But getting two birds with one stone seems to me like a good thing."

"Well, they're cute at times and they're a pain in the ass at times. I mean, I'm glad we decided to have kids but two at once is just a nightmare sometimes."

"I bet it is."

He was distracted, clearly in the middle of needing to do something. Maybe several somethings. Probably at least two. "You know, you may regret it later if you don't have kids. Just don't have twins."

Hearing my new niece and nephew in the background was a dose of the real world. There are a lot of things missing here, not just the sun. For a full year at McMurdo I didn't see a single person below age twenty, let alone a baby. Except for the small greenhouse, I didn't see any plants. No trees, no wildflowers, not even a blade of grass, only sparse lichens clinging to exposed rocks. I saw no dogs or cats or pets of any kind. During the winter, when the marine life intelligently abandons that wasteland, the only living things I saw that weren't human were a beetle that my friend Katie found in a shipment of lettuce and one inebriated fruit fly.

~

Bugs in the Brain Room

McMurdo Station, Antarctica
Thursday, July 24, 2008

As it turns out, there *are* bugs here! They live in the band room. We were practicing and I swore I saw something fly by. I passed it off as just my mind playing tricks on me, which is all too common these days. A couple of the others noticed too, but they also just assumed their own madness. Then one landed on Jeremy. A fruit fly! A real bug!

The band room is adjacent to the beverage storage area, and these little guys have been living off a two-four of Guinness that froze and exploded, so they were happy little fruit flies indeed. Jen captured one (not a difficult task with a drunken fruit fly, unless of course you're a wintering Antarctican) and affection-ately named it Gwinness, the Guinness Princess. Then she squished Gwinness onto a microscope slide for classification.

~

McMurdo and South Pole workers travel to Antarctica via Christchurch, New Zealand. The first thing many of them do upon returning from the Antarctic is visit the Christchurch Botanic Gardens. I spent three straight days doing nothing but soaking in the myriad of forgotten aromas and sights, textures and sounds: songbirds singing, flowers blooming, water gurgling, grass massaging my toes. The onslaught of scents was the most poignant rediscovery but the presence of children had me stopping to stare, which surely seemed creepy. Fortunately the Kiwis in the gardens are well-accustomed to the peculiar starvings of Antarcticans, who engage the Kiwis' children with play and accost their pets with cuddles.

Katie's beetle survived for about two weeks in a container with lettuce and water. I was fascinated by it, for no other reason than I hadn't seen a bug in six months. I never could have imagined a world void of insects, but it exists. The stations I lived at in the Antarctic were on the coast, so they did have wildlife—seals, whales, birds, and of course penguins (but *no* polar bears—it's a standard Antarctican pet peeve to be asked about polar bears).[37] But Summit Station is in the literal dead center of Greenland. There is nothing alive here but us. It brings new meaning to the word *uninhabitable*.

---

37   I also find it bothersome when people refer to Antarctica as "up there." On the rare occasion when both blunders are combined —"Are there polar bears up there?"—my mind tends to wrap itself into a Mobius knot where "yes" and "no" are equally incorrect and I'm forced to back away in slow confusion with my internal alarm blaring, "*Disengage! Disengage!*"

9

In which I go on a brief rampage and then attempt to set some scientific stuff straight, but ultimately decide that none of it matters in the long, long, long run.

Day 37
Monday, December 10

I am often mistaken for a scientist. People assume that everyone who works at a research station—especially in the Antarctic —is a scientist. They're not. I'm not. Still, I am often asked my supposed expert opinion on climate change. Many of the askers are skeptical, and with all the misinformation out there I can't blame them. Some buy into a conspiracy theory in which the greater scientific community shuns any scientist who opposes climate change and essentially strips them of all clout. I've been asked why this might be, though the answer seems right there in the question. All I can do is offer my opinion, and this is what I tell them:

I work with a fair number of scientists and I haven't met one yet who disbelieves that we as humans are impacting the earth in such a way that it will affect the global climate. Since I've never

met a skeptic, I must logically conclude that the majority of the
scientific community accepts climate change as a reality. And why
shouldn't they? A vast amount of research supports the idea—
unquestionably, to most eyes. And that research is performed,
critically reviewed, and accepted by a vast number of reputable
experts. A scientist who opposes climate change is essentially
ignoring the work of a large community of peers and experts who
are widely well-regarded. It should come as no surprise, then, that
the opposing scientist won't be. Does it mean that scientist is
wrong? Probably.

I think the real problem is that some people oppose climate
change for personal reasons and prey on an uninformed public,
spreading false information to suit whatever personal purpose
they have. I suppose that may sound like a conspiracy theory as
well. But I recently came across an article by one of these naysay-
ers, and I can't come up with any other explanation for his mis-
representation of the data.

I was minding my own business, just doing a little light reading
on climate change. I wanted to know more about the projects that
I'm here to support, and nearly all of them are linked to climate
change. I found myself going down a dozen interrelated rabbit
holes and I kept coming across a hot debate over the recent writings of this naysayer. Then I stumbled on one of his articles, without realizing at first who wrote it. His rhetoric was so convincing
that I did a serious double take. He had colorful graphs of real
data to solidify his perverted point, giving it the appearance of
legitimacy. I read the article several times and had to do some digging before trusting my initial instinct that it was hogwash.

It was hogwash. He showcased individual puzzle pieces that
conveniently promoted his argument, but failed to mention the
full picture that contradicts it. My digging revealed that his
graphs excluded the past 150 years. He was ignoring the entire
Industrial Revolution, the time period that matters most! I was
appalled.

So this guy is either a negligent fool, which seems unlikely
given his clever aptitude for hoodwinking, or he's a knowingly

deceitful bastard. I find it infuriating; he's intentionally misdirecting people, and there is little chance for anyone without a scientific background to pick up on it. Instead, people eat it up and this jerk's purpose of skepticism is achieved. These hacks *deserve* to be shunned by the scientific community.

I decided to fight back in my own way; I wrote a basic rundown of the carbon cycle for the thirty or so people who read my blog. I don't expect it to change anything, but it made me feel better.

~

The Carbon Cycle

Summit Station, Greenland
Monday, December 10, 2012

I am not a scientist. I merely collect scientific data for scientists. I work for NOAA. Summit Station is one of the core locations for NOAA's Global Monitoring Division, which collects data all around the world. Their goal is to provide a long-term global record of atmospheric properties and evaluate the role they play in driving climate change, ozone depletion, and air quality. The hope is that we as a society can learn to manage our impact on these things. I gladly support that.

Scientists believe the primary factors driving climate change are greenhouse gases and aerosols (tiny particles in the atmosphere; think dust, or smog). To manage these effectively, their impact needs to be understood. Many of the instruments we maintain at Summit, as well as the air and snow samples we collect, do just that.

From a widely zoomed-out perspective, climate change is simply energy in versus energy out. Radiation, light, heat—call it what you will—it's all energy. The sun provides essentially all the earth's energy, bathing us in visible light and a bit of ultraviolet. The earth either reflects or absorbs that solar energy. Some of it is absorbed in the atmosphere (mostly by ozone, which absorbs ultraviolet light), some is reflected back out to space (lightly colored surfaces like clouds or snow or sand are best at this), and the remaining sunlight (about half) is absorbed at the earth's surface, heating it up. That's the energy in. But that heat at the surface wants to escape, so at the same time the earth is absorbing light energy, it's also giving off its own thermal radiation back into space.[38] That's the energy out.

So, energy in: sunlight. Energy out: heat. When these are balanced, the earth maintains its temperature.

Enter humanity. Wait. No. I'm jumping ahead. There is more to learn first. Let's start with the air.

The majority of our atmosphere consists of nitrogen (78 percent) and oxygen (21 percent) with just a bit of argon (about 1 percent) thrown in to top it off. These three gases compose 99.9 percent of the air we breathe, humidity excluded. *What about carbon dioxide?* you ask. *Don't all the world's plants need to "breathe"?* True. But carbon dioxide makes up a surprisingly minuscule amount of the atmosphere: 0.04 percent. That's only three thousand billion metric tons! Well, it's small when compared to five million billion. It's the atmospheric equivalent of one M&M in a two-liter bottle full of M&Ms, and if you've ever guessed how many M&Ms are in that bottle, you'll know there are a lot more than you think.

But I'm glad you mention carbon dioxide because that brings us to one of the key concerns of climate change: greenhouse gases. Greenhouse gases are good. Without them the earth's surface would be about 35°C colder. (This is science, so I'm using centigrade, but to us 'mericans, that's about 65°F colder—*brr.*) Greenhouse gases are our down comforter. Here's how they work:

The light from the sun is high-frequency energy, and for the most part, it passes right through the atmosphere—just like it passes through the glass roof of a greenhouse. The thermal radiation from the earth, however, is low-frequency energy, and some of it

---

38 That's radiation as in the outdated hot water radiator in your grand-parents' living room, not radiation as in nuclear fallout.

gets hung up instead of escaping to space—like the glass traps heat in the greenhouse. The primary constituents of our atmosphere—nitrogen, oxygen, and argon—allow this thermal energy to escape, but greenhouse gases do not. Instead, they absorb it and then reemit it in a random direction. Some of this "scattered" energy continues out to space and some is reflected back down to Earth. In this way, these gases act as a nice, warm blanket. Adding greenhouse gases to the atmosphere is like adding down to the comforter; it creates a thicker layer that redirects more thermal energy back down to Earth. Too much insulation and the blanket gets suffocatingly hot, so you wake up in a pool of sweat and throw the damn thing off. Of course, throwing off our atmosphere, were it possible, would also prove suffocating.

Many gases cause this greenhouse effect, but the two most significant are water vapor and carbon dioxide. The reason for their significance is their stability. Other greenhouse gases—nitrous oxide, methane, hydrofluorocarbons, etc.—are less stable; they break down in reactions with sunlight or with other gases, leaving more innocuous compounds in their place. Not so for water vapor or carbon dioxide. Instead of breaking down, these molecules continually enter and exit the atmosphere as part of a cycle.

In the case of water, the cycle is straightforward: it evaporates, it condenses, it evaporates, it condenses. Sometimes it takes a passing vacation through a plant or animal or takes a nap in an aquifer or a long-frozen hibernation in an ice cap. But for the most part, it evaporates from the ocean, precipitates on land, and flows back to the ocean. I'm sure you remember fifth-grade science class. I know I don't.

Though water vapor is the most significant greenhouse gas, we're not in a position to do much about it unless we can learn to control the clouds, the humidity, the rain—basically, the weather. Prediction seems difficult enough. Fortunately, air can only hold so much moisture, so to a large degree this cycle regulates itself.

That leaves us with carbon dioxide, whose cycle is a little trickier. Complex interactions like life as we know it get involved, and we're forced to track carbon in all its guises, not just as CO_2. This is done by understanding interactions between the reservoirs, or sinks, for carbon: the ocean, the atmosphere, the biosphere (plants, animals, and microorganisms), and earth itself (not *the* Earth, just earth: organic soil, sedimentary rock, fossil fuels. You know, the ancient Greek element *earth*). Water, air, fire, earth— carbon is everywhere.

Where the greenhouse effect is concerned we're most interested in the interactions of CO_2 between the atmosphere and the other sinks: the ocean, the biosphere, and earth.

The ocean exchanges CO_2 openly with the air, and the molecules simply pass to whichever has the lower concentration. This is a slow process, however.

In the biosphere, plants photosynthesize, pulling loads of CO_2 from the air in order to grow. (This fascinates me: plants get the majority of their substance from the atmosphere, not from the soil. They create leaves and branches and flowers and fruit from thin air. It's truly magic.) Then animals eat the plants, taking up the carbon, and microorganisms decompose the plants and animals when they die, putting the carbon back into the air as CO_2. The net effect is nullification in the short term, but over *very* long periods of time, some of the dead stuff in the forests and swamps becomes buried, slowly depositing carbon in the earth reservoir. That carbon eventually becomes fossil fuel.

Examples of carbon interchange directly between earth and the atmosphere are few; volcanoes belch CO_2, and certain rocks release CO_2 as they erode. These contributions to the atmosphere are minuscule. But we're changing that: we've joined earth's team —in a big way.

Okay, *now* enter humanity.

We know that when we burn fossil fuels we create two primary products: carbon dioxide and water vapor. *Wait a minute*, you should be thinking, *those are the two worst greenhouse gases!* Yep. The water is trivial; the oceans will take that up immediately, no problem. But we've added a significant path to the carbon cycle that doesn't exist naturally. We're taking carbon out of one reservoir (earth) and moving it to another (the atmosphere) at an incredible rate. And that's the real problem: rate. Once that carbon is in the atmosphere, its path back into the earth is ludicrously slow. It took millions of years for it to become a fossil fuel in the first place.

So where will all that carbon go? Nowhere fast. The oceans will eventually absorb the majority of it, but that will take thousands of years. And that has its own problems. (You've probably heard the term "ocean acidification" being thrown around.) Reforestation might be the quickest way to draw CO_2 back out of the atmosphere, thus sequestering the carbon in biomass, but we're not good at that. In fact, we're much better at deforestation. Plus, I suspect it would take a lot more forest than we have room for— especially with the ballooning human population, which I think is a more immediate threat than climate change.

So what can we do? Commute on a bicycle. Turn down the heater. Stop eating meat. Consider the impacts of your purchases, downstream *and* upstream. And start growing bamboo, lots and lots of bamboo.

What are we actually doing? Nothing, it seems. We continue to burn increasing amounts of fossil fuels and pretend the problem doesn't exist despite overwhelming evidence. In the US, we emit three times as much CO_2 per capita than the global average. We drive huge cars. We heat and cool oversized homes. We wash our clothes after each wearing. We use every kind of appliance imaginable. We must have the latest gizmo, even though the gizmo we're replacing works fine. In short, we are gluttons. But we're not alone in our wastefulness, we're just one of the bigger offenders. The entire world lights its cities through the night, consuming horrifying gobs of energy. And for what? Safety? Commerce? Don't you people sleep?

Maybe some of us disbelieve in climate change because that makes it easier to justify our excesses. Lifestyle is a difficult contentment to downgrade.

I suppose there are also people who are convinced of climate change but don't believe it matters. It's true that historically the earth has warmed and cooled naturally many times. And it's true that the earth has been much warmer in the past than it is today. In fact, in the early Triassic period (during the rise of dinosaurs, if you believe in that sort of thing), the earth is believed to have been around 15°C warmer. But the issue now is not that the earth is warming; it's the *rate* at which it's expected to warm that is ringing the alarm bells.

Here's the deal. Over the past million years, the earth's temperature has followed a repeating pattern, based on subtle variations in its orbit. The earth cools gradually into an ice age and then jumps dramatically back out. This happens about every 100,000 years. Just recently—geologically speaking, that is—the earth recovered from an ice age, so it is currently in the warm part of the cycle. So, it should be cooling toward the next ice age.

It isn't.

During that past million years, CO_2 in the atmosphere also went up and down, plotting a graph that looks identical to the earth's temperature. CO_2 averaged about 220 parts per million, and never went above 300. But now, it's about to pass 400.[39]

So here we are, at the warmest point in the earth's temperature cycle, and we've doubled the down in our comforter—*and* we continue to stuff in more insulation. Something is going to happen, and scientists are busy trying to figure out what. They're expecting the earth to warm rapidly. Perhaps more rapidly than

---

39   As of 2016, atmospheric CO_2 is beyond 400 parts per million, and continues to climb.

ever before. Undoubtedly faster than modern humankind has ever experienced. Many species will be unable to adapt. The extinction rate is already on the rise. There will be more extinctions. Possibly mass extinctions.

Maybe our own.

The dominoes stand poised and our finger swings. That's the geological freeze-frame we find ourselves at, and it's too late to halt the finger. All we know is that we're causing extremely rapid changes to the earth, and there is going to be some sort of outcome. Let's just hope it's not catastrophic.

~

I learned something interesting about Venus today: its atmosphere is ninety-six percent carbon dioxide. I knew Venus was a hellishly noxious inferno of a planet, but I didn't know it was due to a greenhouse effect gone berserk. The average temperature on the surface of Venus is 462°C. Earth's average is only 15°C. My initial thought was, well, yeah, Venus is a lot closer to the sun than we are. This naturally led me to look up Mercury, which is even closer to the sun and, as it turns out, doesn't have an atmosphere at all. Its average surface temperature is only 167°C. Hmm.

Is the berserk greenhouse a possible fate of Earth? I suppose on a cosmic timescale it is. Then again, on a cosmic timescale, our sun is just a calm nuclear-fusion fuse to a supernova time bomb. We're doomed.[40]

---

40   This is not strictly true; our sun is not massive enough to go supernova. However, in five or six billion years, it will become a red giant, growing to envelop Mercury, Venus, and Earth all in a gargantuan blood-orange inferno. So, we *are* doomed.

10

In which I discover that what I've been calling storms were just periods of increased inconvenience.

Day 38
Tuesday, December 11

When I was a kid we occasionally got a snow day, when we would happily put on our snowsuits for a frolicking day off from school. The polar version we call a whiteout, which is similar in that we can't go to work but different in that we go outside by necessity only and it's rarely fun. In fact, it's dangerous.

Summit Station has weather guidelines for safe outdoor travel. Much has to do with carrying a radio, signing out, and using the buddy system, but there are specific rules concerning the weather that can restrict travel or forbid it altogether. This is broken down into three categories, blandly called Conditions 1, 2, and 3.

Condition 3 covers the average everyday stuff: cold and miserable by most standards but pleasant by ours.

Condition 2 is defined as visibility below 2,000 feet or wind chill below -90°F. Looking back at our weather observations so far, I'd say we spend about half our time in Con 2, usually due to obscured visibility from freezing fog or blowing snow, not to mention the dark. In theory, Con 2 restricts travel by requiring approval from the manager and a radio checkout/check-in when going beyond the Big House-Green House-S.O.B. corridor. In practice, manager approval is assumed—otherwise, it would be a constant annoyance—so we just need to let someone know if we're headed to TAWO or MSF and radio in when we get there, which we're in the habit of always doing anyway. We essentially operate by Con 2 parameters all the time.

If visibility drops below 200 feet or windchill below -100°F, we're in Condition 1. All travel is halted excepting "well-coordinated regular tasking or in event of emergency," which is more lenient than the Antarctic, which goes on lockdown for Con 1—no one leaves the building they're in. Here, "well-coordinated regular tasking" basically means careful travel—as long as everyone knows where you're going—between the Big House, Green House, and S.O.B., rendering "or in event of emergency" meaningless because if there is an emergency, those are the only buildings that matter. If TAWO caught fire we'd never see it, and even if we could, we'd let it burn without question.

If someone were to become lost out there in Con 1, the chances of finding them are so minimal that it would scarcely be worth the risk. This is why we have roped flag lines. Then again, we're a family, and we would do anything we could to help each other, within the confines of relative safety. Rule number one of search and rescue is not to become a victim yourself.

The only emergency travel I can imagine at this time of year would be to the emergency generator shack, which is not far, and if it came to needing the backup generator, our efforts would without a doubt be well coordinated.

~

A Moderate Breeze

Summit Station, Greenland
Tuesday, December 11, 2012

We awoke this morning to rattling walls and howling windows. The wind reached forty miles per hour and the temperature was a balmy plus four degrees Fahrenheit.

On my way to the Big House for breakfast, I marveled at the above-zero temperature and neglected to wear my goggles, choosing instead to tuck my head and avert my eyes from the face-stinging slivers of blowing snow. No—it's not snow. Snow is big and soft and fluffy and fun; snowballs, snow angels, snowmen. We don't get snow. This is ice, even at plus four degrees.

The wind shakes the Big House and makes strange whistling and knocking noises as it broadsides the building, which sways on its stilts, giving the eerie feeling of being on a ship. The curtains shift. The toilet water shakes like a bowl full of jelly. The wall clock appears to bob with the weight of time as the minute hand lopes around. Or perhaps it's me doing the bobbing.

Over breakfast the visibility deteriorated from Con 2 to Con 1, so the walk back to the Green House looked something like this:

~

The hike to TAWO was out of the question, as was most of the rest of work on station, so we had an extended breakfast that left little more than an hour before an early lunch.

Me: "Man, the wind sounds like someone's playing a perpetual kazoo over there by the bathroom."

Neal: "Or slaughtering a cow really slowly."

Lance: "I don't want to go back out there. This morning I had to reboot the cloud radar like ten times. Every time you do it, it takes twenty minutes. It's the static; it fries everything."

I don't know why Lance was at the MSF so early, but he was

right about the static electricity: during a storm, it's intense. Touching anything metal while standing outside in the wind results in a painful shock, even through my thick gloves. Holding the railing on the Green House roof is like holding an electric fence. The shocks come rhythmically, about every second. The first time I experienced this, disbelief compelled me to continue torturing myself.

Me: "Well, if it stays like this you won't have to go back to MSF."

Phil: "How's that new flag line, Lance?" Phil and Lance recently installed a new row of flags between the Green House and the MSF.

Lance: "It's nice. It's like a fence!" He sounded excited. I wasn't sure why. I guess at this point any change is something to be excited about.

Phil: "You've got a fence on either side of you now."

Lance: "I just get funneled in there. That flag line from the Big House was horrible. I fell down twice. I don't know if it's because the wind pushed me over or because it was uneven. Now I feel like I'm in a fenced-in yard because there's flags on both sides!"

Neal: "It's your safety net."

Lance: "Yeah— *Don't cross the street; stay in the yard!*"

Me: "Now we just need to get you a collar."

Neal: "I was thinking more like cattle, you know, how they're in those runs to funnel them to their doom?"

Don: "Is there any poo in your field, Lance?"

There was a silent pause as we all looked at Don.

Neal: "Wait a minute. What was the question? *Is there any poo in your field?*"

At this point I was struggling to hold in a laugh; I wanted to hear Don's explanation.

Don: "It's a big fenced-in area; that's a field. And you were talking about cows . . ."

Neal: "Yeah, and you're talking about poo, once again!"

Don: "Everything is poo!"

And that's when I lost it. Among the laughter, Neal got up and headed to the bookshelf. I knew exactly what he was going for.

Me: "Don, I think you just made the quote book."

Neal: "We need to fill this thing out more. There's only one quote in here." He sat back down at the table and Lance leaned over his shoulder to read the quote.

Lance: "*Winter Phase 2, 2012-2013. 'I don't care what it's shaped like, it tastes great!' -Rex.*"

We all laughed.

Me: "Taken out of context that doesn't make any sense! I don't even remember what I was talking about."

Neal: "Well, that's the beauty of it. Phil said something this morning that was clever when taken out of context but I can't remember it now."

Me: "Wait, it was clever when you took it *out* of the context?"

Phil: "It's intimidating, the spontaneity of this group."

Lance: "Yeah, every time Neal picks up a pen now, everyone's gonna be quiet." He turned to Neal. "You know, you don't have to put their name by it. You could just put down the quote."

Neal: "Well, all the other quotes have names by them. They don't know which Don!"

Lance: "*Winter Phase 2, 2012-2013.* You don't think that gives it away?" We laughed again.

Neal: "Okay, I'll quit putting names. *'Everything is poo!'*" He wrote as he spoke, and smiled as he added, "'*-Don.*' I'll quit putting names after this one." We laughed.

Lance: "Oh, hey, Don, that reminds me, I've got a website for you that Hannah sent."

Don: "Oh yeah? What is it?"

Lance: "It's got all these pictures of poo and you have to guess what animal it came from. You'll love it!"

After lunch, I told Don I'd be back to brew beer in the afternoon, since we had no more work we could do. I guess I should have specified that it would be more than ten minutes, because an hour later Don and Lance came into the Green House calling my name like I was a lost puppy.

"We weren't sure what happened to you," Lance said when he

found me in my room, waking from a nap.

"Oh, sorry, I didn't know you were waiting for me. I was just about to head back over. I've got the brew kit right here."

"Neal called on the radio and you didn't answer," Don said.

I immediately felt bad about this. "Shit, I didn't hear it." A guilty glance at my radio told me why. "My radio is off." In case of emergency, my radio should always be on. Especially in weather like this, my radio should absolutely, definitely be on.

Don shrugged it off. "Well, Neal said if we found you to be sure and pry the beer from your frozen, lifeless fingers." At least they weren't too worried. Then again, maybe that's a bad thing.

The weather continued to be horrendous for the rest of the day. The back door to the Green House was engulfed in strangely shaped drifts that grew up from the ground *and* down from the

Snow drifts attempting to conceal the Green House

roof, bringing to mind the mythically gnarled entrance of a yeti cave. Don dug steps down to the level of the door so he could walk to the S.O.B.

The wind settled slightly after dinner, down to twenty-five knots, so I asked Lance if he thought I should try to launch the evening weather balloon. He said he attempts it as long as the wind is under thirty. Of course, this morning his balloon took off horizontally and he heard a metallic *ping* as the sonde bounced off some piece of equipment to meet its demise. So I'm not sure his advice is sound. I decided to give it a go anyway, and Neal brought a camera to film it, convinced it would be entertaining.

As we opened the S.O.B.'s garage door, mounds of drifted snow toppled inside. I trudged through the pile and pressed into the wind. The balloon immediately shifted from above my head and started pulling me straight along. I held on while the balloon bounced and contorted at ground level. I dug my heels and waited for a moment of lift that wouldn't come. Suddenly a cord broke and the balloon disappeared into oblivion. Fortunately, the expensive weather sonde was left safely in my hand to be launched another day. Then, to my surprise, the sonde's damn parachute opened, giving me a wild jolt and Neal a wilder laugh.

We've discussed the irrelevance of the parachute, which is meant to bring the sonde safely down for recovery after the balloon bursts high in the atmosphere. It serves little purpose in an endless empty expanse where there is no chance of the tiny payload causing any damage to anything, much less ever being recovered. In gloved hands, I didn't have the slightest chance of hanging on. The sonde slipped from my fingers and promptly disappeared into the black whited-out void, much to Neal's bursting delight. I had to laugh too. The parachute was suddenly quite relevant, though in a way exactly opposite its intended purpose.

"I'm beginning to think Lance eggs us on because he's amused by our failure," I said.

"I'm amused. That was hilarious!" Neal replied jovially.

"Whose side are you on?"

"I'm just glad I'm not the only one who's fucked this up."

"Fair enough. That *was* pretty damn funny. Let's see the video."

My failure with the balloon freed me up to watch a movie uninterrupted. I didn't have to get up midfilm to close the data collection and transfer the files. We've been waiting for our first Condition 1 to watch *Whiteout*, which features our Tucker. It was purchased from the filmmakers, complete with colored ground-effect lights that supposedly sync with a thumping aftermarket stereo system. They also added a row of overhead spotlights that, when turned on, transforms an average day into a whiteout, as advertised.

Day 39
Wednesday, December 12

The weather improved just enough to get back to our regular routine today, but it's still crummy. We found the precipitation sampling tower blown over, with its guylines still attached and taut. The tower was bent around like a skyward-aimed bow with no arrow. It went back up okay, but I'm worried about its durability—it's just a couple lengths of flimsy aluminum tube. I wonder how long it has survived here and if this is the first time it's been buffeted down.

The tower is about fifteen feet tall and has three little mesh bags intended to catch falling snow. I'm impressed that they created enough drag to fold the whole thing over. We typically clean the frost from these bags daily. Any time there is precipitation we are to collect them, melt the snow, and bottle it for shipment. This project uses a network of collection points across the ice cap to determine how the Arctic climate is affected by annual sea ice extent—the amount of ocean that freezes each year. The theory is that decreased sea ice means more ocean exposed for evaporation, which brings more moisture and precipitation to the region. That precipitation changes the reflectivity of the ice cap's surface, which affects melting and freshwater discharge. Freshwater discharge affects the salinity of the ocean, the salinity affects the density, and the density affects the circulation of ocean currents. The gory details are fuzzy to me, because isotopic ratios get involved again and I lose interest—I'm a big-picture person. The big picture is, if the Greenland ice cap melts too rapidly, it could shut down the Gulf Stream and cause Europe to become very, very cold.

Day 40
Thursday, December 13

We're finishing each other's sentences now.

Me: "A lot of our cheese is—"

Phil: "Getting a little moldy, yeah. I don't remember that happening before. But it only takes one bit of mold in there to—"

Neal: "Spread it around everywhere. But, doesn't that make the cheese better?"

OUR QUIET DAY off on Tuesday caught up to us with a vengeance today. The wind came down and the temperature was still up. We needed to take advantage of the weather and get some big tasks done, so we decided to do the one-meter pit. Our first hurdle: we didn't have enough clean sample bottles, which was a discouraging way to start the day. So we tag-teamed the purified-water triple rinse of more bottles and placed them under the hood to dry, putting the pit off until the afternoon and doing the daily checks and the bamboo forest in the meantime.

Unlike most visits to the forest, which are long and cold, today's was easy and enjoyable at only a few degrees below zero. It was so nice out that I didn't need to cover my chin or mouth with my gaiter. I even brought my camera and stopped to take pictures of the incredible not-quite-day. A fiery orange horizon beneath cotton candy pillows set this white world ablaze with color. Clouds like slate-blue sails with glowing amber edges floated adrift in the pink sea. This is the magical land where diamonds dust the air, emerald falls from the heavens, cotton balls make pilgrimage, and bamboo grows shorter.

"It's more of an orchard, really," Neal said.

"What?" I broke from my reverie.

A lovely day in the bamboo forest

"The poles are all neatly spaced on a grid. A forest would be random. We should call it the bamboo orchard."

As we surveyed the orchard, the clouds slowly blackened and descended to the horizon, pinching the orange band with a red-hot-coal smoke.

The dark ceiling of rare winter cumulus dropped the first flakes that I've seen. It's strange that in this environment consisting almost entirely of snow, so little of it falls from the sky. It certainly accumulates, but I don't know where the hell it comes from. I

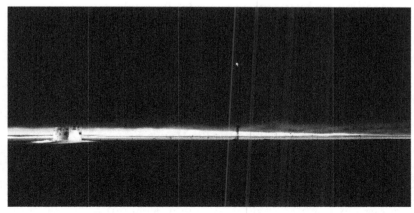

Polar night reclaiming the sky behind the MSF and 50-meter tower

guess it just blows in, or freezes out of the Gulf Stream air. The snowfall meant that on our way back to TAWO we would have to sample the precip tower. Our day was steadily filling.

We arrived hungry at the Big House for a late lunch. Having already squeezed a normal day's work into a long morning, we weren't at all motivated to go back out, but the weather was so agreeable that we ate quickly and rallied. The bottles for the meter pit were dry now, but in our haste, we'd forgotten to clean the tools. After another impetus-sucking delay we hiked out to TAWO, collecting the precip samples along the way, and then dug the majority of the pit before I realized that we'd forgotten the thermometers, which were all the way back at the Green House. With resign and a long-exhaled expletive, I looked up from shoveling and told Neal. There was a long pause. It was getting difficult to believe how many things we had botched in preparing for this job. Our motivation was at an end. We would have loved to say "screw it" and go home, except that the pit was practically ready and to succumb now meant filling it in and redigging it later. Screw that, too.

"I told Lance I'd help him make sushi today, but it's not going to happen, is it?" I asked.

"I told him the same thing," Neal replied.

"You have longer legs," I said without humor.

"I'm slowing by the minute," Neal countered.

I resigned. "I'll go. I think I'm getting my first wind."

Another half hour was lost as I plodded to the Green House and back, and then we were in the pit again. The sky cleared as we sampled, and by the time we finished, the temperature was taking a plunge. We were already late for dinner, which is rare, and my stomach was letting me know. "I can *not* wait for dinner," I said as we began the trudge back to the Big House.

"Me, either," Neal agreed. "I love sushi. I can put back a lot of sushi."

And he wasn't kidding. At the end of the meal, in an effort to squeeze in as much sushi as possible, Neal left to "make some more room." Since the Big House bathroom has a saloon-like half door, we were able to heckle him from the table. When the first sound came, Don repeated the noise and yelled, "Sounds like a chicken in there!"

Lance and Don have been spending time at whopooped.org—I'm afraid to know how much—and Don said the most difficult poo to identify was the chicken, even though he has chickens at home. "But the best part is that you have to feed the animals and when you raise their tail, then bits of poo fall out and it goes—" Don made a farting noise like a four-year-old.

Neal returned from the bathroom and reported. "It was all thunder and no lightning."

"I'm trying to figure out which is the thunder and which is the lightning," I said.

"Thunder is the audible part."

"I was thinking that, but the lightning analogy is rough. Maybe the lightning is the part that comes down from the heavens?"

We all sat back with full bellies as Neal managed a few more pieces of sushi and then began sipping on the leftover juice from the pickled ginger. "Ginger is good for settling your stomach," he said. I'm sure he needed it, but he got too comfortable and accidentally took a large swig, followed by a larger *whoop*. Then he continued our theme of boyhood zest:[41] "I'll give you all the money in my pockets if you snort this wasabi."

"You don't have any money in your pockets," Don pointed out.

"That may be true, but I bet you don't either, so you can double your money!"

---

41   "Zest" sounds much better than "immaturity."

11

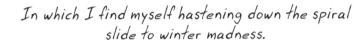

*In which I find myself hastening down the spiral
slide to winter madness.*

Day 41
Friday, December 14

We've discussed the idiocy of ICESat at length. The conclusion
I keep reaching is that I refuse to do it unless the temperature and
weather are really damn good. Phil drafted a summary of the
safety issues that doesn't inspire continuation of the pursuit, at
least not in the winter. The take-home message is that all the
safety equipment, while providing slight peace of mind—I think
he called it "intellectual confidence"—really doesn't do jack shit to
help us in a real emergency—he definitely called it a "pseu-
dosafety effect."

We assessed ICESat and discovered that in addition to having a
gimpy rescue vehicle and a useless stack of frozen communication
devices, the emergency sleeping bags are also inadequate due to
age and a frightening lack of insulation loft from years of being
stored compressed. Phil brought all this to attention in his email
and posed several suggestions: fit the polypod with a small diesel
furnace heater and a high-power VHF radio that would run on
the marine battery; provide new winter-quality sleeping bags and

store them uncompressed in the polypod; introduce a prescribed temperature cutoff point for vehicle operations; and require that the transponder breadcrumbs are operational for winter off-station travel. I say let's make ICESat nice, warm, and fuzzy by doing it from the comfort of an enclosed, heated vehicle.

We woke this morning to the fabled "really damn good" weather, so I was willing. The temperature had come back up and the air was calm with a light fog. Neal and I gathered everything together immediately and headed out. Naturally, the whole thing fell apart from there. My snow machine stalled inexplicably on the way to the snow-sampling location—twice. The samples irritated the hell out of me because I couldn't remove the damn perf strips. I was miffed enough that I used my teeth on one, contamination be damned. By the time we finished the samples, the freezing fog had thickened, reducing visibility to not much. We paused to discuss the conditions and reluctantly accepted the possibility of bagging the whole thing if we had to, but we were determined to go on. Damn if we weren't going to get this heinous overblown task out of the way on such a warm day.

My machine stalled again as we followed four closely spaced flags to the start of the transect. Then we couldn't find the next flag. Visibility had suddenly dropped to absolutely nothing. We had to stay close to each other just to maintain visual contact. I pulled up next to Neal in the unearthly and disorienting Ping-Pong ball, and my machine stalled again.

"I guess that says it," I sighed, finally accepting the omen on its fourth call.

"Damn it," was all Neal could reply.

We turned and began retracing our tracks, which, owing to their continuity, were much easier to follow than the flags that emerged only occasionally through the fog. Neal was ahead of me, with no polypod to haul, when my machine stalled again. I watched as his taillight disappeared, swallowed by a palpable haze. I flashed back to our inability to see during the previous ICESat. There was no panic this time, just a feeling of exasperation toward the absurdity of this task. I radioed Neal. Useless. He couldn't hear his radio over his snow machine. I managed to restart my machine, but as soon as I started moving it stalled again. *At least I have the polypod*, I thought, *with the frozen electronics and the crappy old sleeping bags*. I made a mental adjustment. *Stop being cynical*, I told myself. *At least it's a relatively warm day, only ten below zero . . . and I can't see a damn thing.* Useless.

I radioed again. "Neal, Neal. Rex. Copy?"

"Rex, this is Phil. Have you been separated?"

As I was keying the mic to reply, a headlight eked fuzzily through the fog. "I've got him. Thanks, Phil."

"I'm glad you could see that you couldn't see me!" I told Neal as he pulled up.

"Just like the last time," he said, a faint smile in his voice.

We swapped the polypod over to Neal's machine, and I took the lead at a turtle's pace that my machine managed with only occasional protest. Back at the Green House, we packed all the electronics back inside to warm up for another try tomorrow. When we plugged the GPS card in to clear it, we found that the data was corrupt because the battery had died because Neal connected it to the charger backwards because the negative battery cable has a red crimp instead of, well, *any other color* because some muppet put it together that way. Red means positive. Negative should be black, or green, or even bare copper, but never, ever red. I cursed and scribbled as much black ink on the bloody red crimp as I could.

It was easy to dislike ICESat after that first miserable round, but now I'm beginning to despise it. It's a huge pain to get everything together and a royal annoyance to get shut down halfway due to circumstances beyond our control. I would have gone through the roof if we'd finished the entire thing and *then* found the dead battery. There's just so much logic against ICESat and so little for it, despite the whole paragraph in our operating procedure emphasizing that right now it is "more important than ever to maintain our ground measurements" during the interim between the nonexistent satellite we're ground-truthing for and its successor, scheduled for launch four years from now. I can only think of one word for that business: extrapolation. Surely the slight blip of data we're collecting doesn't amount to squat compared to the swaths of information gathered by satellite. Seriously: compare the old ground data to the old satellite data, and the new ground to the new satellite, find the difference, and *bang!* Your new satellite is calibrated to your old one. Now extrapolate the interim in swaths instead of blips.

At lunch, Don reiterated the offer he'd made me after our first ICESat traverse.

Don: "Hey, I wasn't kidding. I'll go instead of you. I don't mind."

Me: "That's good because I've decided I'm boycotting ICESat. If you wanna go, more power to ya. I'm done with that shit."

Neal: "Don's looking for a vacation."

Me: "It actually wouldn't have been bad today. It was warm, at least."

Don: "Are you gonna try to go again tomorrow?" He directed the question at Neal, probably guessing what my answer would be.

Neal: "If it's like it was before it got foggy, yeah. I mean, warm and not windy."

Me: "It's just frustrating and pointless."

Don: "You're so negative."

I thought about that for a moment as I walked over to the cupboard and opened a package of cookies.

Me: "You know, that's usually not true. But today: yes."

Don: "You'll feel better after your cookies."

Me: "I feel better already. I felt better as soon as you said you'd do it!"

Neal got a good laugh out of that.

Don: "I might regret what I said."

Neal: "Have you ever been out there?"

Don: "I haven't been anywhere. The farthest I've been is . . ."

Neal: "TAWO?"

Don: "TAWO."

Me: "The view out there is lovely."

Neal: "Yeah." He said it dreamily, thinking I was just joking around. I guess my negativity permeated the words with an unintentional sarcasm.

Don: "What's lovely? The fog?"

Neal: "You can hear the waves lapping up on the beach. And there's a lot of wildlife out there."

Don: "Did you meet any women?"

Neal: "I lost count of all the women we saw out there."

Me: "Yeah." I said it darkly, then got up and headed back to the cupboard. "I think I'm gonna need another cookie."

Phil: "Just put them on the table, Rex."

Me: "You want one?"

Phil: "No, I don't want *one*." He grinned. I laughed, welcoming an uplift in my mood.

The electric kettle boiled and Neal got up to make himself tea. After a while of rummaging through the boxes and bags of miscellaneous styles and flavors, he finally burst. "What the—? Why do we have so much caffeine-free tea? What are they really trying to accomplish?"

Phil: "Fucking hippies! It's because every new person up here asks for something different."

And then they don't return to use it, leaving a plethora of odd choices, none good.

Don: "There's chamomile, if you wanna be gay!"

We all got a laugh out of that one,[42] and Neal headed directly to the quote book. Then he started fucking with me.

Neal: "So, Rex, do you want to go out and snow sample today?"

Me: "Hell, no! Why the hell would I want to do that? I already did that today."

Neal: "Only half."

We're supposed to "try" to collect the ICESat snow samples on the same day as the weekly ones, but that doesn't seem likely to

---

42   I should clarify here that none of us are against homosexuality, nor do we believe in stereotyping. But, we strongly believe in jokes about stereotyping.

work out very often. We just did the weeklies a few days ago, and having the samples too close together doesn't provide useful data.

Me: "I'll do them tomorrow when I go out to TAWO. What's today?"

Neal: "It's Friday."

Me: "That'll be fine. Did we sample on Monday or Wednesday?" The days are starting to spin around in my head.

Neal: "Wednesday."

Me: "Then there's no point in doing it today at all."

Neal just smiled at my justification.

Phil: "Well, then, a little caffeine-free tea and some naptime this afternoon?"

Me: "Hell, yeah. I think I better do some yoga too—to help my happy."

Neal: "Rex has crossed over to surly mode."

Phil: "Does seem like it, doesn't it?"

Me: "It happens sometimes."

Don: "You need some calm tea." He smiled mischievously as he passed me a tea bag.

Me: "Fucking calm tea doesn't do shit. Calm, my ass. This would just piss me off more. Thanks, though, I do appreciate it."

Neal cracked up at my off-kilter gratitude.

Neal: "That was the least sincere thing I've ever heard you say."

The strange thing was that I meant it; I appreciated Don's gesture, even in jest. But Neal was right: it sure didn't sound like it.

I wish I could say that the rest of the day went swimmingly and my sour mood lifted after a nice nap and some soothing yoga. But the rest of the day continued exploring the theme of everything gone wrong, and the only thing resembling swimming was the wet pile of laundry that I had to haul to the Big House to dry. I was tired, frustrated, and grumpy, and in a momentary outburst I cursed aloud at my parka for letting the wind through a gap between the hood and the fuzzy liner. Was it then that I realized I was being ridiculous? Or was it crawling around in the back of my mind already? I know I have surly moments from time to time, but today was absurd. It's time for tomorrow.

Day 42
Saturday, December 15

The fog lifted overnight revealing a clear sky, so Don was able to go on ICESat with Neal. I thanked him, even though by volunteering he undermined my boycott. It was a pleasant day at -30°F, and the wind only picked up slightly while they were out there. They finished quickly, though Neal still frostnipped his forehead a touch, making me wonder if he's had enough frostnip over the years to simply be more susceptible to it. He's spent many winters in the Antarctic—four that I know of at Palmer and at least a couple at the South Pole—and once you frostnip, it's easier to nip the same spot again. Then again, in this climate frostnip is likely to get you whether you're susceptible to it or not. At the midpoint of my winter in Antarctica I ran the "half-done run" in a side-wind blizzard. To my amazement they didn't cancel the event, and to my further amazement I frostnipped the lobe of my right ear while it was covered by a gaiter *and* a winter hat. But I got a free T-shirt. It had a typo.

When I asked Don how ICESat went, he just shrugged. "It was okay. It's not very exciting."

"No. It's not," I agreed.

"It wasn't bad, though. I don't know why you don't want to go."

"I'm sure it's not bad on a nice day like this. It's not because it's cold and miserable that I'm boycotting it, it's because it's fucking stupid and because it's unsafe, especially at sixty-five below."

Clearly, I've still got leftover grumpy from yesterday. Oh, well.

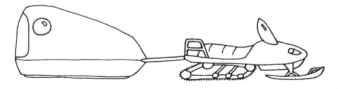

THIS EVENING WE saw a faint wavy band of aurora that stretched from horizon to horizon. It was nice but not worthy of my expectations. Overall, we're all disappointed by the lack of anything notable. Some solar maximum.

Day 43
Sunday, December 16

The freezing fog returned today with more tenacity, except that it's leaving an inexplicable view of the calm night sky. It's just a dense, opaque surface layer, encouraging a heavy glaze of hoar-frost that's coating everything.

We were lounging in the Big House after a late breakfast—it being Sunday—and Phil noted that our weather forecasters were right about the fog. But I was baffled by it.

Me: "It seems weird that it would fog up when it's getting warmer. I would expect it to be the other way around."

Neal: "It increases the moisture-holding capability of the air, so it makes sense. Warmer air can hold more water."

Me: "But I was thinking that fog happens when warmer air with more moisture gets cooled down, and it forces the water out and that's what makes the fog. Just like dew, you know?"

Neal: "We need Lance here to explain meteorology."

Me: "We do. I'll forget to ask by the time I see him."

Phil: "I think that the other fact is, apart from the atmospheric side of it, you're looking at that cold snow surface, so that's causing the moisture to precipitate out."

Me: "Oh, only near the surface. Right." That's exactly where the fog was. I initially assumed it was just settling there. It just seems heavier than clear air for some reason.

Phil: "Like Neal said, that warmer air rolling in holds more moisture, but there's only a degree or two difference between the air and the dew point. Near that cold snow surface the air drops those couple degrees. I think that's why we always get freezing fog right down close to the surface."

Me: "That makes sense. I guess that's the same reason a river valley collects fog sometimes."

Phil: "Right."

I wish the fog would lift. It has been inky black without the moon, as I anticipated, and with fog obscuring the horizon—the only place we see any light—I realized that there's an intensity of darkness *beyond* inky black. The moon is now past new and should be rising low in the south, but there is nothing to see through the haze. If there was, maybe I'd be out taking pictures. I guess it's just another mellow Sunday to look for things to do.

Back in our office, we stared at our computer screens, and Neal confirmed the deficit of available activities.

Neal: "Man, do you know how boring this place would be if I didn't have work?"

Me: "It's true."

Neal: "I mean, it's fun for a day."

Me: "It *is* nice to have a day off now and then."

Neal: "Yeah."

Me: "But it's really hard to fill."

I've found that baking bread fills up a few hours nicely. The last time we brewed I saved some leftover brewing grain and also hop sediment, and today I incorporated both into the bread. I baked two loaves and used different amounts of hops in each, unsure whether it would be any good. I'm glad I experimented because one loaf was great, the hops adding a subtle fresh-floral flavor and a touch of bitterness, mostly in the crust. The other loaf: not so much. Too much hops made the crust puckeringly bitter and basically inedible. The heart of the bread was still good at least, but maybe only for a hophead like me.

I spent the rest of the day sorting through the extensive collection of music given to me by one of the divers at Palmer. I've been meaning to do that for three years, so it felt like a major accomplishment—until I dashed all my efforts by accidentally erasing the entire library. A day wasted, or a day filled?

NEAL: "WELL, A new scientific study just came out that said men who do housework, i.e., 'women's chores' like washing dishes and vacuuming—"

Lance: "Are more likely to drink chamomile?" He laughed.

Neal: "They have less sex than men who don't."

Lance: "What?"

Neal: "Even though the women are more sexually satisfied by men who do housework."

Lance: "Instead of having sex?"

Neal: "Yeah. The women are happier, but the men are getting less sex if they do women's chores."

Lance: "Did they do this survey at Summit?"

We all found this amusing. Phil especially cracked up.

Neal: "Well, maybe that's skewing the data a bit. So, I refuse to do any more cleaning or washing dishes while I'm here because it's definitely cramped my sex life."

Phil: "Mm-hmm."

Lance: "What was their definition of housework, and what was their definition of sex?"

Neal: "That wasn't fully explained. They just said 'traditional women's chores,' which I would assume is washing dishes and cleaning and breastfeeding."

I never tire of Neal's quick, dry wit.

Me: "Does that suggest that men who do housework have less sex drive?"

Neal: "It just said they're getting less sex."

Me: "But *why* are they getting less sex?"

Neal: "Because they're too busy washing the dishes!"

Everyone laughed, and Phil retorted in a high-pitched voice.

Phil: "Don't touch me with those soggy hands!"

Neal: "The girls I've lived with, that's when I got most of my sex: while they were washing the dishes."

Don: "While *they* were washing the dishes?"

Neal: "Yeah, I've got nothing else to do."

Me: "There's nothing good on TV . . ."

Don: "I take it you're having your experience solo while they're washing the dishes?"

Neal: "No comment. I just watch from afar and do what comes

naturally."

Lance: "How far?"

Neal: "It's actually my neighbors who are doing the dishes."

Lance: "Does the same thing happen when we're doing the dishes?"

Neal: "You know, Carhartt overalls are the great equalizer. Everybody looks the same in 'em." I laughed at the suggestive implication in Neal's dry delivery.

Don: "Some of those girls down on the ice look pretty good in their Carhartts."

Me: "Yes, they do. Of course, now I'm wondering how many of the girls I admired from afar—all wrapped up in their red parkas and Carhartts, you know—were actually men with a feminine gait."

Neal: "You'd've known."

Me: "True. A gait is like a name tag, isn't it?"

With everyone in the same red parka and Carhartts, how else are we supposed to tell each other apart?

Day 44
Monday, December 17

I'm extremely tired today. It took me forever to get out of bed so I barely made it to breakfast in time for the morning meeting. Afterward, in a daze, I did the radionuclide filter swap and let Neal know it was done.

"I just did the RN like five minutes ago," he informed me.

"Hmm. I wondered why the numbers were nearly identical."

"Yeah, even the date!"

"Shit."

The radionuclide monitor is a simple device that pumps outside air through a filter, which we collect and replace every other day. Our operating procedure says:

> These filters will be analyzed for the natural radionuclide tracers ^7Be and ^{210}Pb. ^7Be is formed in the upper atmosphere when cosmic rays split atoms, while ^{210}Pb is formed

by the decay of ^{222}Rn, which is emitted into the atmosphere from rocks and soils.

Because we have no rocks or soils and we're not in the upper atmosphere—not quite—Summit Station is not a source of either of these tracers. Their presence here means they came from somewhere else, so their concentrations are used to study atmospheric mixing.

Neal suggested that I change the filter back, but I decided that changing the log was much easier, which is lazy and perhaps not good practice but I didn't see how it would make any difference since both filters had five minutes on them at that point anyway. We should probably ditch the other filter and start fresh next time though.

We had some rare excitement today, which was a nice break from the norm. We dismantled an air pump that feeds three *ometers*. We replaced some shattered internal bits that had seized the motor and tripped the breaker, which also took down the pumps for two other *ometers*, since they're on the same circuit. An impressive five birds with one stone.

Repairing the air pump and getting everything running again was so inconceivably exciting that we forgot to take the Monday snow surface samples for Noone. Fortunately it's not a big deal to be off by a day or two.

When I got an unusual second wind in the afternoon, rather than go back out to TAWO for the samples—which, in addition to the second wind also would have required a functional memory—instead it motivated me to troubleshoot the Green House washing machine's dysfunctional spin cycle. It's a juxtaposition: motivating oneself in order to be lazier. I think everyone else has given up now and just carries their laundry to the Big House, but I have persevered in the Green House, each time rolling dice on the sodden schlep to the other washing machine.

I opened the machine's guts hopeful and closed them frustrated. That's what motivation gets you around here.

LANCE WAS DISHING up his dinner. Phil queued up behind him and started fucking with him, but Lance wasn't having it.

"C'mon, move along, move along." Phil taunted. "You're holding up the line here. Damn sleep all afternoon and then hold a guy up who's been slogging away."

Lance quickly adopted a calm demeanor, like someone who had slept all afternoon. "Why have you been slogging away?"

"Well, I've really just been making enough noise to make you think I've been working."

"Are you suddenly in a hurry now?" Lance taunted back. "Are you hungry or something?"

"Well, you know."

"I'd've let you go first if I knew you had places to be."

"I do. Horizontal."

Day 45
Tuesday, December 18

I'm exhausted again today and I did little until late afternoon, when the weather was acceptable for snow sampling. I finished that and, remarkably, managed to piggyback some yoga onto the same motivational effort. I was quite proud of myself. Still am. Perhaps the key is simply to maintain momentum. But it's easier said than done: through every task, the desire to be finished and resting pulls so strongly at my thoughts. Is it the excess melatonin? My body's need to conserve energy?

Tomorrow will be a big day for me and I'll need all the gumption I can muster. It's my turn for rounds and the weather balloon, my night to cook dinner, and our typical day for the bamboo forest. I really need a decent sleep tonight.

Day 46
Wednesday, December 19

Neal was on a mission to finish the bamboo forest. He was so rushed that he fell over on the way out and got all twisted up in his skis, much to my amusement. Later, while we were midforest, he nearly did it again—twice. As we removed our skis outside the Green House, with our backs to the piercing wind, I remarked on his energy level. "Man, you were really motivated today."

"I was only motivated not to be out here," he replied.

"Oh, now I get it."

I can't blame him. It wasn't terribly cold but the wind made it miserable. It was strong enough to necessitate goggles, which I still haven't mastered the art of. Neal told me about a guy he knew one winter at Pole who conceived several iterations of a strange snorkel-like contraption to funnel his breath away from his face. Apparently it rarely kept his goggles from freezing over.

Long before we finished measuring all the bamboo poles, I could see next to nothing. I kept writing over numbers that were already there and having to ask what the last measurement was. It's a testament to Neal's will to be indoors that we still made it back in record time.

I suppose Neal's clumsiness on skis today could be partially blamed on the disorienting fog that continues to encapsulate us. It has persisted for the past six days and is bafflingly impervious to temperature changes. That leaves just two days until the end of the world, according to the Mayan calendar, and at this rate we won't even get to see it. Imagine all the spectacular cataclysmic events that are likely to occur because the mythology of an ancient race has us living in the final days of their fourth "world" but they have rudely refused to extend their calendar into the fifth. Volcanoes, meteors, floods, celestial collisions, supernovae, locusts! And all we'll see here is fog.

It's a common topic for us lately, since the Mayan calendar ends on the winter solstice—no sheer coincidence—and for us that's Midwinter, by far the most important day of the year. It marks the midpoint of our extensive night. At that imperceptible moment of reversing current, our horizon will begin to drift back toward the dawn. Darkness is such a defining characteristic here that this moment is far more significant than any other—barring perhaps the dawn itself. But, though the dawn is set, the moment we'll first behold the sun remains uncertain. The solstice we can count on.

For some reason we all thought tomorrow was the solstice, but it's the twenty-first: Friday. I have no idea how we all screwed this up in our heads, but it doesn't matter. There are only two dates we need to remember: the sunrise and the day we fly out of here.

We've all agreed to subdue Christmas and concentrate our festivity on the solstice and the coming of more light to our bleak icy world. Just returning to the roots really, to the original pagan celebration that was twisted long ago during its assimilation into Christianity and is now completely diluted, deranged, and fucked up by capitalism.

Day 47
Thursday, December 20

We decided it was Lance's fault for our anonymous misconception over the dates. He said last week that he'd be cooking beef Wellington for a nice solstice dinner, and since Thursdays are Lance's night to cook, reason actually prevailed. Our only mistake was to trust a winter-over to know what day of the week it is. "How about a nice solstice *eve* dinner?" Lance suggested, resolving our dilemma. We all agreed that since the world will be ending tomorrow, we might as well have our fancy meal tonight.[43]

Neal removed the phyllo dough crust from his beef Wellington, as well as the crustlike skins of his sweet potato slices. Lance didn't assail him with sarcasm this time, maybe because he was distracted by the bottle of scotch that Phil brought out for the occasion.

---

43   Still, for the most important day of the year we basically botched it, didn't we?

Lance: "I'm going to put on clean underwear tonight so I'm ready for the end of the world."

Neal: "Will that be your midseason underwear change, then?"

Lance: "No, no, I'm just going to turn them inside out."

Don: "So the crust is on the outside!"

Phil: "And we're right back to poo." He said it with humor, but also with resign.

Lance: "I'm worried when I get home I'll have irresistible urges to yell out *POO!*"

I felt the time was right to bring up the stoic Antarctic woman who comfortably informed an entire table of strangers all about her polyps.

Lance: "They put a hot poker up your ass? Man, I hope I never get that."

Don: "Oh, if you live long enough, you'll get polyps."

Lance: "Well then let's hope the world *does* end tomorrow."

Me: "Speaking of, and in the spirit of it all, tonight should we watch some drawn-out apocalyptic thriller and drink every time they use immense amounts of special effects to make up for the shitty acting and plot?"

Neal: "Let's just not watch *Whiteout* again. That was awful."

That got me thinking about the all-obscuring snow globe of freezing fog that finally lifted late in the day, unveiling a beautiful starry sky, a half moon, and a wonderland of thick frost. The frost is thicker than I've ever seen it; some of the flags look like giant cotton swabs with bits of blue cloth trailing out. The half-inch-diameter rope that's strung across them has grown as big around as a melon in spots. *Mmm,* what I wouldn't give for a nice ripe melon right now. Our fresh food is practically depleted, and all the good stuff has been gone for a while.

"Our first night there, Rex and I finished up all the leftover happy hour pitchers, right?" Neal looked at me expectantly.

"Um, sorry, I was off over there somewhere." I gestured vaguely. "What are we talking about?"

Day 48
Friday, December 21

A week or two ago a scrap of flower-print plastic appeared tucked between my window and the wall of snow that covers it. It's a flake of wrapping from the colorful broom handle Neal uses to clear the roof vents. Without escape, this unsuspected—but not unwelcomed—winter bunk companion will accompany me indefinitely. I sometimes find myself staring at it; a final wisp of faux-tropical color in my midnight-white world.

And then I realized: my window—I'm not sure when it happened. I watched so closely as it became buried, awaiting the final seal with eager trepidation, and yet was somehow distracted when the crucial moment arrived. Much like watching oneself go mad without recognizing the point of conversion due to the madness itself.

Oh shit.

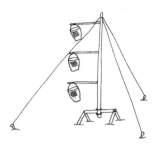

THIS MORNING ON rounds I noticed the precip tower was a bit bowed and the guyline was getting tight again, making it difficult to disconnect and lower the tower to clean the collection bags. While I had it down I attempted to gently bend the cold aluminum straight, but I felt it lurch at the midpoint, where a sample bag "branch" required a bolt hole and was therefore a weak point. It was holding together, but I could see a crease in the pole, so I mentally crossed my fingers as I raised it. It crumpled like a cheap toy.

I entered the Green House with half a mast, sample bags, and guylines a mess in my arms. I grinned at Neal. "I have a present for you." Not willing to admit my active role in the dilemma, I adopted a more passive one, telling Neal that I lost grip of the guyline and the tower dropped harshly, something we've both done before. We already suspected the mast was weakened by the last storm, so my "final straw" story was credible.

It was an inconsequential lie, but I immediately questioned myself: Why did I tell it? It's not like me. I usually have no problem owning up to my mistakes. We all make them, and I've found it's almost always better to admit them. It wasn't that I felt guilty; I think I was just embarrassed. I should have known better than to try to bend a cold, flimsy, weakened aluminum tube. I simply wasn't thinking. I just hope it's a singular event; it will be a long winter indeed if this kind of thing happens every time I'm not thinking clearly.

~

Midwinter

Summit Station, Greenland
Friday, December 21, 2012

It's the winter solstice—Midwinter's Day, as we call it in the polar regions. It's a celestial and psychological turning point, so tonight we'll be celebrating with homemade pizza and homemade beer. In fact, it's time to get gulping. Cheers!

~

It feels like the holiday season, even though we don't actually get any time off—our tasks remain unchanged. But things are just a little more relaxed. I can't explain it; there is simply ease in the air. Phil decided to cancel the morning meeting today since it's the holiday, so perhaps the day just felt less official. Whatever the reason, it's nice.

12

In which I revisit my Antarctic winter writings and find myself rooting for my own insanity.

Day 49
Saturday, December 22

My left eye still twitches occasionally. I'm tired most of the time. I struggle with insomnia. I'm exasperated by simple tasks. My mood overswings readily and I experience the emotions more strongly. Big ups. Big downs. I can't motivate myself to do anything unnecessary like yoga or even just ten minutes of stretching. I realize that I'm getting grumpy. It's okay. Expected. I can still laugh at it because it's funny, in a morose sort of way. But that may not last long. It's definitely the heart of winter, which means the foggy glissade into mental dearth is well underway. It generally only affects the little things, but it's disturbingly pervasive. Frustration comes easily and is exacerbated by increasing ineptitude and sloth.

We're only halfway through this short deployment and already I'm beginning to look forward to leaving. I'm starting to get bored, which is why I left Palmer. I loved Palmer, but my deployments grew increasingly unremarkable as it became more familiar. By the end I had done everything there was to do a dozen times before. My experiences were amazing, but as it turns out, unsustaining.

Walking through a penguin colony, following fluffy little chicks as they hatched and grew throughout the season. Rappelling into a crevasse, surrounded by wild formations of deep blue ice, a sliver of light above and a gulf of darkness below. Seeing immense swaths of glacier break free and collapse thunderous into the bay.

An adélie penguin colony near Palmer Station

Daysailing on extravagant cruise ships. Driving a small inflatable boat alongside colossal icebergs. Watching humpback whales burst out of the water with mouths agape, mere meters from the boat.

I look back on those early memories with great fondness.

A humpback whale feeding near Palmer Station

Unfortunately, the sense of wonder faded in the repetition. During my second season I began to feel like I had seen it all before and there was little left to explore, though I still found enjoyment. By my third season, the novelty was gone and I found myself wishing there was a mountain bike trail, or *something* I could do repeatedly and continue to be energetic about. But there wasn't. Except under special circumstances, the furthest you can venture from station is three miles, and that's by boat. By foot you can go about a mile, but only in one direction. There was simply nothing left for me to explore and I lost interest. There are people who return satisfied year after year; the camaraderie and subtle differences between deployments are enough for them. I am envious of that, but I guess I'm just not wired that way.

Kira hates to hear any of this because she came along during my second season and she can't help but take it personally that I consider my first season to be my best. She doesn't understand that it's not a reflection on her. Sometimes she can be too much of a romantic. The real world isn't like that. It's not all butterflies and ponies and moonlight and skipping through meadows. I tell her that falling in love was fantastic and it made my second season incredibly better in that one respect. But in all others it was inferior. I tell her that even Rebecca, Palmer's station manager for many years, told me at the end of my first season that it was the best she'd ever had. The weather was unusually good, the crew was incredible and entirely in sync, the wildlife encounters were top-notch. The stars were aligned. It could only go downhill from there.

And now I should find it no surprise that Summit Station is getting monotonous. How could it not? It is literally a featureless plane. Again the novelty has worn off, and this time there is nothing to do in my spare time—no boat rides, no hikes, no wildlife to watch. I feel like I spend all my time on my ass, just staring at stuff: a book, a movie, my computer screen, this journal, my dinner, my companions, the flake of flower-print wrapping trapped in my window. The boys are great and I truly enjoy their company, but if I'm not working I'm just sitting around wanting to *do* something.

I'm also getting more irritable. I don't know if it's showing yet, but I'm tired of all the annoying little nuances. I hate having to put on all those clothes just to walk to the next building. I'm tired of having dry, cracked, bleeding lips. I'm tired of waking up every night unable to breathe and having to unload a kaleidoscope of gooey greens and dry crusted reds from my dismally dehydrated nostrils. I'm losing focus, having to read everything twice, and my mind wanders off track during conversations. The solar max I was excited about is a bust so far. I haven't seen a good aurora in over a month. Of course, I don't want to go home either, because that means going to work full time for the first time in how many years? Six, I guess. Seven?

To find myself imprisoned in this melancholy is frustrating. I'm normally a happy person. I forgot about this perk of winter, this sort of meaningless trudge that's not quite depression but shares a part of the road.

I can't help but be reminded of my winter in the Antarctic. Friends and family who were following my blog told me they could see the decline as my mental and emotional stability flushed into the black hole. I'm sure they could. Having never revisited it myself, now seemed like an opportune time to read through it. Curiosity ensnared me: would I see in it what they saw?

~

Summer's End

McMurdo Station, Antarctica
Thursday, February 28, 2008

Summer is at an end. The population is down from a thousand to two hundred and it is remarkably noticeable. During mealtimes only eight or ten tables are occupied, instead of the usual fifty or sixty. Everyone has their own room. Everything is quiet.

I have a couple friends and a small handful of acquaintances who will be staying the winter, but for the most part I'm starting over again meeting and getting to know people. So far everyone exudes the usual pleasantness that is rampant here. For example, I met an extremely agreeable fellow the other day who goes by the name "Grump." I'm assuming it's a sarcastic nickname because he walks around in slippers adorned with flowers and bells. I have a feeling things are about to get even stranger than they already were.

~

Oh, if only I knew . . .

~

McMellow

McMurdo Station, Antarctica
Tuesday, April 1, 2008

Things are changing. The days are quickly becoming short and the shadows are remaining long. It's hard to think of this as autumn because it's like none I've ever known, but it's not winter yet and it's certainly not summer anymore either. The open water I'm accustomed to seeing from my perch at the Arrival Heights lab is rapidly freezing over. The temperature has been staying consistently below zero. "Little Red" jackets are being replaced by "Big Red" parkas. Rambunctious parties are being outnumbered by quiet movie nights. I actually have time to read before bed.

The changes bring on an interesting blend of emotions: excitement and boredom, intimacy and loneliness, comfort and longing, introspection and extroversion. I think it's safe to say that spending the winter here will change me.

~

This foreshadowing of contradictory emotions is funny to me now. At the time, I didn't even know there was something to foreshadow.

~

The Last Sunlight Disappears

McMurdo Station, Antarctica
Wednesday, April 23, 2008

Today the sun will breach the horizon for the last time. Unfortunately, the western flank of Mt. Erebus obscures the horizon where the final direct rays cross the sea. Still, the sun winked a seductive farewell as an orange splash across the ice.

It's a shame to lose the sun because in the past few weeks I've seen some of the most amazing sunsets of my life. Oh, and because it's going to be dark for a long time.

The final flight left a week ago, leaving 125 people on station. We are the intrepid handful who will remain here at least until the next flight arrives, in four months. Now begins the cold dark winter.

~

Gentlemen, start your engines!

~

Invisible Snow?

McMurdo Station, Antarctica
Thursday, May 22, 2008

I had a dream the other night that a spider was crawling all over my hand and arm. I was so amazed to see it that intrigue shadowed discomfort. This is something I've been aware of during my time here, but the point hadn't yet been driven home like this; aside from people, *there is not a single living thing on this island!* Sure, in the summer there were skua and seals, and the occasional penguin, but those intelligent creatures have left this forsaken place in its dark wintertime, leaving only us who hope an airplane will eventually come to take us away. There are no budding trees, no squawking jays, no whistling grasses, not even a single buzzing bug. *No bugs!* It seems absurd.

Another thing I miss that folks in the northern hemisphere are probably taking for granted right now is rain, or even just the natural sound of flowing water. Shouldn't every mountainous island have a babbling brook and an ocean break? I guess the reality is, nearly everything I see here is water: the sea ice, the snow-covered hillsides, the frost on the railings, even the clouds. But as much as I mumble incoherently to the snow and ice, it never makes a sound in return.

Occasionally though, there is an otherworldly beauty here that makes it all worth it. One of the most mesmerizing things I've seen is invisible snow. I realize that statement contradicts itself, but allow me to explain. Last week, the air was clear and still and the sky cloudless and star-filled. The temperature was dropping and frost was forming on railings, doorknobs, flagpoles, bicycles. But it was also forming out of thin air into weightless microscopic flakes. Floating ice crystals too small to be seen by the naked eye were reflecting the light that shone down from a full moon. The air around me was sparkling, like a shower of moonlight pixie dust in a cold, demented fairyland. Tiny specs winked, appearing for an instant and disappearing immediately into a void of perfectly clear air. I stood there staring for several minutes, occasionally reaching into the glittering nothing. I can only imagine that I looked like an escaped mental patient, grasping at visions in the empty space around me. It was surreal.

~

Okay, I'm having strange dreams and claiming to mumble incoherently and I *look* a little crazy, but I still seem to be enjoying myself.

~

A Short Status Report

McMurdo Station, Antarctica
Thursday, June 5, 2008

The weather has warmed considerably in the past few days. Currently, it's above zero. It makes me realize how acclimatized I am to the cold. Suddenly a walk through town is tolerable and could actually be considered comfortable. Of course, acclimatization has its own physiological implications.

As to the status of my mental health, well, let's just say it comes and goes. The cold and dark are already having a noticeable effect on me, particularly my energy level, but occasionally my mental capacity as well. I'm still enjoying my time here, but I'm getting very tired and a little, um, distracted? Forgetful? Just a little off, I guess.

~

Let the madness begin!

~

Welcoming June

McMurdo Station, Antarctica
Thursday, June 12, 2008

In the winter we get a two-day weekend once a month. We just had June's, and man, was it a doozy.

FRIDAY

The party began at the far end of my hallway. Its theme was "redneck," and it featured old tires, duct-taped couches, torn white T-shirts, and a screen door on a dorm room, which is humorous in and of itself but also begs the question: What the hell is a screen door doing in Antarctica?

Everyone enjoyed the rule that you drop your empty can wherever you finish it, until the power went out and all the rednecks had to go to work. This included me, since most of my instrumentation doesn't last long on battery power. Fortunately, the weather was too foul for me to drive up to Arrival Heights, so I did that on . . .

SATURDAY

It took me about half the day to get everything squared away.

Then consumption resumed. I went to happy hour at Gallagher's bar, followed by a "martini bar" party at the BFC—technically the Berg Field Center, but referred to locally as the Building Full of Chicks, owing to its disproportionate number of female employees. By the end of the night I was inebriated and therefore impervious to cold, allowing me to enjoy the walk home to my dorm through a snowy windstorm. Extremely fine flakes swirled like a murmuration of tiny snowbirds, diving and twirling in unchoreographed harmony. Abandoning my normal brisk pace through such weather, I slowed to a stroll, arriving home hours after midnight and well into . . .

SUNDAY

Naturally I wasn't feeling my best when I woke. Fortunately there's an easy fix for that: just throw down two ibuprofen, swallow, and then realize they were sleeping pills. Oh yes . . . I did.

Needless to say, Sunday was uneventful. I hurried to get my daily checks done before the pills took hold and then spent most of the afternoon in a vague battle to maintain consciousness.

~

". . . and then realize they were sleeping pills." Wahahahaha! You idiot!

~

Midwinter

McMurdo Station, Antarctica
Saturday, June 21, 2008

Things are getting strange. We have been cordoned off from reality, and a blurry veil is being pulled over our world. We are becoming bleary-eyed, sluggish, and foggy-headed. We cling to routine to keep ourselves on track. The whole thing is difficult to explain. It's subtle, so I don't always notice it, but there is a zombieness to everything. As a group, we accept it, and it makes our community stronger; it's comforting to know that we all share the same strangeness.

At this point we're halfway through the winter, which makes me wonder: How strange will it get?

~

Now I wonder: Did I really want to know the answer to that question?

~

An Orientation Ending in Disorientation

McMurdo Station, Antarctica
Monday, July 14, 2008

Welcome to the galley. Walk in, grab a blue tray and a plate. Place the plate on the left side of your tray. At the nearest counter, cut a slice of fresh baked bread and place it in the lower right corner of your tray. Next go to the hot line, then to the cold line, filling your plate. If you remember, a decision can be made here to go to the deli/sandwich line if nothing else appeals to your buds—*if* you remember. Try not to use a bowl for anything unless you can fit it on your plate or you didn't grab any bread, because you'll need that top right corner of the tray for two beverages: one water, one 50/50 blend of apple and cranberry juice. These are attained simultaneously in a specific manner; the water pours into the cup in your left hand at twice the rate that apple juice pours into the cup in your right, so when the water cup is full, stop pouring apple juice and switch to cranberry. Fifty-fifty, every time. Grab a fork and knife and place them to the left of the plate. While grabbing the knife, remember that you need butter for your bread and return to the bread line (also every time), all while trying to ignore the desserts.

Now that you have your meal, enter the seating area. Do not sit in the lower section. In the summer this area is primarily full of Air Force personnel, firefighters, and generally stiff-shirt-looking types. In the winter there is no reason because there are no Air Force personnel and it turns out the firefighters are okay, even fun. But you're institutionalized and it would just be weird to sit down there. Do not sit at the IT table: they have their assigned seats and your presence would not be welcomed readily. In fact, it's best not to even look in that direction (however, it *is* encouraged to think of ways to subtly change or move the IT table and try to imagine how far it would go before they noticed and gauge what their reaction might be). Instead, sit at one of the four upper-level tables nearest the exit. If there are only full tables and empty tables, feel free to "porch it" at one of the full tables by grabbing an extra chair and joining the end of the table. Available space will require that you turn your tray from a landscape layout to a portrait (hence the near homonym "porch it"). Be aware though, that this may sometimes lead you to wonder why there are eight or nine (the record) people crammed into a six-person table that is surrounded by five roomy, empty tables. Don't worry—the simple answer is that you are all mindless sheep.

Okay, you're done eating and your social skills have degraded to an absent stare, so it's time to leave. Take your used utensils, plate, cups, and blue tray and deposit them in the appropriate locations while saying hello and thank you to your community dining attendant (i.e., pot scrubber). If you have any remaining food, dirty napkins, or other waste, be sure to dump them into the proper receptacles: food into Food Waste and napkins into Burnables. There should also be an Aluminum Cans receptacle nearby, should you need it, not to mention the other trillion garbage categories at a typical dormitory waste station: Light Metal, Fabric, Mixed Paper, Glass, Plastic, Cardboard, Batteries, Aerosols, Non-Recyclables—and don't forget all the categories available at various other locations: Sanitary Waste, Sharps, Construction Debris, Heavy Metal, Nonferrous Metal, Electronic Scrap, Hazardous Waste, Wood. I know, it's overwhelming, but all this crap has to be shipped back to the States to be burned, buried, recycled, reused, or sold, so please sort your garbage as best you can according to the official "Trash Matrix." Don't fret about it too much, though, because you're bound to make plenty of mistakes (for instance, bottle caps go in Burnables—who knew?), which is why a whole department is dedicated to resorting your improperly sorted mess and making sure it makes it onto that cargo ship in the proper containers.

Oh, and there's also a Skua bin to satisfy all your thrift store donation urges. Skua (named after the gull-like bird, to confuse you) is a great way to get rid of crap that you think (incorrectly) someone else here may want. Go ahead and put those gasoline-soaked boots and jeans in Skua. Throw your favorite '80s cassettes in there, and those twenty-year-old freeze-dried rations you've been saving for the end of the world (guess what, you're there!). These items are certain to spend eternity here where there are no little bugs to work diligently at their decomposition.

Um, what was I talking about?

Screw it. This concludes your orientation.

~

Yes, this is the stuff! And it sounds all too familiar: the institutionalization, the irrational trifling habits, the forgetfulness, the wandering, unfocused mind.

~

Losing Our Marbles

McMurdo Station, Antarctica
Sunday, August 3, 2008

I noticed early in the winter that most folks were developing fatigue and lethargy, myself included. Shortly after that came an eerie mind-numbing quality to life. And now, our brains are malfunctioning. Processing feels short-circuited. Words are fleeting, memory short, train of thought easily derailed—often catastrophically and for no reason. These have become the norm. So, when we're having a bad day, we're really bad; useless, in fact. I've had a couple of those during which it was an effort just to focus on simple tasks, or hold a cohesive conversation. It happens to everyone, and the longer we stay, the more we're affected.

We're not actually dumber, though, just slower. I can still do things just as well (I think), but I get caught up in the (normally) mindless stuff. For instance, while I was researching this blog post, I caught myself repeatedly clicking my "McMurdo Station Intranet" bookmark and cursing that it was taking so long for Wikipedia to load. Or I'd copy a term that I wanted to search and then find myself staring vacantly at Google and wondering what the hell I was just doing. I had a couple more examples, but I've forgotten them.

Mealtime conversations are entertaining. Our common lack of focus leads to endless topic shifting, sometimes midsentence. Stories are left hanging without conclusions due to the insertion of simple comments that spark new lines of thought or sidetrack the tale-teller. Sometimes fifteen minutes and as many topics will pass, and someone may have the presence of mind to ask, "Were you telling a story earlier?" But no one will know. At the mercy of our own psychoses we often zone out and stare vacantly across the room. At a typical table of six, you can only expect four or five to be aware at any given moment. The others will come around shortly, but you may not notice because it's your turn in la-la land.

So what's the deal? There are many things at work here: darkness, cold, long work hours, monotony, isolation. It's both physiological and psychological, but the darkness and cold seem to be the real workhorses of winter malaise.

Darkness—or rather, lack of sunlight—causes fatigue and mood variations, especially depression. Scientists believe this is due to high melatonin and low serotonin levels in the body, though they don't have a full grasp on it. Body chemistry is complicated, I guess. But those of us who live in the Pacific Northwest get it; we're run down and stir-crazy after long months of thick clouds and incessant rain. It's called seasonal affective disorder. The Antarctic version is the same, just more intense.

But it's the cold that really does a job on us. When we're having a "winter moment," we tend to blame it on T_3, a hormone that helps control how quickly the body burns energy. The body adapts to extreme cold by increasing its metabolism to stay warm, and it uses T_3 to do it. The problem is, the body needs T_3 for other important stuff too, but with metabolism maxed out for the cold, there's not enough T_3 to go around. This is where it gets spooky. In addition to controlling metabolism, T_3 regulates chemicals in the central nervous system.

Here's what my harebrained research has turned up:

If you don't have enough T_3, or if its action is blocked, an entire cascade of neurotransmitter abnormalities may ensue and can lead to mood and energy changes.

Neurotransmitter abnormalities? That doesn't sound good.

In extreme cold, T_3 gets used so much to keep the body warm that the brain is left with a less than adequate supply of the hormone. This can cause the "Antarctic stare," *common particularly among winter residents, forgetfulness and lack of focus, as well as increased anger, irritation, and depression.*

Holy shit, I have *all* of those symptoms.

T_3 is created in the thyroid gland. When demand for T_3 is too high, the thyroid can't keep up. This is called hypothyroidism.

Some of the most profound effects of [hypothyroidism] are in the mental arena. Hypothyroid people sleep easily and do not get full refreshment from their sleep. During waking hours, they experience fatigue, apathy, and "brain fog" (short-term memory problems and attention deficits).

Holy shit, I have all of *those* symptoms.

Hypothyroidism also weakens muscles, including the diaphragm. As a result, breathing can become less efficient. Snoring may start or become worse.

Holy shit. I've started snoring. I know because it wakes me up, which is great for my already fitful rest.

Here are some other fun symptoms I found for hypothyroidism: chronic mood disorders, bipolar spectrum syndrome, attention deficit disorder, and premenstrual syndrome.

That's right, I live on a remote island full of moody bipolar psychos with ADD and chronic PMS. We're fargin' looney tunes down here.

So, to recap, we have an overload of melatonin (fatigue), a shortage of serotonin (depression), a haywire biological clock (insomnia), and a T_3 shortage (neurotransmitter abnormalities—!).

In four weeks, normal people will return to station and refer to winter-overs as "toasty," as in, "That guy is *toast.*" We'll be considered strange and misunderstood, but we'll have fun exaggerating our affliction in order to be avoided by those who have invaded our peacefully bipolar world.

Comments:

Lyn: What's your most passionate topic of conversation these days?

Me: Staring at the wall. Or travel. Yes, definitely travel. Travel, followed closely by staring at the wall.

～

Holy shit, *I* have all of those symptoms. Again. And they're only likely to get worse. On the upside, maybe *neurotransmitter abnormalities* can explain my persistent eye twitch.

I remember it took me a long, long time to pull that blog post together, and I had to keep putting it on the back burner until I had it making a reasonable amount of sense. What I didn't know was that when the "normal people" returned, there would be no need to exaggerate my affliction.

～

Groundhog Week

McMurdo Station, Antarctica
Monday, August 18, 2008

Ever seen the movie *Groundhog Day*, where Bill Murray relives the same day over and over again? That's exactly what is happening here, except that it's *Groundhog Week* and instead of funny, it's mind-numbing and depressing. My work tasks are repetitive on a daily basis, which is bad enough. On top of that, after-work events are scheduled weekly, so they're repetitive weekly. My week looks something like this:

Monday is "entertain drunken Katie" night, because she has Tuesdays off due to her skewed kitchen staff schedule.

Tuesday is either pool league or bowling league.

Wednesday night is soccer.

Thursday is whatever didn't happen on Tuesday, which confuses the shit out of me.

Friday night is band practice.

On Saturday, if there isn't a party already planned, then one forms.

Even Sunday, our only day off, is repetitive. I sleep until eleven—something I haven't been capable of for many years. I have brunch, go to work for about an hour, then sort through pictures while I burn a movie to DVD. I put the movie on and promptly fall asleep (why I still bother to burn one every week is beyond my reasoning capability). I wake for dinner, and then meet Brody, Casey, John, and Genevieve in the lounge to watch exactly two episodes of *Deadwood*.

Other folks have different schedules of course, but they're equally repetitive; instead of soccer on Wednesday, they may work in the library; instead of band practice on Friday, they may go to "Art Bar." You get the idea; we're all becoming habituated zombies, incapable of remembering a change in routine unless our calendar reminds us, and still we forget.

Today should have provided a spectacular and much-anticipated event to break the monotony. Instead, a thick layer of clouds shrouded the horizon, veiling the sun on the day of its glorious return. Damn bastards.

～

Feeling a little depressed and irritable, are we?

～

If It Wasn't for the Dark, Would You Love the Sun?

McMurdo Station, Antarctica
Tuesday, August 26, 2008

It has only been a week since the sun made its first appearance after over three months of absence, and already it's staying up for five hours a day. It's exciting to see the light again; it means the end is near, and that lifts spirits—if only it could lift the fatigue. Unfortunately, the return of light isn't making us any less crazy. In fact, it seems to be making things worse initially; many are having trouble sleeping again now that the light is back to influence their circadian rhythm. I've certainly had some insomnia myself, which exacerbates the constant fatigue.

~

There's just no pleasing some people. You'd think I'd sound a lot more excited about the return of precious sunlight. I guess a notch up doesn't show much when you're at the bottom of the scale.

~

Winfly

McMurdo Station, Antarctica
Sunday, September 7, 2008

They're back. Our five-month isolation is over. About 170 of them so far and another fifty on the way today. They're tan, refreshed, and energetic. They're loud, annoying, and intrusive. The first flight more than doubled the population and they outnumbered us immediately. I was initially excited to see new faces and old friends. I had a blast catching up on that first day. But Andre— one of the winter-over firefighters—was right; he said to give it three days. That was three days ago.

Now I realize more than ever that I'm toasty. I'm tired, grumpy, distracted, unmotivated, and easily annoyed. I'm annoyed with myself for being annoyed; it's annoying. I'm apathetic. No, apathy isn't exactly right; I just don't give a shit. For example, with other winter-overs, I openly discuss my general grievances about the newcomers even if they're well within earshot. I have no filter, no tact. I avoid the galley, or at least refuse to sit at a table with no winter-overs, or even sit at a table other than the few I've been using all winter. If those aren't options, I'd rather take my meal home and eat alone. I feel a strong bond to anyone who's been here with me through the long dark, whether I knew them well or not. I have no desire to meet new people. These are the traits I was told I would have but didn't believe it, even just a week ago. I also have a headache but I think that's unrelated. Unless one of those bastards brought some sickness here and my lethargic immune system has also been overrun.

Ethan came in on the first flight (not my brother Ethan of course, but my coworker and friend* from last summer here). When I first ran into him outside his office, he was writing on the dry erase board: *29 days to go*. I had fifty-one. *Bastard. I gave him a hard time about it, but I was actually amused. Later, I told several friends. Not surprisingly, the story made it back around to Ethan, but much agitation had been incorporated. What irks me is that I can't be sure if someone else added the agitation, or if I did it unwittingly. Maybe I sound agitated all the time.

Okay, so it's not all that bad. I won't say that I'm exaggerating because these are my true feelings, much to my surprise, but they are not all feelings I am proud of or feelings I would normally have if I wasn't so T_3'd. It is a taxing effort on top of a fatigued body and psyche to willingly accept this tremendous change in a longstanding routine. It's a huge burden on the mind to keep up with this new pace of simple conversation without taking repeated zone-out moments to catch my mental breath.

Still, I'm excited to see a lot of returning friends (and even mere acquaintances, provided they have a signed and stamped seal of approval from a fellow winter-over). Many of them brought things like strawberries and pineapple to win us over. It is amazing how wonderful fruit is right now; I can't even describe it. I had a private dinner with several winter-over friends and a full bowl of freshly sliced bananas, apples, oranges, pineapples, and strawberries. Every one of us was moaning at the taste of these long-forgotten delights. A passerby would have thought we were having an orgy in there. I don't even think the sounds were coming from my voice box; I think it was the joy of a hundred thousand taste buds jumping up and screaming for more.

So yes, there are moments of joy, but there seem to be a lot more of annoyance. Along with all these new people comes queues. Wait in line for a plate, wait in another line for food, wait in line at the store, wait in line at the bar. I guess it's what these summer-only people are used to, but I've spent nearly twice the time at a much lower population, so I remember the lines for everything but only with resentment and impatience.

On the upside, these changes mean that my time here is finally coming to an end. I have seven weeks left—not that I'm counting (forty-seven days)—before I reenter the real world and start doing strange things like forgetting to pay at restaurants, or look-ing for the proper waste bin to throw something away, or spend-ing unnatural amounts of time in the fruit section. Then, several weeks after that, I'll once again be a regular citizen of the world, only changed a bit by experience. Maybe a big bit.

~

Man, talk about moody. Is there an emotion I didn't cover here? Or one that hung around for more than a few sentences? Maybe I shouldn't be making fun of myself, knowing that I'm cur-rently headed straight down the same road to lunacy.

It seems to me now that the madness was at its best at this point—when the returning population first arrived. The stress of that change had an intense effect. The contrast of fresh legs made my toastiness much more apparent than it was when solely sur-rounded by equally deficient minds.

On a side note, I never forgot to pay at a restaurant, like so many do. Twice, though, I caught myself walking around the restaurant with an armful of dirty dishes, trying to figure out where I was supposed to put them.

Now that I think about it, it's possible that I also forgot to pay and never realized it.

~

Things Forgotten, Things Ahead

McMurdo Station, Antarctica
Tuesday, September 16, 2008

The days are getting back to normal again. There was sunlight for about eleven hours today, with the sunset and dusk extending well into the evening. But my thoughts are elsewhere—much warmer places—so I've riddled this post with pictures from my New Zealand trip last year. They have nothing to do with the text around them, but represent the constant background hum in my mind.

Lake Tekapo, Canterbury

Warm thoughts aside, I'm settling into this increased population thing now. It was much more stressful than I expected. Since we winter-overs are all unstable, the influx of people is like being crushed by a breaking wave and then having to ride out the whitewater whirl of emotions. We will have another population jump in a month, a much bigger one, and I hope to be better prepared for it, though I have my doubts. Honestly, I think it's going to suck.

Routeburn Track, Otago

I still find myself avoiding the crowds and trying to sit with winter-overs at meals, but I've accepted the new noise standard somewhere in the low levels of my brain, the only levels that are functioning. I've even enjoyed meeting some of the returning

Christchurch Botanic Gardens

folks, although I try to avoid FNGs—or "fingees"—at all costs. These fucking new guys are far too excited for me.

But despite the languor, my schedule remains as busy as ever. I'm exhausted. I can't wait to take a long nap in the grass. Several of them.

~

I can't help but notice that the contradiction of words and images in this post is completely bipolar.

~

New-Mown Grass Smells So Sweet

McMurdo Station, Antarctica
Friday, September 26, 2008

First, allow me to apologize for my lack of concern for timely blog posts. It coincides beautifully with my lack of concern for anything else. Apathy is biting down hard. My thoughts are miles away from this place. I'm over it. And now I'm sick too (damn new people). But it's Condition 1 outside and I have nothing better to do until the wind dies down.

So, I've been amusing myself with Andre's blog, which is hilarious. I especially love his description of our mid-winter polar plunge:

> *Most people will surface immediately and then actually levitate themselves up out of the water in a defiance of the laws of physics not normally seen outside of a* Road Runner *cartoon. ... The cold is unbelievable. It's kind of like being covered in menthol and getting clawed by a thousand menthol-intolerant badgers.*

Classic Andre humor! Alas, now he has escaped north with many others. Our numbers are dwindling. Andre's blog now contains pictures of fellow winter-overs back in the real world. It's bizarre. They're so out of place. They don't belong. And it's hard to imagine myself back in those "real-world" settings. Looking at Andre's pictures, I immediately keyed in on several things that are so strangely distant in memory: animals, trees, water, even a side-walk and a fence. But one thing stuck out even more: Andre's hand in the grass. It appeared laid-back, nonchalant, normal. But I know better. He was aware of that grass, not just sitting in it. He felt the forgiving texture between his fingers. He savored the organic aroma. I'm certain he was absorbing that grass, soaking up its livelihood. It's haunting.

I'm almost there, four more weeks (twenty-seven days).

～

Yes, I can certainly see it: winter's grip is there. The emotional circus has me not quite myself, and those who know me would see it clearly. It's the recurring undertone of depression and irritability between bouts of normalcy. That's what stands out to me now, though admittedly, I was hoping for something more dramatic. I'm not sure why. Maybe because it felt more dramatic than it sounds. Or maybe because I'm enjoying rooting against myself.

～

"We'd Like to Go Home Now"

McMurdo Station, Antarctica
Saturday, October 4, 2008

We should have had three flights of fresh people in by now, but the weather this week has been horrendous, and flights have been canceled for five straight days. This is great news for me because I haven't had to deal with the population jump yet. Then again, I'd feel differently if I were going home. A lot of winter-overs are scheduled to leave, are more than ready to leave, *need* to leave, and some of them are getting downright irate.

～

Perhaps I should have anticipated the real possibility of finding myself in the same situation, instead of being surprised when it happened.

~

Use Your Damn Blinker

McMurdo Station, Antarctica
Friday, October 10, 2008

Bamma is back! And she thoughtfully brought me pad thai from a restaurant in Christchurch. It was *amazing*, for the three seconds it lasted. Thanks, Bamma!

The weather finally broke and we've gotten three flights in the past two days, bringing the population up to about 720. The galley is packed. Finding an empty table is nearly impossible, which means I will have to start settling for atypical, foreign tables. It's crushing.

We, as fellow winter-overs, are now brutally aware of each other's toastiness and are more and more able to recognize the affliction in ourselves—like being at the controls of an imminent crash but unable to switch tracks. Against my will I mumble disapproval under my breath as people gather and stand in the busiest corridors, undermine any flow that once existed in the food line, turn blind corners without pausing to consider traffic. I've begun to wonder if there is a deeper subconscious that develops among winter-overs. Even when no one seems to be around (a rarity now) someone will still round the bend intent on collision. I don't recall this happening in the winter. The intersection of Highways One & Two in Building 155 was never so dangerous, even at peak mealtimes. Did we develop a subconscious traffic pattern? I don't know, but there was flow. It worked. It's gone.

Gone, just like our filters. Things spout from our mouths without concern for consequence. Some little annoyance that normally wouldn't even provoke irritation will start a chain reaction in the nervous system ending at the lips with some exasperation. Shawn told me today that he saw the line for food and unconsciously blurted out some expletive. Several people heard it and moved aside. So that's a plus.

Yesterday I got to see another returning summer friend. Eric has been following my blog, and he noted the conveyance of my mental decline. He said he half expected me to throw something breakable after every sentence (sarcastically . . . I think). He approached me with care. I didn't realize my ranting made me sound so dismal, so I just want to say that I'm still myself; I'm still generally happy, easily amused, and enjoyable to be around (I think . . . I hope). I just want to capture this winter-over state honestly, while I'm experiencing it, because it is downright bizarre.

The sun is now up most of the time. It settles behind the mountains for a few hours at night, but the sky remains light. I love the sun. And hate it. It's fantastic to have it back, a beacon in the sky over a desolation of white, but at times it's too bright. It can be an immense amount of light in a snow-bleached landscape, far too much for the twilight levels my eyes are accustomed to.

~

I seem continuously unable to settle on any one emotion. They even seem to come upon me randomly and without any period of transition. I remember it taking many weeks—months, even— back in the "real world" before I felt I was fully back to normal.

~

Engine #2

McMurdo Station, Antarctica
Wednesday, October 29, 2008

We boarded the Air Force C-17 at 1:30 p.m. on Monday. We waited. Trouble on engine #2. We waited. We taxied up the runway, and then back. Still trouble. We waited. By 8:30 p.m. dinner was over, so they brought us pizza on the plane. We waited.

We arrived back at station at 10:00 p.m., still unsure what was wrong. Our room keys were hanging on the housing office door. A note from RaJa—one of the few remaining winter-overs—said she was glad I was staying in town with her a little longer. Another from Bamma said she had beer and pizza waiting for me.

I needed a beer.

Tuesday passed. No information. Summer folks expressed their condolences. Winter folks laughed. Wednesday started out looking bleak. The rumor mill brought multiple strands of conflicting information, but eventually a new bag-drag time appeared on the scroll, shortly followed by a transport time.

We arrived at the airstrip just in time to see a snow-covered C-17 having its wings and cockpit windows brushed clean with a kitchen broom. It was worrisome—I'm certain the shape of those wings is important. But after some warm-up and a practice acceleration down the runway, engine #2 was declared healthy, and soon we were in the air.

The single tiny window of the cargo plane was dirty but the view was epic. The sun was setting behind us as we flew along the Transantarctic Mountain Range. The last light caught low clouds over the jagged and icy landscape, transforming all into a pink sea. Soon only the shadowed, ice-covered mountains remained.

During the busy final weeks of my stay, I slowly regained some energy and mental capacity. I attribute it to everything: the return of the sun, the warmer temperatures, the increased energy of the station, and especially the greeting of returning friends. I became much happier to still be there and sometimes even felt a desire to stay (though minuscule compared to the monumental desire to leave). I realized that over the winter I had developed a strong sense of ownership that dissolved many inhibitions I felt as a fingee the previous summer. Instead of an overwhelming world of strangers, McMurdo had become a familiar world filled with friends.

After 372 days on the ice, this will be my final Antarctic entry in this blog. I will be landing in New Zealand in just a few hours, only two and a half days late. For all I know this is the last I will see of the frozen continent, and so my departure is bittersweet. The friends I've made here are close and amazing and I know I will keep many of them. I hope to see them all again.

~

Aw, it's a happy ending.

And now I find myself back in the middle of the story, but in Greenland. I'm reliving much of the winter murk that I've already experienced, but additionally finding myself with much less to do. Still, I know the irony: though I want something to occupy my spare time, I likely couldn't muster the effort to pull my gaze from the fuzzy blank and actually do it.

I guess all I need to do is continue to eat, sleep, work, and allow the madness to take me once again.

13

In which the cold reaches a bewildering low, the guys start showing signs of losing it, and I stop sleeping, against my will.

Day 50
Sunday, December 23

I didn't get up until nine this morning. When I got to the office Neal said, "Lance is at MSF. I'm going back to bed." Phil and Don still weren't up at ten so I signed out to TAWO with a sticky note on the bathroom mirror. I thought, *if something goes wrong out there, hopefully someone will need to pee before I freeze to death.* In hindsight it would have made more sense to radio Lance and sign out with him, even though he was signed out himself. But I accept that logic is no longer my strong suit.

I had a late lunch, my schedule skewed from having no morning meetings the past couple of days. We're definitely in holiday mode. In the afternoon I brewed beer and then continued reading *Big Dead Place*, which I picked up shortly after hearing of Nick's death. I've been meaning to read it for several years, but now I feel the need to push through it and move on to something more uplifting. Maybe a polar winter is not the best time to read his book. Nick had a keen eye for the bureaucratic nonsense that pulses through the US Antarctic Program, and reading about it is amusing but also aggravating. Kira would say that's because I have a problem with authority. Maybe she's right, but only to a certain degree. It's not that I don't want to do the shit I'm told to do, it's a lack of tolerance for asinine rules and nonsensical status quos—I don't want to do the *stupid* shit I'm told to do. Perhaps more accurately, I want the freedom to either do shit or not do shit, without people forcing their unsupported opinions on me.

I'm all for safety, and I understand that procedures are necessary and that the least common denominator must be accounted for. That's not what bothers me. It's the way "The Program"—as Nick likes to call it—sometimes goes about it.

I bought a power kite when I went to McMurdo. I had recently picked up kitesurfing and I wanted to try snowkiting. After some investigation I learned that the Kiwis from New Zealand's Scott Base—only a kilometer away—snowkited on the sea ice at the rugby field. I also heard that the The Program had an official procedure for flying a kite—a fact that I considered to be *stupid shit* in and of itself.[44]

Rumor has it, an American was caught snowkiting near the airfield during a landing, so the procedure was put in place. It deemed only one location permissible for flying a kite: Hut Point, a peninsula of exposed rock scree that drops precipitously to pressure ridges of jagged sea ice. Would I fly a toy kite there? Sure. But it was the absolute last place I felt safe launching a power kite, a kite designed to haul a person across water or snow. Now, I can't be sure that the procedure was put in place because of snowkiting —the McMurdo rumor mill is admittedly outrageous and not to be trusted—but the rulemakers must have seen the Kiwis flying power kites on the rugby field, and to have a procedure just for toy kites seemed absurd. Yet there was no mention of power kites. So, I couldn't help but perceive that the procedure was essentially

44   As of 2018—when I asked a friend to search the Antarctic Program headquarters—the kite procedure seems to no longer exist. Perhaps it never did. See rumors, next paragraph.

just a devious and cowardly way of saying, "No, you can't do that."

That's what bothers me. If the kiting procedure simply said "No snowkiting," I would have been upset and disappointed. But sidestepping the issue felt deceptive and manipulative. That approach makes people suspicious and distrustful, especially when the rules are enforced by a "We'll fire you" attitude. It's no surprise that the community often resents the management. Like an ironhanded parent, The Program's rulebook feels exhaustive and overly conservative, and it governs your personal time, not just your job. Many times during my McMurdo contract, I heard myself whining inwardly, "But the Kiwis are allowed to!"

So, like a rebellious teen, I put on my personal green ski coat—conveniently similar to the Kiwis' standard green parkas—and gave it a go on the rugby field. I got away with snowkiting, but I got in trouble for parking at Scott Base; my government vehicle was obviously not there on official business. I had driven it two unauthorized miles.

I'm sure The Program would claim that snowkiting is an unacceptable safety risk, yet I'd be surprised if any of the rulemakers kitesurf, or know much about it. I bet a lot of them cycle though, and that's why the annual cyclocross race can include a flight of stairs that the community encourages people to ride a bicycle down. Perfectly safe. I saw some spectacular crashes and it astounded me that the ultra-safety-oriented management allowed it. This is the kind of contradictory nonsense that Nick was so good at digging up and pointing out. And though he treated his cynicism with masterful humor, I still find the bullshit he unearths to be frustrating.

The rumor now is that Nick was blacklisted from The Program by the new contract holder because of *Big Dead Place*, and that's the reason he committed suicide. But if there's one thing I learned in McMurdo, it's to never believe a damn thing anyone tells you. No matter how convinced they are that it's the truth, it isn't.[45]

---

45   In fact, there are rumor-mongerers who inject far-fetched tales just to watch them spread and twist through the mill.

That said, I do believe it's probable that Nick was blacklisted: that fits The Program's paranoia bill nicely. But I have a hard time believing that an intelligent man such as Nick would find that reason enough to commit suicide. In his book he mentions having bouts of depression that sound severe; that seems a far more likely suspect.

Nick reveals these periods of depression during his description of the psych eval. He utterly fools the test on this very point—a point I would consider critical for someone about to winter in the Antarctic. From his test results the psychiatrist interprets that he is not familiar with depression and even shows concern that if he faces depression, he won't know what to do. The test results missed the mark entirely.

It's like Neal said: the test is a nonfilter. It may work adequately on the ideal cookie-cutter citizen, but a typical Antarctican has bent, broken, and tossed that mold over their shoulder with a dismissive shrug. They cannot be characterized and categorized easily, or perhaps at all.

Nick, probably knowing he didn't fit the mold, approached the psych eval like this:

> *I answered all questions on the test false if they mentioned "dread" or "worrying" or, in dealing with people, trying to "put them right," and I made a point of favoring "social engagements" over "alone time" because solitude is widely disapproved of and is favored only by criminals. In questions of authority I chose the most spineless possibility unless—when snitching on my fellow workers, for instance—a firm moral conviction impervious to peer pressure was called for.*

Supposedly the test allows for this premeditated deceit and compensates for the skewed result, but it obviously didn't work in Nick's case.

As I read on, I reached a nicely compiled list of some of the more bizarre true-false questions on the evaluation. One of them stopped me cold, my jaw agape:

I often feel as if there is a tight band around my head.

In the midst of a mild freak-out, I scanned frantically back through this journal. Sure enough, three weeks ago I said it, almost word for word. So it's official: I'm fucking nuts.

I STOPPED IN our office after dinner and found a large note filling my computer screen: *No morning meeting tomorrow.*

"I think Phil is enjoying his sleep-ins," Neal suggested.

"So am I. *And* I'm enjoying not having morning meetings."

I moved to the lounge and noodled around on the guitar a bit while waiting for everyone to show up for the movie. I was glad to learn that there is a guitar here. I'm even more glad now because it gives me one more thing to kill time with. I've always found playing music to be a nice temporary escape from reality, though in this case it feels more like an escape back *into* reality.

"It's a little early for 'Here Comes the Sun,' don't you think?" Neal asked when he wandered in.

"Yeah, I guess so. Wishful thinking, I guess." I swear my subconscious is taking over: I rarely play that song.

Don clattered about in the kitchen next door, asking questions about a popcorn popper that neither Neal nor I knew the answers to. Suddenly he was shouting, "Shit! Shit! Shit!"—immediately followed by the fire alarm. Neal and I rushed in to find him frantically waving at the smoky air above a mountainous bowl of popcorn that was spilling over onto the counter and floor. I resisted the urge to point but made no attempt to hold back a maniacal laugh.

Neal joined me heartily. "Don, I think you made enough!"

Not fifteen minutes later, as all five of us watched a movie together, I was thankful for the persistent aroma of burnt popcorn. Apparently we've reached the point where loud farting is not only acceptable but encouraged. Don lifted out of his chair to release. Neal retorted immediately, to Don's delight. Phil raised a leg to point one at Don.

"What, are you guys playing Battleship?" Lance asked.

"Battleshits," said Neal.

I'm beginning to agree that an all-male phase *is* a bad idea. It's like third grade, with an average age over forty. I'm not as amused. It's childish, honestly. I'm going to smoke these bastards out silently.

Day 51
Monday, December 24

I couldn't sleep again last night, and it was hell getting up. When I caught up with Neal at TAWO, the radio crackled. It was Lance checking out for his daily venture on top of the MSF. "Phil, it's Lance. I'm going up on the roof." Phil responded in a high-pitched voice with an unintelligible ramble.

"I think Phil is losing it," Neal said.

"Oh, yeah?" I hadn't considered this.

"He's canceled all the meetings for four days, and he's starting to act weird."

"Maybe weird is Phil's natural state, and he's just getting comfortable," I offered, even thinking there may be some truth to it.

Neal laughed. "Maybe."

I hope Phil *is* losing it. I'm losing it, and I don't want to be the only one! Neal is right, though: Phil has held a lax routine lately. But to be fair, we had Midwinter and then Saturday and Sunday, and now it's Christmas Eve. It's a long holiday weekend in that sense, and I suspect we'll get back to our morning meetings soon enough. As for weird, I think that's just Phil's way of having fun. Besides, Phil is weird in his own way just like Neal is weird in Neal's way and I'm weird in my way and so on. I hope. It would be worrisome to lose our leader to madness.

"Hey, did you remember to do the RN yesterday?" Neal asked.

"I have no idea . . ." I paused and considered. Had I swapped the filters? "Nope, I really have no idea."

It turns out I'd forgotten. But it also turns out that it's not just me who's getting forgetful: just as Neal was asking me to remember the RN, he was forgetting to check the model number on the TAWO power strip, which we had been meaning to do for over a week. Of course, I was forgetting too, but that's missing the point.

We went through the daily routine of instrument checks and couldn't do much more than that. TAWO was in a cloud of smog, traceable immediately back to the generator, so any air or snow samples would be contaminated. Instead, we began the trudge back to the Big House for lunch, during which Lance exemplified that his memory is going, too.

Lance: "Remind me to do that bobbin."

Neal: "Whenever is fine."

Lance: "No, because if you don't remind me—I could have done it by now but I totally just *pfft*. If you just remind me."

Me: "Bobbin?" I had a vague notion that Lance was fixing some clothing for Neal, but I thought he was hand stitching. "Have you been using that sewing machine in the Green House?"

Lance: "Yeah. I started on Neal's pants, but the bobbin ran out halfway around one cuff. And then he brought me another pair and asked, 'Can you fix these next?' and I was like, 'Nope, the machine's broken.'"

Don: "But you should have plenty of thread."

Lance: "Well yeah, but there's none on the bobbin!" His joke implied the disproportionate enormity of a simple task like threading a bobbin.

Neal: "If Lance is driving his car down the road and it runs out of gas, he's just like, 'Oh, it's broken.'"

Me: "Be careful or he'll sew your pant legs together."

Phil: "I had that happen to me once at a New Year's party that I got shitfaced at. Fell asleep on the sofa and woke up in the morning with a mighty hangover and I could *not* fucking walk. And I couldn't figure it out. They'd stitched my pant legs together up to the knee."

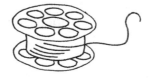

THE TEMPERATURE HAS dropped dramatically over the past few days. There is substantial bite to -65°F, even without any wind. I found this out after lunch when we took out the garbage, which accumulates on the Big House's small back deck until the pile is too big. We all pitch in to move the bags into a homemade wooden dumpster built on an aircraft cargo pallet. Don tossed the bags over the railing and we passed them to the dumpster. I wasn't expecting it to take long so I didn't bother with my overalls and just wore jeans. My legs started to sting after only five minutes. I should know better by now; at sixty degrees, five minutes is long enough. But it took considerably longer because the bags Don tossed over for the long drop began breaking open on impact. When we were finished and I was back inside, I jumped up and down to warm my legs back up. After walking to the Green House and taking off my jeans, my skin was still pink from my boxers to my socks. Stupid. At least nothing nipped.

I closed out the remainder of the workday finding, cutting, and drilling a length of conduit to fix the precip tower. Breaking the tower brought unwanted attention. When you need input from scientists, they're nowhere to be found, but break their chintzy tower in half and they're nitpicking everything else. The precip tower scientist wants to know why we're no longer filling out her weather observations spreadsheet. The answer is that we already fill out a station weather observations log that contains identical information. The format is the only difference. But I couldn't tell her that her spreadsheet is redundant and that I don't care if it's easier for her to have the information in both formats and that I'm only required to provide the data and that means in whatever format is easiest for me. Unfortunately—despite my winter demeanor—I still retain my core good-natured self, so I offered to copy-paste into her damn spreadsheet but suggested she start using the station weather observations log instead. I guess this is my penance for lying about the true cause of the tower's demise.

SHIT. I THINK I was supposed to call Mom yesterday. She wanted to pass her phone around so I could chat with the whole family. I thought she wanted me to call next Sunday, but that doesn't make sense for a Christmas gathering. This is how the winter works on your mind: it leaves reason more or less intact but introduces confusion and forgetfulness.

Day 52
Tuesday, December 25

I don't think this is what Irving Berlin had in mind when he wrote "I'm Dreaming of a White Christmas." It was cold as hell this morning, with a stiff breeze to drive it home. As I began my traverse of the inhospitable white nothing to do rounds, I thought, *Do I really need to do this on Christmas? Surely we can miss a day?* Then Phil radioed that the windchill was below -100°F so we were in Condition 1. I happily turned around.

~

Merry Christmas!

Summit Station, Greenland
Tuesday, December 25, 2012

Christmas morning at Summit Station:

Temperature: -66°F

Windchill: -101°F

Motivation: somewhere between -66 and -101

Comments:

Me: I don't know if it's bad karma to comment on your own blog, but we've reached a new phase low and I thought it noteworthy. The temperature is now -74°F, windchill -108°F, and anyone who says it's all the same below -20°F is full of shit, even if it was me during a relatively balmy Antarctic winter.

~

"Has this ever happened to you?" Lance tried to pour his beer into a glass, but it was frozen in the neck of the bottle.

"What did you do?" I asked, splaying my arms, palms upward.

"Nothing, I just walked here from the Green House."

"Holy shit, that's all? I wouldn't think it'd be possible for it to freeze that quickly."

"It's colder here than the South Pole because of the humidity. It cuts, man. I've done the bamboo forest at Pole when it's eighty degrees and twenty knots and it's worse here at forty degrees because it's more humid. It's crazy!"

"What?" I said in disbelief.

"Pole is dry as fuck. Hell, it's colder in Seattle when it's thirty degrees and raining than it is at Pole!"

That can't be right, I thought, *it's not humid here, it's incredibly dry.* But Lance is the meteorologist in the group, so I'm sure he knows what he's talking about. Still, I was curious and looked into it: our humidity has been between fifty and ninety percent since we arrived, which blows my mind. My cracked lips and drywalled nostrils protest this information adamantly, and they're not entirely wrong. If you warm this air to room temperature, the humidity would be less than one percent. So it feels dry as hell because there's very little moisture in the air, but it's still enough to help suck the heat right out of you. It's the worst of both worlds. I couldn't find any actual data for the South Pole, but everything I came across said the humidity there is practically zero, so Lance makes a good point. And I know from experience that thirty degrees and raining is a lot colder than ten degrees and snowing, though I'm not sure that's relevant and I don't care to think about it hard enough to decide.

We spent most of the day hanging out in the Big House drinking wine and nibbling hors d'oeuvres. Tracy phoned to wish us all a merry Christmas and sing us a carol, which was sweet. She had thoughtfully left us a Christmas gift when she was here at turnover. It was the only gift that would be opened here—Santa wisely avoided this forlorn chimney. The array of chocolates Tracy gave us seemed a perfect match to the day. One, labeled "beef jerky milk chocolate," had the description, "Close your eyes. Breathe. Let the plains of Wyoming roll on your tongue as you snap the chocolate in your mouth. Beef jerky, smoked paprika, and deep milk chocolate deliver the power of the magical cocoa bean." I guess chocolate goes with anything.

Outside, the temperature continued a slow descent. The weather screen had Phil's full attention. Each time a new low appeared, he ran to the office to take a screenshot while we continued to banter.

Lance: "I just started reading *No Picnic on Mount Kenya* and that first chapter is just . . . it's just *us*. Because, it's all about a POW camp and how they have nothing to do. It starts out when somebody wakes him up and he says, 'Dammit, that would be one less hour I'd have to spend here if I could have just slept!' But he decides that he's gonna climb Mount Kenya with a couple other guys and all of the sudden they have this goal and time is flying by. Stuff is happening, you know, and he's actually excited to wake up every morning. But all these other people around him don't have goals, so they're just . . ."

Don: "They're in a prisoner of war camp?"

Lance: "Yeah, right at the bottom of Mount Kenya."

Me: "How were they going to climb the mountain if they're prisoners?"

Lance: "Well, that's the whole thing. They've gotta figure out how they're gonna get out, *and* how they're gonna get everything they need. They're tailoring wool suits out of blankets and making ice axes and crampons out of whatever they can find. So for six months or something they've been stoked to wake up every morning because they're busy and they've got this thing and all of the sudden—"

Me: "They've got purpose."

Neal: "Motivation."

Lance: "Yeah, they have a reason to be there rather than just waking up every day and going to roll call." He paused a moment. "It really doesn't sound that bad, though, because they get mail and they get books. I don't know, I was actually thinking, I mean, it's not as bad as it is here. We don't get mail."

Neal: "We don't have a mountain to climb."

Lance: "It's kind of funny how he puts it in perspective. The whole point is, he's thinking: 'Well, once we escape there's wild animals to worry about, and food, and it'll be rainy and cold, and we won't have any of this or that.' And he realizes it kinda makes being in prison with his warm blanket and three meals a day—"

Me: "Sound pretty good."

Lance: "It sounds *really* good. But everyone else is bitching about being there. So it's funny how he's analyzing all this stuff."

Me: "Well, it's nice having room and board, but it's still prison."

Lance: "But that's the thing with the POW camp, because he brought this up too: in a regular prison you have a sentence, so you know when you're gonna get out. But in a POW camp, it's whenever the war ends, so they have no light at the end of the tunnel."

Me: "We're not allowed to leave, either, so it's kind of like a sentence." I leaned forward to our snack platter and grabbed some cheese on a toothpick, then leaned back and continued to sip my wine.

Phil: "Well, hold on. There are similarities, but it's a very different thing to be in a place by choice."

Lance: "Yeah, but what's weird here is there's no fence, but you still can't leave!"

Phil: "You could. You've always got the choice."

Lance: "But you could walk and walk and walk . . ."

Phil: "Oh, I'm not thinking of that long walk for the choice."

Neal: "You could always just max out your credit card and call Norlandair."

Phil: "Well, that's one choice."

Lance: "No, I don't have a limit that big!"

Phil: "The other choice is to call PFS and just say, 'Come and fucking get me!' and I think they'd have to."

Me: "Would they *have* to?"

Phil: "I think so."

Neal: "Or break Don's legs. Or set a building on fire. Any building." Neal is right, that would get a plane here pronto.

Don: "Well, if you're gonna do that you might as well burn the S.O.B. because—"

Neal: "It needs to go?"

Don: "No—it would burn the best! There's lots of flammable stuff in there."

Phil: "Let's start the emergency generator first, and get the power switched over, so we don't freeze to death before the plane can get here."

Me: "We could just keep warm next to the burning S.O.B. Do we have any marshmallows?"

Don: "It wouldn't be long before we'd be a mess without the S.O.B., with or without that other generator. It'll run a little while and then it's gonna be out of fuel."

Phil: "Correctomundo."

Don: "And then what are we gonna do?"

Phil: "Five-gallon cans, mate, one at a time."

Lance: "Bucket brigade?"

Phil: "Yep."

Don: "Where would you get it from? Pump from one of the fuel bladders?"

Phil: "That aviation tank, my man."

Lance: "Doing that all day would keep me warm at least."

Don: "Please don't burn the shop! It's only another month. Break my legs instead!"

Day 53
Wednesday, December 26

Everything is broken. Not Don's legs. Those are fine. Everything at TAWO is broken. The air pump we fixed last week—which should have lasted at least a year—failed already. So that's five instruments down right there, again. Additionally, the GPS base station isn't working, and Neal snapped the air sampler's telescoping mast in two, probably because it's still below sixty out there and everything is brittle. He sleuthed out the replacement mast, but it was broken too, which means the true replacement mast was the one we were using and someone swapped them out without bothering—or remembering, maybe—to report it. Neal managed a kludge of the newly broken and the shouldn't-be-broken that seems to work. We'll have to be careful with it though.

On the up side, the precip tower replacement went together beautifully, though it's a little top heavy since the upper section is now galvanized pipe and the lower is still aluminum tube. I have faith that it will last until we leave, but not much longer. At that point it will be someone else's problem. It's poor karma, I know, but my regard is fairly deficient at this point.

So we're up one and down seven.

Day 55
Friday, December 28

I haven't been able to fall asleep the past two nights. Could it be the around-the-clock iota of reflected sunlight that is permeating the night sky? The moon is full, bringing with it an intense illumination for unpracticed pupils. It arcs through the sky in such a way that its silver agents of espionage silently ninja my room through some obscure slice of my otherwise impenetrable window. They project a bright stripe, first across my face and then down the rest of my length as if I'm being slowly scanned for signs of drowsiness. After failing to detect any, they continue exploring a deliberate path across my closet, door, and wall before spelunking back out into the darkness, just in time for breakfast.

The moon has been circling a clear sky for the past few days, and the wind has dropped to a light yet arctic northerly. The temperature was a piercing -70°F this morning, and it froze the drain for the Big House kitchen sink, rendering it unusable. I'm frozen too—I've been wearing long johns all day, outdoors *and* in.

By lunch the temperature dropped another five degrees and we watched as it continued a slow descent. Phil was jumping up again to take a screenshot for every new tick down the scale. No one was motivated to go out in such cold, so we lingered. It reached -83°F.

Then we remembered instant clouds, which roused Don, Neal, and me to take advantage of the calm, biting cold for a bit of fun.

We started with coffee mugs of boiling water and quickly

Instant cloud fun at -80°F

upped the ante to full pitchers for bigger effect. A strange whistling sizzle fills the air as projectile droplets of near-boiling water vaporize and immediately freeze into a fan-shaped cloud. Very little liquid traverses the entire arch to reach the ground, even when flinging a full pitcher. Nearly all is converted to a cloud that drifts slowly off with the breeze.[46]

This was something I wanted to try during my winter in Antarctica, but I somehow never got around to it. That winter was so different from this one. With over a hundred people on station there was always something going on. I filled my schedule to overflow with after-work activities: pool, soccer, music, trivia night, volunteering in the library, travelogues in the bar, bowling in the bowling alley. There was a freaking bowling alley![47] The options for things to do weren't endless, but they were many and varied. In comparison to Summit, my perspective was utterly reversed: I looked forward to those few days when I had no commitments and I could laze around doing nothing. Now I'm dying for something to do, and tossing up a few pitchers of instant-cloud was a great respite, if only short-lived.

This general boredom has been drawing my mind magnetically toward fun, warm, summery things to do. My yen compass points south. I can't wait to get on a bike again, go hiking with Kira, go rafting with the gang back in Oregon. Lately I've been killing time on the internet looking at new toys and rivers to run and how far you can get from Corvallis in a day's drive. I'm definitely tired of being here. There's just nothing to do.

---

46   If you'd like to try this at home, the water *must* be boiling, and the air temperature *must* be very, very cold. Depending on where you live, you'll probably need to go to someone else's home, hopefully far, far away from the comfortable climate you've sensibly chosen to live in.

47   A two-lane bowling alley with old pin-placement machines incapable of loading themselves. Community members worked as pinsetters for a little extra cash. They wore long brightly-striped socks to advertise their presence behind the pins and sometimes returned notes in the finger holes of bowling balls. Scathing criticisms garnered bigger tips. Sadly, McMurdo's bowling alley no longer exists.

ME: "IT's WARMING up outside. It's only seventy-five!"

My facetiousness fell on dead ears as I entered the Big House for dinner. I'm okay with it though: it means the boys are also feeling the saturnine effects of winter, and we're all in this together. Or, I'm not as funny as I like to think.

Don served steak with potatoes and beets in an effort to use up the last of our freshie supply, which is practically depleted. We're down to a bit of bok choy and whatever potatoes and beets Don didn't use.

Don: "I shouldn't've boiled these beets: they turned to mush."

Phil: "Boy, and they were mush already."

Don: "Beets usually keep the longest."

Me: "So the beets have gone bad too?"

Phil: "Oh, yeah, they had wrinkled skin and felt like mush on the inside."

Me: "Ew." I poked at a cube of beet on my plate. It was a little soft, but looked okay.

Don: "These potatoes don't seem like they got done."

Phil: "They take a long time up here; it's amazing."

Me: "Longer than beans, you think?"

Phil: "Maybe not." He laughed, remembering my failed attempt with the black beans.

Don: "I thought it'd all be done about the same time, but the steak seems plenty done."

Neal: "Hey, but thanks for *beefing* up our leftovers, Don. Ha, ha." At least Neal's joke was intended to fall flat and he could count it as a success.

Neal: "What? Nobody?" Or, Neal is not as funny as he likes to think.

Don: "It's not melt-in-your-mouth quality, but it's tasty."

Phil: "It's all good, Don. I think I'm going to write to Tanya and tell her you actually *can* cook."

Don: "But then she'll want me to cook!" He grinned a boyish grin.

Lance: "What does Tanya do?"

Don: "Fixes teeth."

Lance: "Is she a dentist?"

Don: "She works for the dentist. She was a dentist in Russia, but she's not licensed in the United States, so she can't work with blood: she can't pull teeth; she can't drill teeth. She puts on braces, but mostly she makes dentures."

Me: "Blood's the dividing line, huh?"

Don: "Can't work with blood."

Neal: "Can't prescribe drugs either, right?"

Don: "No."

Lance: "That's why Don's up here!"

Me: "Is that why the clinic inventory is off?"

Phil: "Could well be."

Don: "What kind of good stuff do you have in there? I need to know before I can take it."

Lance: "They asked me what we should do as a group and I said we should have more functions. So, how about the drugs?"

Phil: "There's good stuff in there. When there's shit I have to sign for, it means it's good stuff."

Don: "I have a pain."

Day 57
Sunday, December 30

I had trouble sleeping again last night. I even did yoga yesterday, hoping it would help. It didn't. At least it's Sunday and I got to sleep in. The mornings are the worst part of this insomnia. I lie awake until the middle of the night, finally drifting off into intermittent sleep that eventually grows heavier but always too late—always when my alarm is poised to fire. In the mornings I often rise from this deep state, making it that much harder to get going.

Today I got to sleep through it, but that also meant I missed some aurora this morning that Neal said was decent, even though it only lasted a few minutes. Hopefully that means we'll start seeing more; there's been nothing for weeks. NOAA claims we've most likely reached or even passed the solar maximum, which makes it the least active in a hundred years. I'm starting to feel gypped.

When Neal and I arrived for lunch, we found Don sitting at the table and looking contemplative.

"What's up, Don?" Neal asked.

"Oh, you know. I'm just thinking about killing people."

"That's going in the quote book!" Neal said enthusiastically, but then he hesitated. "On second thought, maybe that's a bad idea."

Perhaps foolishly, neither of us stopped to consider Don's statement as a warning that he might go homicidally berserk. After all, it's always the person you least expect.

Don filled us in. A maniac in New York killed his sister, then set the house on fire. As firefighters arrived, he started plucking them off with a rifle. Two were killed. The firefighters were forced to stand down and let the police deal with the shooter while the blaze brought down six more homes. It happened on the morning of Christmas Eve, so we're a little late in hearing the news. What bewilders me is that this criminal already spent almost twenty years in prison for killing his grandmother with a hammer! Why is such a heinous lunatic left alive to kill again? We should sentence degenerates like this to the crime they committed. One hammer could have saved several lives.

Day 58
Monday, December 31

I'm writing this in the middle of the night because I still can't fucking sleep. It's so aggravating. I thought for sure a good New Year's Eve drunk would help me pass the hell out. No. Instead, it's an on-and-off, foot-on-the-floor insomnausea.

Don and I got started in the afternoon. We cracked the first beers and caught a hankering for nachos. We decided that one large tray was definitely too much, so we made two smaller trays and failed to realize that they summed to the same area as the large one. It was incredibly too much, but just the same, we enjoyed crunching it down as we slurped our homebrew. At dinner Phil brought out a bottle of Akvavit from Denmark, passed along from the Phase 1 crew. Like my previous experiences with Akvavit, it flowed freely and went down easy. By the end of the meal, which quickly became fun and festive, we were all tipsy. Don was particularly jovial, even more than usual.

I left to launch the evening weather balloon, which I've done so many times now that it requires zero thought: the motions are purely robotic. For that reason—and because I was somewhat intoxicated—I had no qualms performing the task while somewhat intoxicated.

When I returned, the party had moved to the Green House, where we were planning to watch *The Castle*, an Australian "parody of parodies," according to Phil.

"I only watch it when there's an Australian around so they can interpret!" Lance said.

"You probably need somebody who's had some refresher lessons, and that ain't me," Phil replied.

"Well, Don wanted to know if there would be subtitles so we would understand!" Lance grinned.

"Nice," I chuckled. "Aussie isn't *that* bad, though. South African English is much worse. The first weekend I was there I went to Kira's brother's bachelor party and I could only understand half of what they said. And some of it didn't make any sense even when I did understand it. Like, they have three versions of now: *now, just now*, and *now now*—and they all mean *later*!"

"Island time!" Lance laughed.

"Exactly!" With my intoxication mounting, *my* English may have been getting more difficult to understand, but I didn't let that stop me.

"Oh, and Welsh!" I continued, excited to have another story. "I was traveling with this group once, with a couple of Swedes and a German and a Canuck, and there was this Welshman and his accent was horrendous. No one could understand a word he said.

The Swedes would always look at me for a translation into normal English, and half the time I just had to shrug. It drove him nuts! He would get all pissed off and say, 'Way da fok ya dun unnastann meh?'" I laughed at my own terrible drunken impersonation and then continued, "One morning he told me, 'O'v joost add da loovliest crap!' And I was like, 'Huh?' because I didn't want to hear about his morning crap, but he just kept on about how huge and lovely it was and how it had chocolate and bananas and it took me forever to figure out he was talking about a fucking *crepe* that he'd eaten for breakfast!"[48]

"And we're right back to poo," Phil said. We all laughed. It's becoming his catchphrase.

We continued to chatter as we sat sipping on some scotch that Lance brought. We were waiting for Don to return from his evening generator checks when the power went out. In my inebriation, I giggled at the thought that Don had fucked something up in *his* inebriation. But I quickly sobered by the thought that he may be injured, or we may be up shit creek. A power outage is an emergency here, and when the lights go out unexpectedly, it's no different from a fire alarm.

The sobering effect of an alarm is amazing, especially if you've spent time on an emergency response team. At Palmer, nearly all the support staff are required to be on at least one team. Most end up on several. I served on two search and rescue teams—ocean and glacier—and the fire brigade. We rarely got any excitement from search and rescue, but we regularly got false fire alarms. We'd be in the bar on a Saturday night and someone would set off the alarm above the toaster in the galley. It was always the damn toaster. The adrenaline surge was immediate and effective. We would all instinctively bolt for our fire gear and I would show up on scene feeling stone sober and thinking, *I can't believe I was drunk only five minutes ago.* Even after the alarm was called off, sobriety remained. The evening's former mood could never be

---

48   I still revisit this memory every time I come across a crepe, and I have to resist calling it a "loovly crap."

reattained.

Lance and Phil immediately went to check on Don. Neal began dressing to go check TAWO. I told him I didn't think it was worth it to go all the way out there. TAWO can run on a battery backup through several hours of power outage, and our mental state was not one for travel. He agreed and updated his purpose to dressing for the cold that will quickly creep into the building without heat. Neal has also spent many seasons on the fire brigade, and I'm sure he simply felt he should do *something*. I felt the same, so I sort of circled aimlessly, unsure what to do. I turned on my radio and grabbed my headlamp, then continued my uncertainty. The power returned momentarily, cycled several times, and then stayed on. Phil, Lance, and Don returned shortly afterward. Don was grinning ear to ear and apologized repeatedly. "I'm not even sure what happened. I pushed the wrong button," he said. I assured him that I push the wrong button all the time—but of course, it generally goes unnoticed. Don's smile faded and he shook his head, now hanging like a bad puppy's. "I pushed the wrong button."

Day 59
Tuesday, January 1

We were all in a bad way today. Don was still unsure what triggered the power outage last night. "Nothing I did should have caused the generator to shut down," he said, puzzled.

We sat at the lunch table nibbling food that didn't want to go down. Don could only get a few bites in and had to stop for his churning innards. "Did you puke?" he asked me, acknowledging our collective hangovers.

"Yeah," I answered, "but it was in the middle of the night, which is weird for me. Usually once I'm out I stay out. I think I woke to a noxious nacho miasma that was so foul it triggered the puke. Seriously."

"I puked while we were still watching the movie. It was that Akvavit. It was so good."

It *was* so good. And so *bad*.

"I had a great time though," I said. "That was a lot of fun. It was worth it."

"Yeah, it *was* fun, but I don't think I'm gonna be drinking any-thing for a while."

I can't say I blame him. I spent most of the day in a zombie state, coddling a hangover and running on minimal, ineffective sleep. All day I looked forward to going to bed, closing my eyes, and absolutely shutting down. And now of course, here I am finally horizontal and absolutely wide awake. I'm getting damn sick of this.

14

In which I complete the plunge into winter's icy waters, only to be pulled deeper by other forces equally beyond my control.

Day 60
Wednesday, January 2

"Of all the things, this is what I want to turn over the most," Neal complained. "And I don't mean I can't wait to teach the new techs how to do it; I mean I can't wait to never do this again." I agreed as he continued, "'We don't want our samples to be contaminated, so we want you to put on this ridiculous clean suit that gets contaminated just by putting it on. And we want you to wear these thin plastic gloves that you can't fit real gloves under, only liners, and then go out into the Arctic and the first thing we want you to do is "wash" your already cold hands in this freezing snow. And *then* we want you to go ahead and try to open ten of these stupid plastic bags with your numb fingers and pack them full of snow. Oh, and we're going to give you cold metal tools and expect you to write shit down too.'"

I wanted to laugh at his spot-on delivery, but the humor of it was lost in the truth of it, so I laughed at his misfortune instead. Then I realized it was *our* misfortune and I reverted to laughing at his spot-on delivery.

I can't decide if snow sampling is worse when it's "warm" and windy or cold and calm. Both are heat sucking. The weather has continued to be exceptionally calm and pleasantly clear but stupefyingly cold. I'm not sure the temperature has climbed above sixty since before Christmas. I'm also not sure I should wish for warmer weather because then I'd be wishing for tempestuous weather. It's a no-win situation.

Halfway back from TAWO, we swapped: I took the sled with the snow samples and the large crate of air flasks, and Neal took the lead. I slung the towline over my left shoulder and under my right arm, then switched, then switched back. The crate seemed heavy for a payload of air, but it was actually the sticky snow that was conspiring against me. This place is full of baffling surprises. The wide expanse of white stuff would seem like a Nordic skiing utopia, but it's all sandpaper: there's no glide. In fact, every time we ski the bamboo forest I naturally start swinging my raised ski into an expected slide and instead encounter a halting grip, which feels like yanking on a mob of claw-dragging cats. Lance explained it like this: skis work on the principle that friction melts a thin film of water between the ski and the snow, providing slip. But here, at these ludicrous temperatures, it's just too damn cold for that, hence the adverse cats. We don't truly *ski* the bamboo forest, we walk it with long sticks strapped to our feet. You have to lift the ski to move it, which is counterintuitive. But I'm too lacking in neurotransmission to unlearn my ways, so I keep going in for the slide and being surprised by the cats.

Hauling the sled over this snow is little different from dragging it across packed sand, which doesn't bother most of me, but it overwhelms my lungs. My legs, each swinging five pounds of expedition boot without complaint, keep radioing up to say, "What's the holdup, lungs? Bring us some oxygen, would ya?" My breathing was still laborious halfway through lunch.

DON: "I WONDER how this would taste?" He looked back and forth between the mashed potatoes on his plate and the shaker of fairy dust in his hand.

Neal: "Only one way to find out."

Phil: "Does fairy dust go with potatoes?"

Me: "Of course. According to Don, it goes with everything. What *is* that stuff, anyway?"

Phil: "It's nutritional yeast."

Me: "Yeast? That's a topping?" I had never heard of this before.

Don: "It's supposed to be good for you. But I haven't had it the last couple days."

Phil: "Yeah? What's been wrong with you?"

Lance: "You feeling okay, Don?"

Don: "I was afraid it would make me fart."

Neal: "You *should* be afraid of farting."

Phil: "No, *you* should be afraid of him farting."

Me: "I'm afraid of him farting."

Neal: "Well, if *he's* afraid of it, maybe he won't do it. If *I'm* afraid of it, it doesn't change anything."

Day 61
Thursday, January 3

I woke up in the usual way—stunted whistling breath through my nose—so I was immediately pissy. I'm fed up with this continual bloody-flake-walled congestion. It's kicking the downed horse that is my bedtime insomnia and morning lassitude. It's an aggravating way to start the day. So I was angry. But by breakfast I was jovial and even perky, which is strange for me even under normal circumstances. Approaching lunch, as we skied out to the bamboo forest for the umpteenth time, I became extremely grumpy for no reason. As we went on, my frosted goggles eliminated my ability to see the notepad I was writing on. It pushed me over the edge. I mumbled expletives through my frozen gaiter while scribbling illegible notes in the margins that I hoped would later help me decipher the equally illegible data.

After lunch came boredom. I sorted through dozens of live concerts, given to me by Phil, to isolate the ones of decent sound quality that I deemed worth keeping. This turned my boredom to a real sense of achievement, a much bigger sense than was justified, but it waned quickly back to boredom.

In fact, boredom is becoming more and more pervasive as the days go by. Every day is a skipping record. The black circle spins another revolution, the sonic wave traces a few crests and troughs —meal, work, meal, work, meal—then the needle scratches while I attempt to sleep and the freakish hormonal carnival continues on another loop.

I'm so bored. I'm so bored that I insist any poor bastard who reads this journal be bored too, so I'm going to make the remainder of this entry incredibly dry; not British humor dry, just plain boring. And grumpy, let's not forget grumpy.

The oxygen sensor was in alarm when we arrived at TAWO yesterday morning. It was audible from outside the building, which I guess is good since it keeps us from entering a potentially oxygenless room. But it was painfully ear-piercing as we waited outside with the door hanging open to let some known good air in, which of course also let the frigidity in. The oxygen level was fine all along. We reset it. But the damn thing was right back in alarm again this morning. Refusing to be fooled or sonically assaulted, this time we waltzed right in and silenced it, then promptly blocked it from memory.

The NO_x instrument appears to be malfunctioning, but we've been unable to contact the principle investigator and we hesitate to tear into it without approval, even though it's probably just an internal fuse for the photomultiplier.

We finally isolated the GPS base station's problem to a broken cable, which we replaced, mostly. We forgot to anchor it down and remembered later that we forgot. But we figured at least it's working again and we don't need to do the anchors right this minute.[49]

We got word today to begin our End-of-Season Report, any protocol updates, and the turnover schedule. During a phone conference with Katrine, I tried to emphasize that we need to take it easy on the new techs during turnover by simplifying as much as possible. Though I believe what I said, it was admittedly more for my own run-down toasty benefit than for their fresh jaunty one. I don't want to do ICESat and the meter pit early this month just so we can do them again at turnover, which will be early next month. I don't want to do them again at all. Besides, if we add those to turnover, we'll have two new techs leaving on the plane with us. Those tasks are best left until after their chance of escape has passed.

That was a pathetic attempt to convey the tedium. Boring: perhaps. Grumpy: a bit. Dry: not nearly enough. Let me try again . . .

The oxygen sensor is broke. We ignored the damn thing.

The NO_x is broke too, and so is its PI.

The GPS has been broke. We finally fixed it but failed to finish the job.

Katrine gave us a bunch of paperwork to do. We put it off.

I considered writing a post in my blog but chose boredom instead.[50]

~

The Freezer Trench

Summit Station, Greenland
Saturday, January 5, 2013

Before my first voyage to the last continent, while training for one of the instruments that would be in my care, a boisterous

---

49 Or the next minute, or the next hour, or the next several days . . .

50 Now watch as my future self hijacks my past self's mood by ignoring chronological order and inserting said blog post, which was written two days later and several notches higher on the wave.

Antarctic veteran sarcastically prepared me for the dating scene I would soon encounter. "Don't worry, there's a beautiful woman behind every tree!" He laughed and then assured me that despite the shortage of women, there would still be plenty of "Antarctic tens" once my standards were acclimated. I'm sure that if I were a woman, he would have been telling me that "the odds are good, but the goods are odd."

His demeanor shifted slightly, and there was suddenly an element of sincerity when he asked, "Do you know the most amazing thing about Antarctica?"

I should have anticipated his wit at this point, but still I fell wide-eyed into the trap. "No, what?"

"The number of ice machines per capita."

And though he joked, it's preposterously true. At McMurdo, with an average annual temperature of one solitary degree, in an environment inundated with naturally occurring ice, there's an ice-cube machine on every floor of every dorm. Summer temperatures sometimes reach 40°F, so having access to an ice-cold beverage is of dire importance. For the same reason, but with some logic incorporated, McMurdo's frozen food supply is kept in freezer containers to get it through those boat-drink-inducing warm spells.

Not so here. Atop Greenland's ice cap it is exceptionally rare for the temperature to crawl above freezing, even in the summer. Our food stays frozen year-round in a glorified snow cave we call "the freezer trench." Grocery shopping means putting on all your cold weather gear and heading out the back door of the Big House, down the stairs, and under the building to a wide hatch, much like the lid of a chest freezer. A stairwell then leads you thirty feet below the surface, where the freezer trench walls and ceiling are cut from packed snow and then framed in plywood. Lining the walls are long shelves on which you'll find everything from halibut to Cheerios. I thought the sparkling coat of crystals on the ceiling was charming until Neal suggested that it probably consists of five hundred people's accumulated breath. I washed my neck gaiters that evening.

Unfortunately, we're down to dry, canned, and frozen foods for our final month. We used the last of the freshies—a few heads of wilty bok choy—earlier this week. Everyone still manages to cook good meals, but I'm already looking forward to fresh food.

I have five weeks remaining in this deployment. It doesn't sound like a long time, but under the unusual circumstances of a polar winter, it will feel like an eternity. In fact, it's best not to think about it; that's a closet-of-the-mind doorway for the winter gloom monster. It's best to be in the now, even though the now is a little screwy.

~

Day 62
Friday, January 4

We recalibrated the oxygen sensor in TAWO's vestibule this morning, hopeful that it will alleviate the daily state of alarm at 22.2 percent oxygen, which it seems to think is life-threatening.[51]

KIRA AND I have been trying to figure out how we'll be able to see each other after this season. I'll have been to Baja and back to Oregon before she returns from Palmer. She'll have to fly from Chile to Virginia and then back home to South Africa to get her things together for the move to Oregon. She wants to spend some

---

51 In hindsight, it may have saved us some trouble if we had thought about this for a moment: it's reporting correctly but alarming falsely. Doesn't sound like a calibration issue . . .

time with her family and friends there before moving so far away, which I understand and fully support, but it means we'll be apart that much longer. Already we haven't seen each other in four months, and we don't want to wait three more.

It's difficult to spend so much time apart, especially when different time zones and schedules make it hard to find time for live conversation. Additionally, these remote field stations are absorbing worlds; their isolation and self-sufficiency nurture this feeling that the outside world is on an altogether different wavelength. Outside contact is unnecessary and can be awkward and even jolting. It becomes easy to let go; the strange here and now takes over.

From my end I guess there's not much to tell Kira anyway, but she fills me in about goings-on at Palmer and I find myself not missing it, which is comforting. I miss the people, but I'm confident I've made the right decision in discontinuing my contracts there. I greatly miss Kira, of course, and I wish we were together one way or another. We're literally on opposite ends of the world. But it's better this way. I would not have been happy at Palmer a fourth season in a row, and Kira and I will reunite soon enough.

It seemed such a strange thing to me at first, when I learned of couples that do this: spending months apart while one does a deployment here and the other a deployment there. But now that I've grown accustomed to this life of contracted employment in the remote places of the world, I understand. It's not easy, but it's a lifestyle choice. And that lifestyle is addictive: it offers adventure, travel, extended time off, and a unique camaraderie. Naturally, people find partners under these circumstances, and though there may be a relatively high rate of failure, those who make it work simply choose to do so, and I find that endearing.

It's sometimes easy to forget that the guys also have significant others back home. I don't even know them except for Clair, Neal's partner, who I've spent some overlap time with at Palmer. Like Neal, she's fantastic and fun. They've done three or four consecutive winters together at Palmer now, so this is a departure from their normal routine. Neal took this position largely because it was a good opportunity.

I asked him recently, "What are you and Clair doing after this?"

"Well, she just got a contract at Palmyra that starts right after I get home, but I don't know what I'm doing yet. I've applied to a few different things. I'm kind of excited about the winter manager position at Palmer, but I don't think I'll get it at this point. And I applied to the tech position on the ships, and I'm also looking at doing another year at Pole."

"Another year at Pole?" I asked, surprised.

"Yeah, but now that would mean I wouldn't see Clair for like a year."

"No shit."

"Well, I mean, we'd see each other for about a week between Palmyra and Pole."

I did the math in my head, slowly. "Wait, that would be more like a year and a half."

"No, she'd come to Pole for the winter."

"Oh, gotcha. Shit, that's still a long time."

"Well, it's all up in the air right now."

I'm not sure if any of it has landed yet. But it makes an extra month or two away from Kira seem comparatively trivial. Still, I can't wait to see her, so today I bought her a round-trip flight to Oregon from Virginia. It will only be a week, but that will have to tide us over. She's really excited about it.

Saturday

I'm not sure of the date. I can't figure it out right now. My brain is beginning to feel like toothpaste. It's Saturday; that much I know.

An incredible storm burst out after lunch yesterday, breaking a ten-day streak of clear calm cold, and today it intensified into a flag-shredding maelstrom. It's raging at nearly forty miles per hour, which is more than enough to whip up a miserable blinding frenzy and set the Big House to rocking. It's about a two-flagger on the polar storm scale, meaning I can't see anything beyond two flags. I guess it's a sliding scale though, because this seems just as bad as the no-flagger when I got my truck stuck on the roadside between McMurdo and Arrival Heights. Those flags were placed wider. I wish they had been placed straighter.

It being a good day for indoor work, Neal and I finished the first draft of our End-of-Season Report, as asked for. Turnover is approaching and now we've officially begun the too-long march toward an end-of-the-tunnel light that has not yet made itself apparent. It seems that writing the EOS now is premature. More stuff is sure to go wrong; we still have a month remaining in our tenure.

That's a whole month yet of hearing things, like the recently discovered mystery alarm that beeps faintly somewhere around our office every evening at about 9:30. So far I've eliminated the radiosonde lab and decided it's louder in the office than in the lounge, but I still can't find it. It seems to stop just as I'm getting warm—like a reversed proximity alarm. It drives me completely bonkers. Whenever I hear it I can't help but frantically start look-ing for it, no matter how tired I'm feeling or how little it matters, like a zombie marionette that jumps to life when Pavlov's dogs salivate. I can't decide if it's a former science technician's lost watch, reminding him or her to close the radiosonde, or an inten-tionally placed joke meant to drive the upcoming winter phase tenants completely bonkers. I don't understand why I didn't notice it earlier in the season. Wait a minute—it could be Neal fucking with me. That bastard. He still won't admit to hearing the stenographer in our office.

As it turns out, I'm not the only one befuddled by strange noises. Last night Lance and I were in the Big House having some scotch when something starting ringing. There's only one phone there and it has a regular old desk-phone ring, and that's the only ring we ever hear. None of us carry a cell phone; there's nothing to connect to. But this was a distinctly different ring, like a classic cellular. Lance was oblivious at first, making me wonder if I really was the only one losing it. I hesitated to point it out and risk dis-covering that it was only in my head. Fortunately for my own mental state, Lance was just a little slow on the uptake, which I'm sure can be attributed partly to the scotch and partly to having been here over five months now. Soon our sad, withered, combined acumen was searching for the source of the unlikely noise.

"How am I supposed to find it if it never gets any louder or quieter?" Lance asked.

"What? It does for me, but it's like a moving target. I can't figure it out."

It took far too long for Lance to realize it was the iPod in his pocket, which was connected to the Wi-Fi, and which Hannah was calling him on. So it turns out there *is* something to connect to, and if I could be bothered to carry around some sort of Wi-Fi device, I could connect to it and have strange noises coming from my pocket too.

But more importantly, I'm not the only one who's losing it.

AS THE STORM continued to shred flags outside, I sat down to dinner with everyone but Don, who hadn't arrived yet. The phone in Phil's office started ringing and as he got up to answer it, Lance quipped, "Don wants it delivered!"

But Phil returned stating simply, "I get a lot of wrong numbers."

It's strange, but true. I haven't gotten many here but I got them at Palmer a lot. Most of the callers didn't believe me when I said they'd called Antarctica. The satellite connection links the Antarctic stations directly to headquarters in Denver. That includes all the phone and internet services. I assume it's the same here: it's a Denver exchange and therefore a local call for folks in the US. It just goes through a lot of expensive routing.

Don announced his arrival to dinner with: "This place sucks!" Though he wore his usual broad smile. He was covered in snow.

Phil: "Good day to be inside, mate."

Me: "Am I gonna be able to make it back to the Green House in slippers?"

Lance: "Well, it's easy going that way. If you just jump off the Big House deck, you'd probably have to grab onto the Green House weather tower on your way by!"

Neal: "You must have made it *here* in slippers." He made a good point.

Me: "Yeah, but it seems much worse out there now. I didn't get covered in snow."

Phil: "Could you hear the wind picking up out in the shop, Don?"

Don: "I thought it was gonna get blown down! It's really hammering on us." He finished brushing himself off and began removing his boots and parka.

Me: "It's been swaying pretty good over here too."

Lance: "Out at MSF my computer screen shakes and I'm like, *Shit, am I getting dizzy or . . .*"

Me: "I noticed yesterday that TAWO moves, for sure. Not as much as here though."

Neal: "I don't think I should try to launch a balloon tonight."

Lance: "Oh, just put extra helium in it, don't use a parachute, and you'll be fine."

Neal: "I'll be fine." He wasn't buying it.

Lance: "You'll be fine."

Neal: "How's the balloon gonna do?"

Lance: "I don't know. But I have faith."

Phil: "I gave up faith for Lent."

After dinner, I carefully ensured that all my layers of clothing were overlapping and I cinched down anything I could before going outside. With the gale howling across my left shoulder, I twisted my coat around to the right. This angled my big fuzzy hood against the wind, which can cut through gaiter and goggles both. The hood reached halfway across my encapsulated face, covering my left eye. Despite my care the storm still penetrated every crack, its favorite the small gaps between zipper teeth, which suddenly seemed plentiful. With my chin tucked to my chest and only one eye to peer into the blur, I postholed through rapidly growing drifts on my trudge between buildings—in my slippers.

Day 64
Sunday, January 6

Another Sunday. Another week completed. Another advancement through the tunnel. I gladly slept until 10:30, my biological clock certain that the morning is the middle of the night. The storm continued outside with less conviction. It calmed considerably since yesterday, but that's not saying much considering the havoc it caused.

We had to repair, or rather, rerepair the GPS antenna cable. This time it broke loose completely, possibly because we never anchored it down. Honestly, there's no doubt that it was possibly because we never anchored it down. We had all intentions of anchoring it but forgot. It shouldn't go without saying that this time we anchored it immediately.

The storm bent the lower section of the precip tower mast. Only a few degrees, but I didn't dare try to bend it back for fear that it would snap. The tower is still functional, it just leans a bit. I warned the PI that it should probably be replaced with something more substantial soon. I'm beginning to doubt that my handiwork will last until turnover. Every storm will lessen its chances. Soon I may be trying to construct an entirely new tower out of scavenged parts. That's not something I want to do.

When I reached TAWO, the deck was a mess of gas cylinders that had come loose and toppled. A few stood, a few leaned, a few lay, a few lay on top of those few. One sat waist-deep in the snow ten feet below the deck. I decided to leave them. I wanted to take a picture but didn't have a camera, and they're all empty anyway, and it didn't look like a one-man job, and it's Sunday for Christ's sake, and a million other reasons I could come up with to go back to the Green House and take a nap.

I returned to find Don getting fired up about the washing machine. "This place sucks!" His usual smile was strangely absent.

He had the panel all opened up again, double-checking the door-latch indicator switches we'd already bypassed. "It started to spin then stopped. What the fuck?" It was the most irritated I've seen him.

"I can sometimes get it to go on the second or third try," I offered.

Later, while passing through the S.O.B. to launch the evening weather balloon, I noticed Don's overalls hanging in the stream of hot air that blows out of the generator shack. Their damp aroma filled the air. It smelled like defeat.

AT 9:45 EVERY evening, Neal's alarm goes off to remind him—and me—to close out the radiosonde. It's an old digital watch alarm just like the mystery alarm in the walls. *Too* like the mystery alarm. He's conspiring against me, I'm sure of it.[52]

"I closed out the sonde for you," Neal told me after we finished watching a movie.

"Holy shit, I completely forgot." I wondered how I had missed it but knew there was no answer. Then I wondered if this had ever happened before. I didn't think so. Finally, I realized that Neal had to walk right in front of me to close the sonde. "Wait, how did you do that without me even noticing?"

"Well, my alarm went off, I waited ten minutes, and when you didn't get up, I did."

I was oblivious to the whole thing. I never even saw him get up. "Sorry, man. Thanks."

My mind is lost in a fog-choked chasm.

---

52   And I'm checking off another psych eval true-false question: *I believe I am being plotted against.*

Day 65
Monday, January 7

I lingered in the Green House after Neal left for rounds. I wanted my bladder to be as empty as possible when I met up with him at TAWO. We had a lot to do and the last thing I wanted to deal with was having to pee out there, especially in shitty weather. So I delayed, drained the tank at the last minute, then geared up, gathered the snow sampling equipment, and headed out into a freezing windblown fog. The storm, which started as a warm (-15°F) howling wind and blowing snow and abated to a cool (-30°F) high wind and haze, changed to a cold (-50°F) high wind and heavy fog. I waded unwillingly through it a third of the way to TAWO before realizing I had forgotten my camera—I still wanted to take pictures of the tattered pile of cylinders—so I turned around, angry with myself. Back out again, my goggles frosted over double-time and my hood wouldn't stay cinched, so it was like a parachute I had to pull through the wind. My mood darkened further. Almost immediately after reaching TAWO, I needed to pee. Now I was downright ornery.

"This is bullshit," I said to no one as I plodded out to the pee flag, postholing through ice-crusted snow drifts half of the seldom-trod way. There are only a few designated outdoor locations for this, thus minimizing our impact. Human waste is dealt with differently at every polar station. McMurdo is large enough that it has a full wastewater treatment facility. Biologically clean water gets pumped out to sea while solid waste "cakes"—essentially soil at that point—are shipped out. I remember the winter waste technician kept beakers on his desk containing tomato sprouts that had risen from the cake. Some found it weird and gross; others found it fascinating. I'm sure Don would have approved. Field camps around McMurdo often use fifty-gallon drums for human waste. These are eventually sent back to station. The lab at Arrival Heights actually had a "rocket potty," which incinerated its contents. At Palmer, its population small and its impact minimal, human waste simply passes through a masticator—essentially a garbage disposal—and is pumped into the sea. There, pee flags aren't necessary because you are always within stumbling distance of the tidal zone. Don't pollute, dilute, as they say. Here at Summit, and I believe at the South Pole also, human waste gets flushed into an underground holding cave, where it will freeze into the ice cap and slowly work its way to the sea, keeping geological time, twisting, breaking, and dispersing as it passes the millennia.

It's an everyday task whose motions should be robotic, but in this wasteland, in a state of mental degradation, and wearing twenty layers of clothing, even peeing requires a thorough thinking through: *put your back to the wind, unzip your parka halfway up from the bottom, unzip your overalls from the top, all the way down, pull up your fleece pullover, pull down your long johns, pull up your base top layer, find the fly of your boxers, and be extremely careful not to touch your junk to any metal zippers.*

A thick mist emanated along the length of the arc, blowing rapidly away with the wind and telling me to shift my position slightly for the best lee, though it would matter little. I finished my business and shuddered from having my midsection delayered, even though it wasn't exposed.

This little escapade meant that my first neck gaiter was saturated with moisture from my breath too soon, and between the cylinder overhaul and air sampling still to do, I would be snow sampling with a cold, damp spare gaiter. "This is bullshit," I repeated. When I got back to TAWO, I removed the gaiter and put it back on with the wet part in the upper rear, over my hat so it wouldn't touch my neck—much. This would be okay for the next task, since the work would be warming.

After I took pictures, Neal and I cleaned up the cylinders on the deck and then attempted to remove the suicide-jumping cylinder from the snow below. But it wouldn't budge. We had to dig it out. Together we dragged it under the building to the stairs and then had to gasp for air. It was only ten yards. We pulled the cylinder up six or seven stairs on a dolly and keeled over for air again. Pathetic.

Inside, I swapped out my soggy gaiter for my spare gaiter and mentally prepared for air sampling. No, I prepared emotionally. I've done this a hundred times; there is no longer any need to think: I lug the large aluminum briefcase containing the sampler into the wind away from TAWO. Two glass sample flasks are already inside. I configure the apparatus so it will purge the flasks. I take a deep breath, hold, start the pump, and jog awkwardly downwind about ten meters. Breathe. After five long, cold minutes, the flasks are ready to collect air, and I'm ready to hold my breath again. I take several long deep breaths to open my lungs, then one big one and hold while I run to the case, flip a toggle switch, and then run back. Breathe. In one and a half minutes, I've barely regained my breath, but I prepare for another run. Deep breath, deep breath, hold, run. I check the pressure gauge before closing all the valves, then drop my head and suck in air through a soggy gaiter. Easy.

Inside again, I spun my spare gaiter around and could already feel the wet cold that would accompany me through snow sampling as it crept down the back of my neck.

"This is bullshit."

Day 66
Tuesday, January 8

I'm still barely sleeping. I swear I was awake most of last night. At one point I even gave up and walked around, looking out the few unburied windows in search of aurora. There weren't any.

It's almost as though the busiest days lead to the most sleepless nights. When I'm most tired and need the rest is exactly when I can't get any. The guys can tell how much it's starting to affect me. This morning Neal took one look at me and knew immediately. "Up again last night?" No response was needed that my bleary sidelong eyes couldn't convey.

The storm clamped back down today with increased wind and near-whiteout blowing snow. Maybe it's a new storm, but there wasn't much of a lull so it's hard to say. It's not as bad as it was a few days ago, which makes it worse in a way because it's annoying without being as exciting.

I realized today that I've been feeling very low lately. Both my energy level and my morale have plummeted into the depths of melancholy. The annoyance, the fatigue, the boredom, the feelings of worthlessness and ineptitude: it has all gotten to me. I'm officially toasty. There are still laughs, sure, and I still enjoy the company I'm in, but overall, I'm feeling a bloated depression and a strange sort of hopelessness. Perhaps it's for the lack of control over my own condition.

Until today I hadn't heard from Kira in several days, which has added to my somber mood. I know she's busy, and a few days without correspondence doesn't bother me. But the silence has been brushing the edges of unrest in my mind, though I didn't realize it consciously until now. Was this personal gloom a form of intuition? Did I know somewhere deep in my subconscious what was formulating?

If so, the impact was not softened. Her email today was essentially a breakup, and it blindsided me. I'm reeling from the shock. I guess I won't be sleeping tonight, either.

15

In which everything goes to shit.

Day 67
Wednesday, January 9

I slept better than expected, essentially by convincing myself that everything would be fine, that Kira was just having another knee-jerk reaction. I was wrong. In only a few days, she has convinced herself that this is best, leaving me a brokenhearted wreck. I'm barely able to stagger down the tracks as it is, and now I've been hit by a freight train that I never saw coming. I looked back through our correspondence and decided there is no way I could have seen it coming. Everything is bubbly sunshine and love and sappy serendipity. It's a perplexing about-face. It means the gloom I've felt recently is simply that of a polar winter, and this is simply the worst of timing. I was just wading through the mental muck and suddenly I'm drowning in it with clarity; now it's the colossal boot of devastation that holds me under.

I want so badly to talk to her, but it's near impossible with the time difference and the incredibly slim chance of catching her in her room. So I was forced to email. It was torture waiting for a reply, and even worse when I finally got one. I ran out of the Green House in a total whiteout so I could scream. She's not going to change her mind.

What the fuck do I do now?

It has been mind-numbingly difficult to peel my thoughts away. I spent much of the day trying to occupy myself and my frazzled brain. I reorganized the linen closet and did a lot of vacant staring at the wall. Though that may sound like a joke, it's true. The toasty zone-outs are void of thought, so I welcomed them. It was also my day to cook, which helped.

Maintain the distraction.

I don't mind cooking, and I began the season even enjoying it. But my meals have become much simpler as motivation has waned to a sense of hassle.

Maintain the distraction.

Planning ahead is difficult at best, and remembering to thaw all the ingredients in advance seems near impossible sometimes.

Maintain.

Though there are only five of us, we tend to cook for ten, leaving plenty of leftovers for lunches and weekends, which adds to the preparation.

Distraction isn't working. The loss of her is an intense white noise over everything, and no amount of tinfoil on the antenna will allow another signal to come through.

TIME PASSES. THE roller coaster rolls. The wave exits the trough, reluctantly. While the upswing lasts, let me try this again . . .

I made chicken tikka masala for dinner. It was complex enough to distract me yet simple enough for my feeble winter mind. Phil and Lance arrived like clockwork at five and the three of us sat down to eat. It was strange that Neal and Don weren't there yet. Usually everyone shows up within minutes of each other. I think by three or four in the afternoon everyone is just watching the clock, biding the time until dinner.

Lance: "Who cleaned out the linen closet?"

Phil nodded toward me. "Thanks for doing that, mate. Looks great."

Me: "Yeah. No worries." I was intent on maintaining my composure while my thoughts were miles away, but I didn't have the energy to act content, so my low mood was most likely apparent.

Phil: "Maybe I could ask you to put some labels on everything?"

Me: "I relabeled it all."

Phil: "Oh, did you already? All right, cool. I didn't look that close."

Lance made an overarching gesture and said slowly, "Linens."

I chuckled, then sobered with irritation. "Yeah, I took out most of the bullshit. You know, it was like: *top sheets, fitted sheets, matched top and fitted sheets.* And I was like: Fuck that! Top sheets and fitted sheets. If you wanna match 'em, *you* can fucking match 'em."

Phil: "I agree wholeheartedly. It's been in that chaotic state for I don't know how long."

Lance: "I always try to match the sheets when I put 'em on new people's beds."

Me: "And you can still do that."

Phil: "I try to deliberately mismatch."

Me: "I deliberately mismatch mine too. It's more colorful."

Phil: "God knows we can use that here."

Lance: "Tom didn't want to put any sheets on any beds." Tom was the station manager for the previous phase. I'm not sure I even had a chance to talk to him during that first frenzied week. "He said, 'They can do it themselves.'"

Phil: "Really?"

Lance: "Yeah. So I was like, 'That's not very nice. They come up here and they feel like shit and they just want to go to bed and then they have to make it?'"

Phil: "That's just a standard thing that we do. Always."

Me: "It's a little thing."

Lance: "I always put mints on the pillow because Katrine really likes that."

Me: "I thought the mints were hilarious!"

Phil: "We don't have any more, do we?"

Me: "Put Oreos."

Lance: "Yeah, Oreos!"

I felt my mood lifting. It's so nice to have a solid crew of cheerful people around me. And though my hurt is a constant loud buzz, live interaction helps. Don and Neal showed up before long, and Lance, Neal, and I all grabbed a beer. Soon Phil was pouring out shots of the remaining Akvavit, which I gladly accepted, figuring a stronger numbing would only help me more. Don, on the other hand, was not at all keen.

Don: "I can feel my stomach getting weird just looking at it."

Phil taunted him by pretending to pass him a full shot.

Don: "No! I don't even wanna smell it!" He thrust out his arm in protest and turned his face away.

Lance: "This is funny, Don, did you ever get this shot glass before? 'May your glass always be two *terds* full!'"

Lance laughed, but Don's attention was still on the liquor.

Don: "I might give up alcohol."

Me: "Altogether?"

Phil: "I'll bet you drink some scotch before you go home."

Don: "I might."

Phil: "I'll pour out five glasses, let's just put it that way."

Don: "When we're having our farewell dinner, I might have a swig of something."

Me: "Just not this stuff." I raised my glass to him.

Don: "Not that stuff."

Me: "Yeah, it's not as good tonight as it was on New Year's, when I was already a little drunk."

Phil: "It's strong, isn't it?"

Me: "Really potent."

Don: "Just thinking about it makes me wanna go throw up."

Lance: "How about wine, Don?"

Don: "Wine might be good."

Lance: "I've got one more bottle of wine I'm saving for the sunrise."

Don: "When is that? A few more weeks?" He paused to consider. "That might be good."

Me: "We've got two more cases of beer coming in a few days."

Phil: "And that's the porter?"

Lance: "No, this is the porter," Lance nodded at his glass, and then turned to me. "What do you think, Rex?"

Me: "It's growing on me. It's undercarbonated, unfortunately, but there's nothing we can do about that now."

Lance: "The one we made last phase was just the same."

Me: "Really?" I wondered if the high altitude affects carbonation like it affects cooking. I felt like it must, to some degree, but my head was too foggy to consider why.

Neal: "We've got a bunch of CO_2."

Me: "Oh, yeah, we do! Do we have a keg? If we had something to put the beer in to pressurize it, that would carbonate it."

Lance: "We have a pressure cooker."

Don: "That's what I was thinking."

And just like that we were halfway to a draft beer system. The people you meet at these stations are incredibly resourceful and inventive. There's nothing they can't do.

Phil: "Pressure cookers are fabulous. I use them all the time on the boat. Twenty minutes for a dish that would normally take three hours."

Lance: "That's how you do lentils, or those beans."

Me: "Dammit. Three and a half hours I boiled those sons o' bitches."

I FELT BETTER during dinner but the heartache returned to the forefront shortly after. I can't focus on anything to distract myself. My thoughts just churn in ruinous circles. There is no way I'm going to sleep tonight so I've decided to repurpose the sleeping pill I originally intended for the flight home. Crossed fingers and down the hatch . . .

Day 68
Thursday, January 10

Nothing could have prepared me for today.

I got about forty-five minutes of murky, deranged, drug-assisted, mashed potato sleep. The rest of the night I was wide awake, in continual emotional turmoil. At three in the morning I gave up and wrote Kira an email that took me nearly two hours. I shouldn't have sent it. It wasn't for her; it was for me. I thought writing it out might bed down my thoughts and allow me to sleep at least a little, but it did nothing. I stared at the ceiling for the next two hours.

Eventually the station woke. I heard Don waking Phil to tell him the water was down. *Great*, I thought, *it's going to be one of* those *kind of days*. I had no idea. The storm, now in its seventh straight day, had blown the S.O.B. door open in the night. Everything in the room that could freeze did. That included all the water pipes. I don't think it included Don's overalls.

We have diesel "heat cannons" that blow hot air. They're usually used to warm vehicles that live outside, so the vehicles will start in the cold. Don repurposed the heat cannons, aiming them at the frozen pipes. Then he came to breakfast, during which we discussed what we needed to do until the water was back online. We collected snow into pots for drinking and doubled bags into buckets for relieving—since we can't go outside and pee just anywhere—and figured out how we were going to deal with dirty dishes. At that point it was just a waiting game for the pipes to thaw—or be broken, which would take us down a different path. We were just about to go back to our regular tasking when the power went out.

Phil rushed straight to the emergency generator while Don hurried back to the S.O.B. to see what had gone wrong. It took about half an hour to get the station switched over to emergency power, but getting the primary generator going again turned out to be more complicated.

Neal followed Don, hoping he could help. They noticed a strange peppermint smell in the S.O.B. It was the fire suppression system leaking through a bad fitting. The system contains two CO_2 cylinders—a primary and a reserve—that are designed to purge the generator shack of oxygen during a fire, thus extinguishing it. The peppermint odor is added intentionally so anyone in the vicinity will know to get stepping. Seeing an obvious leak, and smelling an obvious smell, Don and Neal knew that was part of the problem. The primary cylinder was empty and they discovered that the generator had been shut down by the fire system, which detected a fire in Zone 3, wherever that is. There was no sign of a fire anywhere, but Don couldn't turn the generator back on because the fire system had shanghaied the controls. At least, that was the best I could understand it from the radio chatter. They spent the entire morning on the phone with Russ, the head of facilities back in Denver, troubleshooting the system so it would allow the generator back online.

I flitted around, helping where I could, running on just an hour of fucked-up sleep. Phil noticed. "You look like hell. Are you still not sleeping?"

"Not a damn wink last night."

"Let's make a call later and see if the doctor has any suggestions."

Phil still thought I was suffering from insomnia. He didn't know yet. None of the boys knew. I tried to laugh as I revealed to him my real issue. "I don't think they can prescribe anything for a broken heart."

I'm not sure if saying it aloud helped; I was too busy making a quick exit. If I allowed the conversation to continue, the emotion would surely break free and I would have to batten it back down. I was much better off focusing on our generator situation and how

I could help, though there wasn't much I could do. In the end, I basically just did my normal job. With Phil's permission, I went to TAWO briefly to check that all the instrumentation weathered the power outage acceptably, and did nothing more. Beyond that it was an unnecessary risk to go anywhere until the generator was under control.

With all the chaos, we convened in the Big House for lunch later than normal, but Phil was insistent that we do so. He made a nice hot soup for us.

Phil: "Soup. I want to make sure you eat." He aimed this comment more specifically at Don, who had been working hard.

Don: "Is there any water here?" The pipes were still frozen, so we were without power *and* water.

Phil: "Yes, that whole tub there is full."

Neal: "Thanks for setting up the emergency toilet, Phil."

Phil: "Of course. There's one in here and one out in the garage too, by the way."

Lance: "We have more toilets now than—"

Phil: "When we started, eh!"

Me: "I put our water purifier's drain tank—that's all just dirty scummy water—I put that on the toilet in the Green House bathroom so we can use it to flush."

Phil: "Okay. Then that'll last as long as it lasts."

Don: "Well, we'll try to get the water back on for tonight."

Phil: "Let's just eat and chill for a minute and not think about what we gotta do, and then we'll talk the whole thing through."

We paused as we let that soak in and tried to clear our heads.

Me: "Well, adding to when it rains it pours, the O_2 sensor in TAWO is off again."

Neal: "Let's get right on that!" He laughed and I laughed with him, glad for the change of mood.

Don: "Well, that's what's wrong out in the gen shack too."

Phil: "So maybe we can do a swap?"

Me: "The bad for the worse?"

Phil: "Yeah!" He chuckled.

Don: "Well, it's not a major catastrophe. We're not gonna die."

Neal: "What? What about that moment we shared out there?"

Don: "Yeah, I was just thinking: *Get outta here!*"

I laughed at Neal's statement, thinking he was just messing around, but Don's response begged for an explanation.

Don: "The first CO_2 bottle must have gone off when I was over here. Russ says there's a sensor—he doesn't know which one, obviously Zone 3, but he doesn't know which one Zone 3 is. The sensor went off, so the CO_2 went off. What we think has happened is, turning that heat cannon on raised the temperature too fast and triggered the sensor."

Phil: "So, a rate of change issue."

Don: "Yes. Sixty degrees in twenty minutes. The sensor thought the building was on fire."

Phil: "And now the sensor has locked the controls?"

Don: "Yes. See, the fire system overrode the gen panels. It shut 'em off. But now we're approaching it from a new point of view: we're disconnecting the fire system."

Neal: "Yeah, since it's not doing anything for us anymore."

Me: "Wait a minute, the reserve bottle is still good, no?"

Don: "The reserve went off too." He said it with a comical mixture of admission and amusement that suggested he'd set off the reserve accidentally. It made us all laugh.

Neal: "It went off while we were in there."

Me: "Really?" My eyes widened. That was a dangerous situation.

Don: "The first one went off, obviously, when we weren't in there. The second one went off when we were in there, because we were pulling sensors apart and it tripped it again, I guess."

Me: "Oh, man." Now I understood the moment they shared. "So they're both empty. It's weird that there's still pressure in the line to leak out of that fitting, then. You'd think if it went off it would just, *poof,* gone, no pressure left."

Don: "It went off. We know that. We stood there and watched."

Neal: "Well, we didn't stand there very long!" He laughed.

Phil: "Did it set off the alarms? That was curious, that the alarms didn't go off."

Don: "I don't think there was an alarm." He looked unsure and his expression changed to a strained thoughtfulness.

Phil turned to Neal for a second opinion.

Neal: "I don't know, I was running!"

Phil: "But the lights would have been flashing?"

Neal: "The only alarm going off was the Neal Alarm!"

Don: "There *was* an alarm, but not a flashing-light alarm." He still looked unsure. I imagine it all happened so quickly that it was hard to remember details like that.

Neal: "I just saw the gas coming out on the outside of the gen shack. It was . . . there was a leaky . . . I don't know, but it was blowing out of there fast. I yelled and ran out the front door and Don went out the back."

I imagined Don and Neal frantically fleeing the building as it filled with a peppermint haze of unbreathable gas.

Neal: "But I didn't know he went out the back, so I went back in to check. Then I saw him coming around the corner, outside, and I was like, *Okay, good, he's not dead.*"

Don: "You were lying on the ground holding yourself and I thought, *What the hell is going on?*" He laughed.

Neal: "Well, because I held my breath and ran back in to see if you were there and then I ran back out." His excitement grew as he spoke. "And then I was pissed!"

Now we were all laughing.

Don: "There's something wrong with the system. It never should have done what it did, according to Russ."

Me: "Awesome." By which I meant: definitely not awesome.

Phil: "The trouble is, with emergency systems, it's not like you can test the bloody things."

Don: "Well, I've got the heat cannon going in there again."

Phil: "Good!" He laughed.

Neal: "Yeah. What's the worst that can happen now?"

Me: "What the—? What happened to your superstition?"

When we finished eating, Phil shifted the mood of the conversation to official.

Phil: "All right, let's just go through this and see where we're at.

From an administrative point of view, I got Tracy into the loop because we're running on the backup generator. So I'm reporting in every hour. If you're still troubleshooting, I don't need the gory details of where you're at—I'll just report no change. As far as personal things, it's about *us*. It's not about the generators, it's not about the camp, it's about our survival and our safety. Everything we do from here on is oriented toward that. That includes coming in to eat. We're not in panic mode. If every system here fucks up and we have to abandon the station, a plane will be sent for us. But that's a decision others are going to make."

Don: "We're far from that."

Phil: "We're far from that, but we're *not* far from that."

There was a pause of subtle apprehension, but then we laughed it off.

Don: "True."

Me: "We're kinda halfway there, I guess."

Lance: "Aw, c'mon; we've got lasagna!" Frozen lasagna. Which, at the moment, can still be thawed.

Phil: "If you get the generator running today, I agree we're far from that."

Don: "Russ says we'll run on the e-gen indefinitely."

Phil: "They will pull us outta here." He said it with confidence, with finality.

Don: "I didn't get that feeling."

Phil: "It's not Russ who makes that decision. Tracy makes it and I make it." This he said with authority.

Don: "Now, don't get upset."

Phil: "No, no, I am not the least bit upset; I'm just stating what the case is. If we only have an emergency generator, they are pulling us out. I'll guarantee it."

Don: "Well, yeah, we don't have a backup to this one."

Phil: "Correct. Well, we do, out on the winter storage berm somewhere, frozen. But getting it in and going and all that sort of thing—I don't wanna even go there. We're not at that stage yet, but . . ."

Don: "Where we're gonna focus now is getting the gens going."

Phil: "Agreed. But I want to discuss the things we're going to do apart from the generators. So . . ." He paused for a moment and looked at his notepad to regroup. "Carry a radio, carry a spare battery. Everybody stay in contact. Make sure you've got a charger in your room and a radio on at night. Make sure you have clothing ready to put on, so if the place goes dark, we're ready for reaction mode as opposed to just living mode. I don't want it to be a panic situation, but if that emergency generator fails right now, we're into a whole different world. Again, it's about us: look after your-selves, and let me know if there's a change in status of where you're at."

He paused again, and I had a faint notion that last bit was on account of me. My status has changed. Phil learned that today. It means I'll be even less able to focus than before, and it's important for our leader to know that.

"Also, make sure you stay hydrated. That's easy to overlook in these situations when you feel under stress. More particularly you, Don. We're just standing by, and I'm gonna make sure you eat and take breaks, okay? I don't give a damn whether that gener-ator gets going or not, because there are backups to backups to backups. What I care about is that you don't get injured."

Don: "Thanks."

Phil: "As far as heat in structures, you have no heat in S.O.B., is that correct? Other than, you've got that heat cannon going?"

Don: "Yeah, but we have plenty of electricity from the e-gen. More than enough to heat the other buildings."

Phil: "We've got plenty of power, yes. But that's our only source of heat now, and the S.O.B. doesn't have electric heaters." Under normal circumstances the generator would provide heat for all three main buildings via an underground glycol loop that recycles the generator's waste heat into our precious living warmth. "The Green House and the Big House are now running on electric. We need to make sure they don't go cold, so set the thermostat in your room to an appropriate level and make sure the heat is com-ing on. I'll set the heaters in here. As far as fueling the e-gen, Don, we're good to go with the track loader?"

Don: "Yeah."

Phil: "And I'll go out and check the fuel sled. We filled it up, didn't we?"

Don: "It's full. Russ says we should drag it out to the e-gen in case we need it."

Phil: "Okay, excellent. Can we assist you and start doing that while we have some light?" What little light we have won't last long.

Don: "Do you want to do it today?"

Phil: "I'd like to have it in place."

Don: "Right now I need go back out and call Russ. The heat loop is still warm from residual heat right now, but if it freezes, we're definitely done. We need to get some circulation going."

Phil: "Okay. Lance, why don't you and I get the loader out, and we can drag that tank over there and have it ready to go. I'm not concerned about fueling yet, I just want to make sure that—"

Don: "It's sitting over there."

Phil: "Yep. Mainly because if the loader failed for some reason and we can't get that tank over there, then we're in a real world of hurt. So let's get the tank in place now." He checked his notes again. "Moving on to food prep: I'll take care of food tonight . . ."

Lance: "Oh, I can do it."

Phil: "Are you cooking tonight?"

Lance: "Yeah—don't cross me off the list yet. I'm still alive!"

Phil: "All right!" He laughed. "What else? Science. I think we're generating enough power that we don't have to worry about shutting down science."

Neal: "But we're not going to do anything extra like ICESat, bamboo forest, or Whirl-Paks." I got a good laugh out of that one, though I'm not sure how much the others appreciate Neal's disdain for the Whirl-Paks.

Phil: "No, no, no. Until we've resolved the situation, let's just assume we're confined to station." We all understood that in this context, "station" excluded TAWO and the MSF. "I think we're doing good right now, but if we don't get these generators running within the next day and a half . . ."

Don: "I'd say if we don't get the generator on by tonight . . ."

Neal: "We're fucked."

Don: "Well, maybe not fucked, but we'll need to start thinking about turning off everything we can to conserve fuel."

Phil: "Another thing: there are two emergency lights—one in the Green House and one outside the gen shack, so make sure you know where they are."

Don: "Maybe everybody ought to start carrying a headlamp."

Neal: "I've got one."

Me: "Yeah, absolutely." My constant companion.

Phil: "I think we're all carrying headlamps already." He chuckled. "I just want everyone to know where things are. Sleep kits if we need 'em; know where they are." Gesturing toward Neal, he added lightly, "Polypod for you!"

We laughed as Neal returned an innocent look. He *was* innocent, of course—Phil was just fucking with him.

Phil: "Have I missed anything? This is a new situation to me."

Don: "I think everybody should just stay calm. There's really nothing that exciting going on. It's exciting because it's different, but we're okay. I mean, it would get bad if the e-gen quit, but . . ."

Me: "It would get bad in a hurry." It would get damned cold in a hurry, and it's not like we can go out and collect firewood. Even if we could, where would we build a fire that wouldn't asphyxiate us? Outside? I don't think so. The weather would have to improve, a lot. Greenland's climate would have to improve.

Phil: "We have backups to the emergency generator too: we've got sleep kits, we've got food, we've got stoves, we've got headlamps, we've got candles." I pictured us as five human popsicles huddled around a tray of low-burning candles. I'm not sure how we would stay warm if the emergency generator failed. Jumping jacks, I guess. I don't think candles are going to cut it.

Don: "Maybe, Lance, if you wanna go look at the emergency generator, let's say every hour."

Phil: "I think that's a good idea."

Lance: "Sure, now that I know what I'm looking at. It's just the gauges, right?"

Don: "And make sure there's nothing unusual and it's not sucking in a bunch of snow. Just open up both side panels and take a look. That thing rarely runs, so a coolant hose could easily be leaking or something."

Lance: "I'll look for fluids."

Phil: "What else? Anybody have any thoughts?"

We paused to consider.

Don: "Well, I wanna get back out there. I gotta call Russ. We really need some heat looping in the generators, even if we're not making any power."

Phil: "Understood. I don't want to interfere in that world at all. All right. Let's meet again at six o'clock to see what our status is and then we'll pass that on to PFS to make a decision. Thanks everyone."

Lance: "I'm gonna go look for a lasagna!"

IT DIDN'T TAKE more than a few hours for Don to bypass the fire system and get the main generator running and powering the station again. By then the pipes were no longer frozen and things were relatively back to normal. The crisis seemed gone as suddenly as it had arrived. Neal and I sat in our office managing the slew of follow-up communications and log updates, the undesired fruit of the day's events. All the instrumentation is on a battery backup system, allowing it to weather a short power outage, but we still needed to inform all the science groups of the event.

As we worked, I filled Neal in on the Kira situation. It felt good to say the words out loud, and to a friend. "Man, I thought *I* was having a bad day," he replied. Not ten minutes later he got an email from Clair, asking if they should stay together if he were to take the position at Pole. "I can't even make this kind of shit up," he said.

"Damn. But you guys will work something out, I'm sure. You're good together."

"Thanks. Well, maybe things will still work out with you and Kira, too. You never know."

"That would be great but not very likely, I don't think." I know better than to hope, but I'm finding it impossible to take my own advice.

Later in the afternoon I got an email from her that bolstered that hope, though it still left plenty of room for doubt. Nonetheless, it cheered me up. We arranged a time to talk tomorrow. I welcome the opportunity to communicate in real time, to hear her voice and better judge her mood and resolve. Email is so empty of these things.

And if her resolve is set, which I think it is, what do I do about the job? Do I take it and work in the same department as Kira? I'm tempted to bail. If I bail, I can join my dear friends Jason and Kate on a monthlong river trip through the Grand Canyon. That would be incredible. And then? I don't know what. I won't go back to Palmer next year; I've grown jaded and bored with that, unfortunately. Plus, she'll be there. I don't want to come back here either, not for the winter anyway, and to come back for the summer would mean to miss the summer in Oregon, which I don't want to do either. That was a real perk of working in the Antarctic; the endless summer—well, technically. But I'm burnt out on contract work. I'm ready to settle in somewhere. I guess I'll look for another engineering job in the Pacific Northwest. But I realize I already have one, one that may be difficult to top. The job at Oregon State University gives me good benefits, over four weeks of vacation, and the opportunity to travel for work.

At dinner I voiced my thoughts to the gang, filling everyone in on my emotional state. It seemed best that they all know I'm distracted.

"Grand Canyon, mate!" Phil said enthusiastically.

"Dammit, I'd love to, but I think I need to take the job. It's a really good job. I can always quit if I can't handle the proximity."

Phil's advice was fantastic: "Well, then, get yourself a young college girl to parade around where Kira will see you and will want to punch her in the face. Better get one that'll look good with a black eye."

Day 69
Friday, January 11

Kira called at breakfast, surprised that it was still breakfast. "We're at breakfast until nine," I laughed. "It's a mellow start here. We usually don't have full workdays. I think that's probably different in the summer, though."

Broaching the subject at hand was difficult. When we did, the conversation turned somber.

"I still love you and care very much about you, but there are layers of love," she said.

"I don't understand. You love me, but less? Not enough?"

"I love you, but I'm no longer *in love* with you."

This I understand. For her the fire has simply faded to embers. I'm just surprised that I didn't see some sort of sign, but there was nothing, not the least indication that things weren't going great—not even in hindsight. There was little more to say. The rational side of my brain knows she's not going to miraculously fall back in love, especially not from thousands of miles away. But that portion of my brain is hopelessly outnumbered and makes only infrequent appearances, so I beg her, "Please, don't do this now. Wait just a few weeks. Consider it for just a few weeks. I can't handle this right now—I'll fucking lose it. I'm already losing it." She can't have considered it already—I bought her a plane ticket to see me that she was so excited about only a few days ago. None of it makes sense.

"I just . . . my gut tells me this is the right thing. I do love you and this is hard for me too, and it hurts a lot. But I need to follow my gut."

I couldn't help but think: *Where was her gut a few days ago?*

But she promised to think it over for the time I'm here. I cling to the hope that it may yet fall back into place. I cycle through all the reasons I can come up with for it to work out: her family likes me and will dissuade her, she'll arrive friendless in Corvallis and will want to hang out, she has three months to be on her own and realize it was a mistake. These thoughts are all flawed and I know it, but they're little nuggets of hope. Otherwise, the only thing I have to focus on is the extremely slow passage of time.

16

The nadir.

Day 70
Saturday, January 12

The weather finally cleared today, which was extremely welcomed after a long week of heavy storm. The wind dropped to nothing, revealing a pale pastel horizon to the south. A wide ruffled veil of benign clouds stretched to the northern horizon, which maintained its usual twilight.

Neal and I jumped at the opportunity to undertake the grand finale of meter pits: the string pit. At the beginning of each month, we have tied a colored string at snow level around several sets of bamboo poles. Today, after we dug and sampled the usual pit, we scraped back the snow to reveal the strings and carefully measured their depths. It was such a relief to finish it. No more meter pits.

I was exhausted the entire time because, unsurprisingly, I didn't sleep last night. I was a vacant automaton much of the day and even when I could have paid attention, I was too busy trying to hold it together in front of the boys.

On the inside, I'm a tumultuous wreck. My ominous emotions overwhelm everything. But I try to keep them in check and allow as little through to the outside as possible. This is *my* monkey wrench, and I don't want it slammed in everyone else's gears— especially not here, not now. Still, I have to talk it out just to maintain my sanity, and the boys have all been great companions. I've unloaded my heartache-filled mind on Don and Phil and Neal each, and it's good to have their ears. Poor Neal; to him I must sound like a broken record. He's an understanding friend, and I'm grateful for that. Lance and I talk mostly about river trips to take this summer, which is even more helpful than pouring my heart out, because it's one of the few things that distracts me.

Ultimately none of it suffices. The distractions are too short lived and my feelings are too intense to be released as mere words. They roil and writhe with nowhere to go. They've sacked my gut and taken up harbor, leaving my stomach in knots so that now, in addition to the insomnia, I have no appetite.

Until now I was eating twice my usual meal size, my metabolism having doubled in response to my body's need to stay warm. But this morning I could only force down a piece of toast for breakfast, sadly insufficient to sustain me in this environment. I've lost almost ten pounds in only a few days, and the effects are showing. On my way to lunch I carried the Green House garbage to the Big House and then collapsed on the floor for several long breaths.

Phil pulled me aside and said, "Let's have a talk after lunch."

Phil has a knack for implying much while saying little. He's not just saying the words; he empathizes. Having done his share of polar winters, I'm sure he's also been through difficult circumstances and had emotions, heartache or otherwise, amplified by this bizarre situation. Either way, his demeanor is very comforting, very zen.

But I knew this would not be the topic of our after-lunch chat; Phil wanted to discuss medication—to help me sleep.

"We've all been through this before and I understand, but I'm concerned about your energy level and lack of sleep. It's getting to the point where it has become a safety issue, and I'd like to suggest that you or I call the doctor and explain the situation."

"I agree. That's part of the reason I've been keeping you all aware of my status. I'd rather not take medication if I don't have to, though."

"Well, then I think we should see how it goes tonight and then make the call. You need to catch up, and that's going to mean at least two nights' sleep in a row."

"I think that sounds good. If I can't sleep tonight, let's call. I'm going to lie down for a bit this afternoon."

"I don't think sleeping in the afternoon is a good idea because it will throw your rhythm off even more. But I can see you're exhausted today, so maybe just lie down for a short nap."

It didn't matter; apparently I can't nap either. My head just spins.

Day 71
Sunday, January 13

I somehow managed to sleep through most of the night, my exhaustion finally trumping my incessant train of derailed thought. Thankfully, it notched up my energy level. Plus, the sky brushed aside its cloud veil today, so it was considerably lighter for the first time, bringing a pleasant bump in spirit, albeit small. I can't say it was daylight out there, but for a few hours the world seemed very bright to my vampire eyes. Only two weeks to go until the sunrise. It couldn't come sooner.

Unfortunately these minor positives brought little solace on the larger scale. Nothing is happening and the emptiness is consuming me. When our half day of work is over, I begin a nauseating whirligig through the emotions. I can't even focus enough to read a book, so I've done my best to occupy all this spare time in other ways—I've begun looking for housing in Corvallis, I finalized my trip to Baja, I started writing another blog post—but I still can't come even close to filling the day. It's demoralizing. Instead I scour through the past two years on a loop, searching for what happened, for what went wrong, and coming up empty. Then I rake her recent explanations for meaning and come up empty again. It's clear that this is painful to her also, which makes it that much more bewildering. Ultimately I'm forced to accept her gut feeling at face value because I can't find any logic behind it. Hell, I can't even comprehend anything in the emotional realm that makes sense to me.

. . . She says I am outspokenly against having children and that has been hurting her a long time . . .

. . . but I'm not *against* having children, I'm undecided and therefore open to either path, which I've tried to reassure her repeatedly. Too many of my jests she takes to be veiled truths, and I can't convince her otherwise . . .[53]

. . . She says I embrace "surly" as my motto[54] and I play a "poor-me" card to sap energy from her . . .

. . . but we all have our faults, and I accept hers: she saps my energy by looking to me for the approval she really wants from her dad but doesn't know that the approval she *needs* can come only from herself . . .

. . . She says it's her weakness that she wants to fill my negativity, giving out happiness at her own expense . . .

. . . but I'm not *that* negative—polar winters excluded. And I consider her altruism a strength; her weakness is she's so damn fragile that I have to sugar coat everything . . .[55]

. . . She says she finds energy in spirit and nature and that I don't know where to get my energy . . .

. . . but . . .

What the hell is she talking about? I get my energy from zipping through the forest on a bike, or sliding across the water propelled by the wind, or sleeping under the stars on the banks of a beautiful river, or spotting a colorful bird that I rarely see. I wish I could find some happiness in nature right now, but I'm in a

---

53 "I love babies, I just can't eat a whole one!" comes to mind. In poor taste, yes, but come on, it's *obviously* a joke.

54 Great microbrews and great bicycles make great T-shirts. Wearing them doesn't make it my motto—I'm just poking fun at my own occasional flaw. I know who I am and I can laugh about it. That's a good thing.

55 I found that so endearing once.

damned wasteland! There *is* no nature!

What the fuck am I going to do for the next three weeks? I'm going insane!

Day 72
Monday, January 14

I am in hell. There's nothing to fill the day but the hideous churning of my thoughts. *In the morning there is hours and infinity*, the song goes. But my infinity continues through the afternoon, evening, and night. I know I'm being irrational. In moments of clarity I have a strange voyeuristic view of my own overreaction. My heartache is real, but its effect is unrealistic, exaggerated, amplified unbidden by my precarious winter state. My emotions are not under my control. I need to get the hell out of here! My mind needs warmth and light and stimulation to break free of this padded cell the darkness has created for it. I cannot heal like this; I'm only getting worse.

This is my home, the walls painted black. The walls of my mind have blurred and faded to black also—faded to nothing, in fact, for nothing remains to hold up the ceiling, which is collapsing.

17

In which I struggle to manage my heartache while writing off my mind as a lost cause.

Day 73
Tuesday, January 15

I went out to the TAWO tower, where Neal had noticed a kink in the lifeline cable. The field risk manager back at PFS declared it out of commission, pending photos and a professional opinion, and asked us to mark it as such. I didn't want to deal with duct tape out there, so I thought it through and prepped inside TAWO, writing on the roll with a marker: DO NOT USE. I peeled what I needed off the roll and stuck it to the forefinger of my glove before going outside. When I reached the tower, I carefully folded the tape over the cable and pressed the sticky sides together. The tape fell flapping to the ground. I tried again, only to achieve the same result.[56]

Back inside again, I tore off a short length of tape. It was sticky. I folded it, sticky side to sticky side. It was near impossible to get it apart, like duct tape should be. I tore off another piece and went outside. I folded it. Nothing. It opened happily of its own accord.

---

56 I have heard insanity defined as "repeating the same action and expecting a different outcome."

No sticky. I went back inside and grabbed the whole roll. I unrolled a few inches and folded over a tab. Then I grabbed the marker. I went back out to the tower. I wrapped the tape several times in a loop from the cable to the tower. I peeled off a long excess and tied it into an ugly knot, leaving a short tail wagging in the breeze. Then I pulled out the marker. It didn't work. I gave up. *Fuck it. It's just us. We know not to use the damn thing.*

Neal arrived at TAWO shortly after.

"Hey, you don't use the lifeline when you climb the tower, do you?" I asked.

"No, I use the claws."

"That's what I thought. Um, never mind the mess out there. It shouldn't be in your way."

"What mess?" Neal asked.

"You'll see."

Day 74
Wednesday, January 16

Phil told me to "suck it up" today and try not to bring down the group. It was unlike him except that he said it with a smile, and it means I really am beginning to bring down the group. That makes me feel even worse. I've tried to stop talking about her. The boys know what I'm up against and don't seem to mind bending an ear for me, but still, they must be tired of hearing it. I think I would be. But although I can control my words, I can't control my disposition, nor shield anyone from it. I'm trying. I think maybe it's starting to get better. Maybe. I hate to bring down the group; I love these guys. I'll try harder.

This evening brought a much-needed respite from the routine —a new experience, the best kind of distraction. The phenomenon kept me up late and I'm too tired to write about it. Right now I just want to fall asleep. I'll try to do it without the drugs tonight. I gave in on Monday and called the remote doctor, and Phil signed out a handful of pills from our dispensary. The prescription sleep aid he gave me has helped. My sleep is still fitful, but I'm hoping the drugs have encouraged a reasonable rhythm.

Day 75
Thursday, January 17

~

Yukimarimo

Summit Station, Greenland
Thursday, January 17, 2013

Last night we witnessed a rare meteorological event. It was discovered less than twenty years ago by the Japanese Antarctic Research Expedition, who named it *yukimarimo*.

Yuki: snow.

Marimo: pet algae ball. (Apparently, in Japan, this is a thing.)

When conditions are just right—calm air, reasonable humidity, and dropping temperatures—moisture condensates out of the air into a fine and delicate hoarfrost fur over everything. Yukimarimo requires just the right hoarfrost; it must form rapidly so that it develops a "growth charge" of static electricity. Then, when one final condition occurs—a light breeze—the tiny crystals will cling together electrostatically, forming small dust bunnies that roll across the ice-cap desert like miniature cotton tumbleweeds.

The little balls seem to have a life of their own as they invade the flat expanse of our frozen landscape. They take turns dashing several meters and then waiting, like ghost crabs on an endless white beach.

Today the air was calm again and the little buggers were everywhere, resting peacefully. To pick one up meant to disperse it like a million dandelion seeds. Stockpiles of little yukis lay collected in corners or folds of sastrugi, in wide piles as though prepared for a colossal miniature snowball fight. For now, they lie in wait. But when the breeze picks back up just right—too little and they do nothing, too much and they are obliterated—they will continue their nomadic lifestyle, their pilgrimage across the demented white fairyland in search of . . . well, hopefully nothing because that's all they're going to find.

~

I'm mesmerized by the yukis. I spent a long time last night trying to film them on their bizarre mass migration, but it was too dark to get good footage. I've gotten good at night photography, which allows me minutes of exposure, should I need it, for a single frame. But there's just not enough light for video. I think the only answer is floodlights, which I don't have and couldn't be bothered to set up if I did.

Today was a beautiful clear day. I enjoyed it by walking leisurely around the station, admiring cities of half-inch yukis tucked away in sastrugi vales, or solitary two-inch jumbo yukis standing proud on a vast cake topped with snowy icing and a billion yuki sprinkles. I'll admit, I poked many of them. Most of them.

Hundreds and thousands of yukimarimo

Day 76
Friday, January 18

Yesterday was much less haywire on the emotional compass, but this morning, just as another massive whiteout engulfed the station, I got an email from Kira that sent the remaining marbles skittering across the roof of my skull. She can't wait any longer. There's nothing for her to consider. The choice is already made. Deep down I knew this already. Not even that deep, really. Still, reading it hurts. Maybe I've only been torturing myself by asking her to consider. I just don't know; I'm incapable of processing it right now.

The storm flares have eerily traced my mind's composure these past two weeks. By afternoon, the wind was blasting at forty miles per hour. The bamboo is bent and the tattered flags are flayed straight out for shredding.

Day 77
Saturday, January 19

"Come have a look at this," Neal said this morning as I exited my room. I followed him to the Green House back door. He opened it and we were faced with a solid white wall.

"Holy shit," I said, "I guess that's why there's a roof hatch."

The storm buried the lee of the building in under twenty-four hours. From the outside, it was a sculpture. Snow corniced off the roof and ramped downward in ridges and gullies. Much of the formation was impossibly vertical and overhung, twisted and ominous. Don would have to dig it out with the track loader. The question was, What were *we* going to do today?

We can't go to TAWO in a whiteout, which only leaves about an hour of work in the Green House, maybe not even. We're scheduled to work thirteen out of every fourteen days here. I should feel overworked. Instead, I *wish* I had more work to do. If I can't fill the time on a normal day, how am I supposed to fill it on a Condition 1 day? I spent the first half of it wandering around trying not to think of her and failing miserably. Phil found me pacing the Big House like a crazy person, for which I apologized.

"I can tell you were hooked on this one."

"I was, but I feel like the impact it's having on me is over the top."

"Well, places like this will do that to you. It's not as bad as it seems."

It seems bad. Really bad. Far, far worse than it is. I repeated Don's smiling mantra: "This place sucks!" Phil laughed and agreed.

I got proactive in the afternoon and forced a change of pace by making a video for my blog. It's not something I've done, so it took wonderfully longer than it should have. I spread out all the layers of clothing I wear for a venture outside and methodically put them on, explaining the nuances as I went.

When I came back into the office, Neal said, "I thought you were losing it out there! I heard you talking, but I knew no one else was there. I actually got up to see what you were doing."

"Well, I *am* losing it," I told him, "but hopefully I'll go out with a bigger bang than just talking to myself."

∿

ECW: Extreme Cold Weather Gear

Summit Station, Greenland
Saturday, January 19, 2013

"Today I thought I'd give you an idea of what it's like to dress for the nasty weather we have here."

[Maybe this explains why I'm standing in front of the camera in my underwear.]

"I'm started off in a thin wool baselayer and some wool socks. I figure that's better than, you know, starting naked."

[Much better, thanks.]

"Over that, I put on some medium-thick polypropylene long johns and a similar midlayer top."

[Sure enough, at this point, for just a moment, Neal's head makes an appearance in the doorway to check my sanity.]

"To keep my torso a little bit warmer than my legs need to be, I wear a fleece top as well. Very important that it zips way up."

[I flip up the fleece collar and zip it to my chin.]

"On top of that: thickly insulated Carhartt overalls. These things are nearly an inch thick. They've got a lot of insulation."

"Next: boots. If it's not too cold out I'll wear these boots."

[I hold up a pair of fuzzy-lined medium-high boots with rubber toes and a leather top half.]

"Actually, I use these most of the time, and they're fairly insulated. But on a day like today, I go to the big boys."

[Now I hold up a monstrous expedition boot, much like a tall, oversized snowboarding boot.]

"These things weigh about five pounds each and they suck to swing around, but it's better than having cold toes. They've got a thick removable liner and they snug up quick and easy."

[With a quick pull, cinch, and wrap, the first boot is on. As I put on the other, I try to fill the empty air—and like any experienced conversationalist, I begin discussing the weather.]

"We've got a good storm going today. It's definitely Condition 1, probably on par with the worst I've seen here. I don't know what it's doing at the moment, but we'll find out in a minute."

"Now my neck gaiter."

[I pick up the gaiter, then put it down again.]

"Actually, with this hat, I put it on first because the gaiter slides right over it. Then I make sure my gaiter goes around the collar of my fleece top. Everything has to overlap. Now, a heavy, fuzzy-lined down parka. And today: goggles, for sure."

[Now my speech becomes muffled because I've pulled the gaiter up over my mouth and nose.]

"I want to make sure everything is covered but this tiny bit."

[I point out the slit where my eyes peer between my gaiter and my hat. The gaiter overlaps the hat around the rest of my head.]

"Goggles go on, hood goes up, zipper up. Sometimes I'll wear glove liners, or even mittens with hand warmers, but usually these gloves are enough, as long as I'm not going to be out long. I make sure to pull my sleeves over them so the wind doesn't get into my wrists as much. And that's pretty much it. Let's go outside."

[At this point I pick up the camera and walk to the door.]

"These are cryogenic doors ..."

[I say as I open and close the first door.]

"... with an airlock."

[I open the second door to a blueish white haze, and the microphone picks up the sound of flapping flags ...]

"Oh, it's not as bad as it was."

[... just before the wind hits it and you can't hear anything else.]

~

Day 79
Monday, January 21

I've entered the angry phase now, a vast improvement over the sappy brokenhearted lost-puppy phase. I have to keep reminding myself that a part of this is my own fault. I *have* been negative much of the time—she's right about that. But I have a hard time blaming myself. I made a lot of sacrifices for her that essentially compromised my own happiness. I should have learned new ways to find happiness, but I didn't realize yet that I needed to. What I've learned about myself is that I'm dependent on outdoor sports and I was spoiled by my proximity to them while living in Oregon. Mountain biking, kitesurfing, whitewater: these joys were only ten minutes away. In the past two years, while I've been with Kira, I've had little opportunity for any of that, by comparison. It slowly bogged down my positivity.

I need to back up here.

Kira and I met and fell for each other while I was still enjoying Palmer. In fact, chasing Kira was what made my second season fun. Otherwise it was nothing compared to the year before, which is a pill she could never swallow. In that first year everything was a new and intense experience, and the crew gelled in a way that I could never explain and I never experienced again. By the end of my second season, our first together, I was much more ready to go home and do all the things I loved and missed. But I didn't get the chance. I was in Oregon only briefly before I drove to Virginia to be with Kira. I didn't like Virginia—I knew I wouldn't; I knew I'd be imprisoned in the populous rat race with little to keep me satisfied on the outdoor front—but I went there to be with her. Then, back to Palmer, and I was even less happy than my previous season because I was totally over it, *and* I didn't get my fix in the interim. I can see now that Kira took the brunt of my malcontent, and that's my fault.

After Palmer I was stoked to go to South Africa with her and see her home, but I failed to realize that I was expecting travel and adventure and Kira was going for very different reasons: home is not an adventure. Though there were great things to see and a handful of places to do the things I love, both were far from Kira's hometown. There was nothing there for me to quench that thirst, and I grew restless. I suspect that was part of the final blow: Kira loves her home, and I'm sure she was disappointed that I didn't fall in love with it too. Though I loved spending time with her family, I had no good way of occupying my ample spare time. I got bored. I even started taking weeklong exploratory trips by myself. In hindsight, I suspect that hurt her, though there was no reason for her to let it. For the most part she held it all in, trying to cheer me—to her credit, but at her expense, and ours.

What makes me angry is that she has given up without attempting to fix anything. She has simply quit, ultimately claiming incompatibility, which I feel is a cop-out. Relationships not only wax and wane but require work, and we're at the crux. This is the point when the chemicals have all burned off and we have a better understanding of each other. This is when the relationship is forged, when we learn our weaknesses and how they interact and we can accept them and work with them. And in this moment of truth, despite the pain it is obviously causing her, she's decided to let it roll over and die. It's infuriating.

At least my anger is far more manageable than sorrow, which was causing an obsessive depression. I feel like I've suddenly snapped out of it, though my sorrow remains deep. I'm finally able to focus enough to read, so I can fill some time, and I'm excited about a possible room for rent in Corvallis with a fellow kitesurfer.

Also adding to my ascension from the nadir, the sky is getting noticeably lighter. After the storm subsided yesterday morning, the air has been calm, and though the visibility is not great horizontally due to the usual surface layer of freezing fog, the sky above has been clear. The short predawn light has become a long predawn light, filling much of the workday with a soft blue glow.

Midday was exceptionally nice today, and I took a walk out to the skiway to absorb it. With all of station to my back, the full view was of the nothingness beyond. I found it overwhelming, and it spun my emotional wheel round. It was beautifully simple and elegant yet bleak in its vastness. The pale blue illuminated a silent sea, tranquil and easy, nurtured from above by the brightest stars in a universe of limitless possibility. There *is* nature here, meditative and zen, I realized. Here, the blissfully clear mind of the earth connects to the heavens. But, such big things; such timeless, sizeless infinity. Insignificance washed over me. I am nothing in this universe. A blip, a grain, an atom, a wisp, nothing. Elation and depression intermingled, bringing intensity to moments when my eyes beamed and teared simultaneously. Just when I think I have it under control, really I've lost it.

One week to sunrise.

Day 80
Tuesday, January 22

A picture of Neal taking measurements in the string pit made it onto the Polar Field Services blog. Katrine commented: "Is that Neal taking snow-pit measurements? Why so uncomfy looking? Almost looks like someone dropped him in!" It was true; Neal's lengthy frame was lumped in the pit like a crumpled body in an undersized grave, dumped there by mobsters. Usually I'm the one in the pit. I don't remember why that is, but it means less digging, and that's reason enough for me.

Otherwise, I can't think of anything notable that happened today. The black circle spins another turn. At least I'm sleeping again, for the most part. That alone is a huge relief. I've been using the sleep aid sparingly—only on the nights I seem to need it—and that's working reasonably well.

Day 81
Wednesday, January 23

I jinxed myself: I couldn't sleep last night, after a week straight of mostly decent nights. Kira was up there parading a marching band through the most echoic chambers of my skull. I gave up on sleep and wrote a stream-of-consciousness letter, this time full of my anger and disappointment. I thought purging my thoughts onto the page would be therapeutic, but focusing my anger and blame only made me more depressed and negative. I should have just taken a damn pill. Maybe then I wouldn't have felt like shit this morning and my breakfast wouldn't have churned immediately upon hitting my stomach. I had to lie down.

It was terrible timing. We've been waiting for the right conditions to do our final ICESat transect. Though the skies have been clear, we've been socked in on the ground by fog and mist. Today it lifted, but now I was bleary-eyed and nauseated. I asked Don if he would mind going for me again, and as I did, I caught myself playing the poor-me card, adding considerable guilt to my already turbulent state. But he seemed happy to go; he even seemed like he wanted to go. "I sort of enjoyed it last time. It was a change," he said, which I was glad to hear.

As Don and Neal were miles from station in the cold, I began to wonder: How much of this exhaustion and nausea is real and how much is only in my mind? Am I embracing negativity and making it worse? I thought about this and decided that part of it was circumstantial: I couldn't sleep last night, which is certainly not abnormal for me. I couldn't know today would be good for ICESat, so those two are unrelated. But the nausea? Some of it must be manufactured. I really didn't want to go out there. I began to feel a little better, knowing it could be unmanufactured with the proper mental power. But then the guilt came back twofold: Had I "poor me'd" Don into doing ICESat? To some degree, I think I did. But I also know that he wanted to go, at least a little bit, if only for the break in routine. I decided this was a better arrangement for everyone, and I couldn't blame myself for that.

"It wasn't nearly as nice this time," Don said after they returned. "I can't feel this thumb and my hands are all tingly."

"Thanks again for going. I really appreciate it," I told him. "I feel guilty about having asked."

"No, no, I don't mind. Really." Don is such an easygoing, agreeable, and cheerful guy. I love him for that.

"If it's any consolation, I couldn't feel my feet for an hour after the first ICESat," I offered.

A few of his fingers tingled for the rest of the day.

LANCE: "I'M TRYING to figure out if this is my fork or yours. I think I lost my fork earlier."

Phil: "Your sanity, perhaps."

Lance: "Oh, that. That I never had. I'm looking for it, though, if you see it."

Phil: "Good luck."

Lance: "I'm hoping it comes in on this next plane."

THE NEWS REACHED us that a Twin Otter disappeared yesterday in Antarctica. It's not reassuring only two weeks before we fly out of here.

Day 83
Friday, January 25

This stretch of the season is interminable. There's nothing to break the monotony. There are no holidays, no events, no new tasks, nothing. There's nothing to write about: the days are the same. There's little to think about either. My plans are all made, my travel and housing secured. All I can do is look forward to not now. At least we still have lively conversation at mealtimes. If it weren't for that, I don't know what I'd do.

Of course, now I'm having a hard time remembering the details of our conversations. Don definitely brought up poo again at dinner. He was prompted by Neal, of course, our other poo nonaficionado. I can't recall the context, though likely there wasn't any. Actually, being too toasty to remember anything reminds me, ironically, of something Neal said recently about being too toasty:

"One day at Pole, I was eating my cereal—leaning over it, you know—and I watched a hair fall from my beard into the cereal, and I just ate it. And then I thought a minute later, *Did I just eat that hair?* That's how I knew I was getting toasty."

I have to admit that I'm surprised at how affected I've become in such a short period of time. I expected this deployment to be easier than my year at McMurdo. The winter is longer there, and I was already grinding away for several months before it started. It was nowhere near as cold as Summit though, and I didn't have nearly as much outdoor tasking. I think that's the major difference. I gained weight at McMurdo, but no matter how much I eat here, I continue to grow thinner. My metabolism is maxed out, leaving no T_3 for my brain. I wonder if the altitude plays a role here too. I bet it does. Have I said all this already?

At least I slept decently the past two nights, with help from the drugs. My physical state is recovering. Apparently the extra sleep isn't helping me mentally, though. I know it's a long bumpy road before making any progress there. Emotionally, I'm still a mess. But there are small improvements. I still have bouts of anger, but they're tamer. I'm still heartbroken and foolishly entertaining false hopes, but sometimes I can accept that it's done and eventually there will be someone else who makes me just as happy, or happier. This is the real, logical, optimistic me shining through the winter mind fog. I'm meddling with acceptance, and happiness will come—at least I know that this time.

Otherwise, I'm just waiting for a plane and trying to keep up good cheer.

Three days to sunrise.

Day 84
Saturday, January 26

They found the missing Twin Otter. It hit a downdraft and didn't recover. No one lived. Phil and Lance knew the pilot. Today was not cheerful.

Two days to sunrise.

Day 85
Sunday, January 27

I only slept half the night last night without the drugs. My head was spinning every which way, as usual. It doesn't matter; I can do my job in my sleep now and I'm so accustomed to the insomnia that to feel well-rested would be unnatural.

One day to sunrise.

Day 86
Monday, January 28

It's official. I have now completed a winter in both the Arctic and the Antarctic. The framing moments of both—two sunsets and two sunrises—were all obscured. But that's what it is to winter at the poles. These things, like so many others, are not in your control.

We nearly saw the sun today. The slightest sliver between the clouds and horizon gleamed a bright orange glow. It was the most light we've seen in months, and though it's not remotely enough to replenish my sanity, I'll take it.

What was nearly as nice as the almost slice of daybreak was the intensely calm crust holding the world frozen in time. A heaped frost held the flags in a confused stationary flutter, unsure whether they should flop or flail. This time the frost was shaped like miniature snow-covered evergreens composing a tiny horizontal forest that reached windward while a fine powder fluff wrapped around the lee. The sugar coating was as thick as I've seen it, but somehow more beautiful and interesting than before. Perhaps I'm only seeing it for the first time on a new day, under newfound light.

Frost freezing a flag's flutter

I lingered outside, taking pictures of the frost until I was chilled. When I returned to our office, Neal was typing.

"How do you spell *thorough*?" he asked.

I spelled it out. "T-H-O-R-O-U-G-H."

"That's what I thought. Why doesn't my computer like it? Oh, I added an extra *R*: *throrough*." There was a brief pause while Neal and my personal stenographer continued typing. "I'm really going to reveal my mental state now: What's that word you use when, uh, you don't want to be known?"

"Huh?" I asked.

"When you want to be . . . *anonymous!*"

"Oh, right."

"Shit. How do you spell *anonymous?*"

"A-N-O-N, um . . . A-N-O-N . . . Dammit, I'm usually a really good speller."

"Y!"

"I don't want to play anymore."

18

In which an airplane finally arrives to take me away, but only after Greenland entices me with one last seduction.

Day 87
Tuesday, January 29

~

The Goggle Situation

Summit Station, Greenland
Tuesday, January 29, 2013

I've figured it out . . .

When it's dead still and warm out (say -20°F), I can wear my hat just above my eyebrows and lower my gaiter so it only covers my mouth and not my nose. This makes it much easier to breathe, though I can feel frost forming on the hairs inside my nose.

When it's dead still and colder (say -50°F), this won't work because my nose will freeze, so I pull the gaiter up over it and I'm forced to breathe into that, which causes my breath to funnel up both sides of my nose and blow out across my lashes and eyebrows, which soon frost over. This won't work because my eyebrows eventually turn into a unibrow of ice, which begins to freeze my skin. So, I have to pull down my hat to cover my brows, leaving the slightest slit to see through. But my eyelashes still frost over, and occasionally when I blink the top lashes freeze to the bottoms and I can't reopen my eye without removing a glove and applying my warm fingers to the compromised eye. This is manageable at least, but now my fingers are getting wet, which will mean trouble in the long run.

If it's *very* cold, or even slightly windy—which is most of the time —I have to wear goggles for fear that my eyeballs will freeze. They won't, but any exposed skin certainly will. This sucks because now my vision is limited vertically by the hat-gaiter slit and my periphery is gone on account of the goggles. And it doesn't work because my breath is funneling up into the goggles and freezing on the inside, so I can't see anything at all. So I shove the goggles down hard onto my nose to pinch it and I laboriously mouth breathe through my gaiter, which slowly turns soggy and disgusting and eventually begins to solidify into an ice block around my neck. But, some of the moisture pushes through the gaiter and still causes my goggles to freeze over—on the outside instead of the inside, and only a little bit more slowly.

So, the best-case scenario is that I'm on a warm, sunny beach somewhere, wearing nada, as in: nada damn thing.

At these temperatures nothing works, but at least I've figured it out.

～

The sun arrived today. It was brilliant. The full orange orb rolled along the horizon unobscured for the better part of an hour. So I arrived at dinner in a good mood.

Me: "I noticed this afternoon that I was like: *Ah, it's a nice, normal day. It's not too bad out here.* But it's fucking forty-five degrees below zero!"

Phil: "Yeah, it's a comfortable temperature."

Lance: "It's crazy!"

Me: "It was super nice having that sun today."

Lance: "The sun was awesome."

Phil: "A little bit more tomorrow. Twenty minutes more."

Me: "But finally, I actually *saw* it today."

Sun or no, I've lost it. Truly, it's gone. Persuading my mind to perform a moment of recollection is like trying to force a square peg through a peg-intolerant badger. I forgot to close out the balloon for the first time a few nights ago.[57] This morning I was confused about whose day it was to do rounds, because I couldn't remember yesterday. Then this evening I couldn't remember whose turn it was for the balloon, which is ridiculous because all I had to do was remember if I did rounds today.

Lance said, "All you have to remember to do is get on that Twin Otter."

"No fucking way I'll forget that," I told him. That's probably the one thing I have no chance of forgetting.

I like to think it wouldn't be so bad without this breakup's awful timing, but I know from my winter in the Antarctic that much would remain unchanged: the forgetfulness, the insomnia, the mood swings, the reasonless depression. This place isn't so bad, really. It's certainly interesting. But right now I would give anything to be away from here, even to be stuck in a blizzard in Akureyri again. I could be soaking in the hot pools or sipping tea at the cafe among unfamiliar faces. Perhaps that's what I need most: the unfamiliar. The simple stimulation of something new, the raised brow of the unexpected, no matter how trivial. Hell, at this point an apple would be thrillingly new and unexpected.

We've had some extra work to do lately, which helps fill the time, but it's neither unfamiliar nor stimulating.

Katrine asked us for a cylinder inventory so she can order whatever is needed for the summer phase. There's a ton of gas here. TAWO alone has nearly twenty gas cylinders—you'd hardly

---

57   Um, sorry loony tunes, it's not the first time.

think that many could fit in there—not counting the empties on the deck, and the S.O.B. is stacked with banks and banks of helium for the balloons.

The PI for the precip tower asked for a new tower design, though not in so many words. Rather than send someone to replace the tower, she wants to send the materials and have the techs build it, which is beyond our level of provided support. So I'm simply sending measurements of what she already has, which I expected her to already know. She'll have to figure it out herself; I can't design a tower right now.

There's a device nicknamed "Gulper" in the Noone vault that has gone incommunicado, and they've requested we dig into the vault to check it. We'll go great lengths to stave that off until turnover, when we have to visit the vault anyway.

We're also busy cleaning and prepping for the turnover crew and, more importantly, our replacements. We were happy to hear that they've arrived in Iceland. They're scheduled to fly here the day after tomorrow. New faces are both a welcome and scary thought. The change is needed, and exciting, but it's daunting to think of interacting with anyone not sharing this retarded—and I mean that in the true sense of the word, like playing a 45 at 33 speed (remember vinyl records?), which I guess is the same as saying mentally challenged—state of mind.

~

Hi Katrine,

I thought we emailed you the EOS report draft a couple of weeks ago, but apparently not. Anyway, here it is.

Cheers,

Neal

~

Day 88
Wednesday, January 30

It was my night to cook and I thought it would be nice to have some fresh baked bread for the newcomers tomorrow, so I started right after lunch. I made four loaves and had time left over, so I made cookies too, then started on dinner. Tonight should be our last together as just the five of us, and since I can't remember anything anymore, I made a point to take good notes of our conversation. If I'm being totally honest, I kept a small notebook in my pocket and jotted things down during bathroom trips, of which there were plenty since we decided to do our best to finish the remaining homebrew—and since I didn't consider myself on the clock while I was cooking, I got a long head start.

Lance showed up first. "Uh, oh, cookies!"

Don came in shortly after and looked into the kitchen where I was finishing up. "What'd you cook? Looks like a big pot of stuff."

"Yeah, it's a little more than I expected."

Don chuckled, then noticed the cookies. "Whoa, cookies!"

It's the little things; they really stand out.

Phil and Neal arrived within a few minutes, as I was putting dinner out on the counter. The "big pot of stuff" was reconstituted mashed potatoes. It came as a powder, so I had no idea how much to use. I used too much.

Phil: "Holy moly! How many do we have coming for dinner?"

Me: "Yeah, yeah, I know. I might have made too many potatoes. I was counting on Neal."

Neal: "Yeah, well, unless you made, uh"—he quickly perused the dinner offerings—"hey, cookies!" Then he continued, "Unless you made vegan pork chops, then I'm eating potatoes. And cookies." He noticed the bread on the other counter. "Dang, you've been a baking machine today."

Me: "Yep, there's cookies. And I made a shit ton of bread."

Don: "Did you make the cookies from scratch?"

Me: "Hell, no!"

Neal: "But he scratched himself while making them."

Me: "I did."

Neal: "Is that beer bread?"

Me: "These two are beer bread." I pointed to the end of the serving counter, where the boys were now filling their plates. "And over there is asiago." I gestured toward the other counter, where our bagels and English muffins live.

Don: "Can we cut it?"

Me: "No!"

Don: "Why not? What are you saving it for?"

Me: "I'm just kidding, you can cut it if you want."

Neal: "How many times have I told you not to fuck with the mechanic?"

I just smiled.

Me: "Well, I was going to freeze three loaves and pull them out as we need them next week, but if you guys want beer bread *and* asiago, that's cool. I wanna try both anyway."

Don went for the asiago without hesitation.

Neal: "Would you cut me a piece too, Don? I gotta bulk up. Pretty soon I have to start paying for food." He looked at the mashed potatoes he had just added to his plate. With a shrug, he added more.

Lance: "That's what I've been doing. I'm up eighteen pounds. I wonder how long that will last me."

Me: "Holy shit, I'm amazed you put on weight here. I'm probably down eighteen pounds and I've been eating like a horse. I don't know how I'm going to switch back to a small-portion diet."

Neal: "Well, the trick is to start drinking whiskey. Low-calorie, low-carb, and after a while, you forget you're hungry."

Me: "I don't find that to be true. I find myself at Taco Bell at two in the morning."

Neal: "That's because you stopped drinking whiskey!" He grinned broadly and we all laughed.

Lance: "Who wants a beer?"

Neal: "Yup."

Me: "I've got one. Thanks."

Don: "Are you gonna drink all the beer tonight?"

Me: "Gonna try."

Lance: "Oh, is that the goal? Man, I'll drink. I gotta mop and clean the oven tonight, so I might as well get drunk."

I was already getting drunk.

Me: "Don? You want one?" I smiled encouragingly.

Don: "Nah, I'm trying to quit."

When Lance returned with the beer, everyone had finished dishing up and we were seated in our usual places—a comfort that will soon expire. Tomorrow, our seating assignments will be supplanted.

Neal: "Well, at this time next week, it will be our last supper here."

Phil: "I haven't even looked at the calendar beyond today."

Don: "No, it'll be on Thursday. We leave on a Friday, don't we?"

Lance: "Yeah."

Neal: "That's because I think today is Thursday." Neal is losing it.

Lance: "It isn't?" Lance is losing it too.

Phil: "It's Wednesday."

Neal: "I can't believe we haven't been having this conversation all season long, actually."

Don: "You mean: *What day is it?*"

Neal: "Yeah: *What day is it?*"

Lance: "Haven't we been?"

Me: "Yeah, we have."

Phil: "We have."

Now Neal was winning the "Losing It" game. Or rather, losing it.

Phil: "Well, the weather's looking good for the flight tomorrow."

Me: "Excellent."

Neal: "Yeah, but Friday," he chuckled, "not so good."

Phil: "Friday and Saturday both look sucky."

This is not good, I thought. The weather could be bad in Akureyri tomorrow, and then our replacements would be delayed for three days, at the least.

Me: "Shit."

Phil: "That was my thought exactly. Goes to shit on Friday."

Neal: "They better make it tomorrow!" His chuckle turned to

laughter. I wasn't finding it as funny.

Don: "What's it look like?"

Neal: "It's getting windy."

Don: "How windy?"

Phil: "Twenty to thirty knots."

Me: "Shit."

Lance: "Well, that'll be a nice welcome for them!"

For this I managed a chuckle.

Neal: "It'll be perfect timing for us to go out to the Noone vault."

Me: "Fuck." My vocabulary had quickly become monosyllabic and increasingly offensive.

Don: "So, what's the weather in Akureyri tomorrow?" That's what I wanted to know, too.

Phil: "Looks good. They should make it tomorrow, barring something unusual." I let out a big sigh. Had I been holding my breath?

Lance: "It's gonna get noisy tomorrow when they all get here."

Phil: "Noisy in a good way."

Me: "A *get us the fuck outta here* way."

Neal: "All I'm thinking is, I'm putting my bag on that plane and it's not too big of a leap for me to just follow the bag."

To limit the cargo weight on our return flight next week, we've each packed a preliminary bag that we'll send on tomorrow's flight. What I wouldn't give to leave with those bags. Just a straight cold-turkey jump back into the real world. Then again, maybe that's not a great idea.

Me: "Tomorrow's gonna be weird."

Neal: "I'll go ahead and say it now: I'm a spastic pooer whenever I experience new things, so . . ."

Lance: "Spastic? You mean sporadic, or spastic? You randomly poop, or you poop all over the place?"

Neal: "A little bit of both."

Lance: "Let's clarify that."

Phil: "He poops all over the place randomly."

Don: "What do you think causes that?"

Phil: "He's nervous about girls."

Lance: "Well, some people pucker up when they meet a new girl, and some people just relax."

I want to cheat here and say that Neal changed the subject, but that doesn't do him credit, and it would be uncharacteristic. He's no more bashful about making fun of himself than he is anyone else. The fact is, as I mentioned, I'm quite toasty and I'm reconstructing this conversation from quite toasty—and drunken—notes. And right now I'm not clever or motivated enough to hide it by seaming the incongruent bits together.[58] It doesn't matter—our conversation has become often incongruent anyway. In fact, I'm surprised it hasn't devolved into a series of unintelligible grunts.

Neal: "I'm washing my neck gaiters tonight. It's gonna happen."

Me: "When was the last time you washed 'em?"

Neal: "Not this year."

Me: "You never washed them at all?" This struck me as disgusting, and my expression conveyed it.

Neal: "I don't think so. Maybe, like, right after the New Year."

Me: "Oh, shit, I thought you meant all season. But still. I've had to wash mine almost weekly."

Neal: "Yeah, I was on that schedule and the last few times I've done laundry I kept forgetting to put my neck gaiters in. It's bad. I mean, it doesn't matter which way I rotate them, they stink."

Me: "That is so, so gross. Isn't it?"

Neal: "Um, yes."

Me: "When I asked what wasn't here that I should bring, it was always, 'Bring your own fucking neck gaiter!'"

Lance: "You have to bring several up here. I've got like eight."

Neal: "How many hats do you have? Twenty-seven?"

Lance: "Something like that. Enough."

Neal: "I saw you the other day without a hat on and I was thinking, *whoa...*"

Me: "Who *is* that?"

---

58   Please file your complaints at the Foreword.

Don: "It's a new guy!"

Lance: "I'm trying to figure out how to pack 'em all."

Phil: "In your ski bag."

Lance: "I wanna keep wearing them, that's the problem. I'm sending the ski bag out tomorrow, so I gotta make sacrifices. I'm sending out all my underwear, but I'm keeping the hats!"

Phil: "Well, you can just poke a couple of holes in them and they'll work as underwear."

Lance: "Yep, that'll do."

Me: "What do you do in the summer, when you're home?"

Lance: "I wear a hat!"

Me: "You wear a beanie in the summer?"

Lance: "No, a baseball cap. But I haven't had a summer for . . ." He paused to think. "Samoa was the first summer I've had in six years."

Neal: "You're almost as bad as me."

Lance: "It's funny, I just go from winter to winter to winter to winter."

Me: "Man, you guys have it all wrong. Summer to summer to summer to summer."

Phil: "Now, wait a minute, what do you mean we guys have got it wrong? You're sitting here with us."

Me: "No, no. I mean *these* two guys. I just mean . . . I couldn't do it. This is my first winter in, uh . . . several years."

Lance: "I like summers, but I love winters. I love skiing."

Neal: "I haven't had a North American summer since 2005. I've only experienced bits of summer here and there, that's it."

Lance: "I get grumpy if I don't get to go skiing. Not that I don't like to go mountain biking and climbing, but . . ."

Neal: "Yeah, I love snowboarding all winter when I'm home."

Me: "Right, I guess it's just a choose-your-poison kind of thing."

Neal: "It is."

When we had all finished eating and Phil felt the moment was right, he placed the bottle of scotch on the table and grabbed five glasses.

Me: "Mmm, I've been looking forward to this part all day."

Neal: "All season!"

Lance: "This is why I stuck around for Phase 2!"

Neal: "Really?" He knew Lance was joking. "I would have bought you a bottle of scotch if you wanted outta here."

Lance: "Nope. It wouldn't be the same."

That was true. This round of scotch had meaning. Phil emptied the remaining contents of the bottle and slid the glasses around the table.

Don: "No! It's too much like that Akvavit!"

Phil: "Well, someone will have to drink it."

Don: "You can do it."

Phil: "Here's looking up your kilts." He raised his glass. "Nobody pulled the kill switch on anybody!"

We all laughed and raised our glasses. Don joined with his mug of tea and I chuckled, then taunted him lightheartedly.

Me: "That better not be chamomile!" We've been riffing on the chamomile joke ever since Don made the quotebook with it.

Don: "It's just hot water."

Phil: "Don, you're becoming a minimalist."

Neal: "You trying to transition away from being gay for when you go home to see your wife?"

Don: "Well, I was never drinking chamomile. Sometimes I had that orange whatever-it-is. Wild sweet orange."

Neal: "So you're only half gay. Bisexual!"

We laughed. Then I took another sip of my whiskey.

Me: "Mmm, that's good scotch."

Neal: "Makes everything better."

Me: "Thanks again, Phil." Neal and Lance echoed my gratitude.

Phil: "No problem. Yeah, it's kind of a nice little treat."

Neal: "More than kind of. It's one of the three best parts of the whole season."

Don: "What were the other two parts?"

Me: "The other times we had scotch!"

Don knew that's what Neal meant, but he couldn't remember the occasions. He's losing it.

Don: "Well, it wasn't for getting here." He contemplated. "We didn't have a drink for that."

Me: "I could *not* have had a drink at that point. I would have died."

Phil: "Yeah, the first couple of nights."

Me: "First week."

Phil: "I think I've had a headache the first week at altitude every single time I've gone."

Me: "Really?"

Phil: "The first several days, anyway. It's vicious up at Vostok. Holy shit." Phil spent some time at this Russian research station, high on the Antarctic ice cap. Vostok is at a higher elevation *and* a higher latitude than Summit, so the physiological altitude *must* be vicious. Our conversation paused as we all tried not to imagine, I imagine. That's what I was doing, anyway.

Me: "Well, gentlemen, I couldn't have asked for a finer crew. You guys have been awesome."

Neal: "Hear, hear."

Phil: "Hear, hear, and here we go."

Don: "You make it sound so final. I'm pretty sure we'll see each other for the next week."

Neal: "But there will be people in the way."

Phil: "It'll be interesting to see whether we hovel together or separate out."

Lance: "Well, I already know we'll all end up sitting at that end of the table. Everyone always—"

Phil: "Clusters down close to the food, yeah."

Don: "I don't want anybody sitting in my chair."

Lance: "I know! Me, either."

We're so habituated. I should have been stealing their chairs all season so they wouldn't find themselves in this preposterous predicament.

Day 89
Thursday, January 31

Two Twin Otters arrived on schedule today. Thank God. On them were our replacements, plus Tracy, Katrine, and Russ to check in on station and make sure the transition goes smoothly. It was a busy day, and the days to come will be even busier. Not only do we have a ton to do, but we'll be surrounded by extra bodies at all times. The way things are set up right now, we have more people than we have beds, and Katrine is actually sleeping on our office couch. I should just give her my bed since I don't sleep anyway.

Day 91
Saturday, February 2

I'm back on sleep aids as of yesterday. I was getting by without them for a few days, but I really need the sleep if I'm going to keep up this week. We're busy as hell, working from the moment we get up until the moment we lie back down. It's a huge change. There is so much to cover, and I feel bad for the new techs, who are doing their best to absorb everything while struggling with the altitude. They watch everyone else pack into the lounge to watch movies while they learn how to launch the evening weather balloon. I remember being in their shoes. "It will get better. Much better," I found myself telling them, even though they weren't complaining.

~

Hey Phil,

Can you forward us the flight times from the other day (on deck / off deck)? We forgot to put it in the clean air log.

Cheers,

Rex

~

Day 93
Monday, February 4

I've been somewhat detached for the past few days. Having new faces and full workdays helped distract me at first, but it's not enough. The emotional carnival wound itself back up. I'm sad, I'm angry, I'm content, I'm depressed, I'm hopeful, I'm heartbroken, I'm optimistic. It's a zoo, an evil zoo where the exhibits are acid-trip caricatures of my warped psyche. No one wants to see that, least of all me. But it's no longer all a manic depression. The other animals are coming out to play as well.

In my hopeful and optimistic moments, I've been surprised to find myself viewing Katrine in a new light. I knew early on that she was smart and fun and down to earth—all qualities I value highly—but somehow failed to notice that she's attractive as well. I was wearing the blinders of commitment at the time, I guess. But Katrine is my boss, and now also my friend, and I wouldn't dare jeopardize either on a wobbly postwinter whim. Still, I can't help but wonder sometimes if she'd look good with a black eye— metaphorically speaking, of course. It's a good thing; it means I'm starting to move on. It only took a month of insanity.

I realize I was wrong to think that I can't heal here. I was just stuck in the winter mire, which overrides the brain. I'm still affected, still toasty without a doubt, but the spell is broken. It's been lifted by the influx of people, the break in routine, the change of pace, and most of all, the immense increase in sunlight. Already, the sun is up for four hours a day. By the time we leave, it will be up for five, and only a week after that it will be up for almost seven. It's amazing how quickly it returns.

I haven't found my frustration with the newcomers to be nearly as fierce as it was in the Antarctic, even though I find my toastiness to be more severe. Maybe it's because my mind is elsewhere. Maybe it's because I don't have time to think about it. Probably a lot has to do with the population. Even now, we're only thirteen. Mealtimes are more crowded, as is the lounge in the evenings, but though they outnumber us, there are only eight new people to contend with, and three of them I already know. That's a far cry from the two hundred who showed up to shatter the reverie at McMurdo. Eight is manageable. Two hundred is overwhelming. This is much better. I'm definitely a small-population kind of guy.

Day 94
Tuesday, February 5

The call came over the radio: a fox.

"A what?" I asked.

"I think they said a fox," Neal answered, puzzled.

"That can't be right." We're three hundred miles from the coast, going either east or west, five hundred miles going south, six degrees north of the Arctic Circle, and two miles straight up. Nothing lives here. Nothing *can* live here. If there was a fox, it was a very errant fox indeed.

There was a fox. I saw it with my own disbelieving eyes. A pure white, incredibly fluffy arctic fox. It was bounding around the station, surely lost and looking for food. It wouldn't let anyone get near it, which is probably good because there's a chance it was rabid, having wandered to the summit of the Greenland ice cap. Its visit was brief, and soon it disappeared across the skiway.

It was a wonderful thing to see. Life. But a sad thing to know that it cannot survive. This place is not meant for the living. To have come this far off course, the poor thing could not have been sound of mind.[59] We doubted the fox's survival, but still we hoped.

Day 95
Wednesday, February 6

I can't find time to keep up with this journal. It's so refreshing.

---

59   The disturbing parallel did not even occur to me at the time. Surprisingly, arctic foxes have appeared at Summit many times over the years, as have migrating birds. But these visits rarely happen outside the summer months. In the summer of 2018 a polar bear appeared at Summit—an unprecedented event—most likely due to habitat loss. Instead of bringing in a relocation team, the National Science Foundation chose to hire hunters. My friend Marci was there and reported: "After she died we could get up close to her. I felt her thick fur full of ice crystals, rubbed her soft ears and nose, and held one of her massive clawed feet in my hands. I am torn up by this experience." *The Program* strikes again. It's a hypocritical move, to support climate change science but to be deathly insensitive to its effects.

Day 96
Thursday, February 7

Turnover has been a mad dash, the days have flown by, and now the end is finally upon us. I'm still dancing with all the emotions—each in their turn—but I've found that I can look forward to life's next adventure, and I'm able to leave much of the extraneous, irrational depression and discontent behind me. Though not all of it; not yet. The mire, the muck, the fog, the toastiness will take some time to fade.

Tomorrow we fly the hell out of here, and I cheerfully anticipate meeting new people and starting another chapter. And most of all, let's not forget: recovering my marbles.

As I've geared up my mind for departure, Greenland has thrown at me one last spectacle—two in one, really—and strangely, it makes me wonder what the summertime might be like, with more sun and more people and more to do, perhaps. Here at the ends of the earth are the travelers and adventurers with whom I feel I belong. Where better to stumble upon another partner of like mind? If nothing else, I would meet more of these wanderers, these wonderers, and possibly see a few I already know from the Antarctic. The ice cap itself likely has a handful of summertime spectacles to charm me with as well. Plus, when the weather cooperates, I could snowkite. All that would be a hell of a lot better than nothing.

Perhaps.

First I need a break. A long break. This time though, I know better than to say never. There is a reason I'm here, and it's good to be reminded of that.

~

Sundog in the Diamond Dust

Summit Station, Greenland
Thursday, February 7, 2013

Surrounding me are billions of the finest ice crystals possible, invisible to the naked eye and drifting weightlessly in the breeze.

The midday sun sits low on the horizon in full regalia, penetrating the crystal-clear arctic air with an onslaught of piercing light. A brilliant beam catches the faceted face of an unseen ice crystal, and for an instant it appears as a tiny streak of white light. The sky is alive with a rain of shooting stars.

I've seen this before by moonlight—"*The air around me was sparkling, like a shower of moonlight pixie dust in a cold, demented fairyland*"—though I didn't know at the time that it has a name: diamond dust.

What I haven't seen before is the beginnings of a sundog on the horizon. The diamond dust acts as a prism, breaking the sun's light into its colorful components. On both sides of the sun, the surface layer of ice crystals created the ends of an intense rainbow: two crimson-through-indigo pillars with the solar blaze between them. The outer edges of the pillars, where there should have been violet, instead projected spotlight beams of white light along the horizon, like the sun's high beams.

If the diamond dust was mixed beyond the surface layer of air, the sundog would complete a full halo around the sun and could

Greenland offers a final seduction

possibly form multiple halos with fractal-like patterns in between and beyond. Alas, our dust is settling, but a partial sundog is still intense and magnificent. It's a fantastic sendoff.

We only have twenty-four hours left here, as long as the weather holds. It is definitely time for me to go. Without a doubt, I've gone batty with the mental degradation of a polar winter, the battle against insomnia, and several symptoms of seasonal affective disorder. C'est la vie, my friends.

There's nothing to be concerned about. I've been here before and managed. Though I'll be changed by experience, once again, I'll return to normal before long—normal for me, that is. The real question is: Have I learned my lesson? Probably not, but I don't expect to be doing any more polar winters, certainly not in the foreseeable future. It's time to settle down. Just for a while.

~

Day 97
Friday, February 8

As our Twin Otter fluttered noisily above the vast ice cap of Greenland, relief filled me and provided clarity. Summit isn't that bad. In fact, outside forces aside, I had a really good season. The winter had its charm, and that charm was found largely in the companionship I encountered: a warm and bright contrast to the night around me. The boys were amazing and fun in so many ways, and it's them that I will remember most fondly. It's strange now to think that we met just a few short months ago.

As we flew, my thoughts wandered back to our first week alone at Summit, when our friendship and family dynamic began to gel. Suddenly I realized that for Phase 3, that week was happening right now. I rejoiced that the new crew was reveling in that same solace. And I felt for them too. Surely they were still fighting an acclimatization that, for me anyway, would never fully arrive. And did they even know that they'll be fighting a mental battle as well? Theirs won't be nearly so difficult, as the sunlight grows daily stronger, and they will not be plunged into unending darkness. Not this time. Still, the cold, the isolation, and the monotony all play their role. I wondered what they were doing at that moment. Probably having a much-needed rest, just like we did. I imagined the new techs sitting in our old office, enjoying the silence that comes after the whirlwind, and thinking to themselves, *What is that clicking noise? Do you hear that?*

Epilogue

NEAL

Neal: "By the way, if you are deciding to change our names to protect our identities, Clair suggests changing hers to Anabel-Lee. I think mine could be Bosco."

~

Senator "Bosco" Blutarski took the job at the South Pole. For a period of about sixteen months, he and Anabel-Lee only saw each other for a few weeks spread here and there. Anabel-Lee joined him for the winter at Pole, and from that point forward, they agreed to choose jobs that were colocated instead of opportunistic. Later, at Summit Station, under a better aurora than any in the 2012 Phase 2, they got engaged.

PHIL

Me: "Until now, I hadn't thought much about changing any of the names, but maybe you want your identity protected?"

Phil: ". . . I'm trapped in the blinding white hell of Summit once again. I 'think' I've been on site for around three weeks, but it seems like an age. . ."

Me: "So, are you okay if I just use your real name in this book then, or do you want a fake?"

Phil:

~

Harpo " " Marx continues to live life just as he likes it: either traveling or sailing between deployments to Summit, where he now works a consistent three months on and three months off, thus alleviating the need to continually search for the next contract. It also conveniently alleviates any need to grow up and get a real job, which he refuses to do.

~

Phil: "Growing up—How would I recognize this state should it ever arrive?"

LANCE

Me: "Neal said if I was changing the names, he wants to be 'Bosco,' which I find hilarious."

Lance:

Me: "Lance, I know you're in Antarctica and it's the middle of winter, but I need to know what you want your fake name to be. It is absolutely vital that you respond, even though I will be ignoring your suggestion."

Lance: "Sorry, Rex . . . extremely busy . . . I thought it would be funny if we went by our real names: William, Payot, Brian . . . No one would have a clue!"

Me: "Shit, I forgot both you and Neal don't use your given first names either. What a bunch of weirdos."

Lance: "Call me Billy. That will keep people guessing."

~

Bartholomew "Billy" Cubbins continues to work in the Arctic and Antarctic Programs. He purchased a sailboat that he lives on between contracts and is in the process of buying a condo at a ski resort in Idaho. He's still enjoying an endless winter and has managed to ski on every continent but Australia.

DON

Me: "Don, the real question is, do you want a fake name?"

Don: "A fake name?"

Me: "Yeah, you know, to protect your identity and shit. What do you want it to be?"

Don: "Oh, you can call me whatever you want. I don't care."

Me: "You're sure?"

Don: "Yeah, I really don't mind."

∿

Phartiphukborlz[60] did a few more contracts, primarily in Alaska, before taking a real job in the Pacific Northwest. The bad news: he misses the Antarctic/Arctic contracts. The good news: he gets to travel a lot for work. The best news: he's back on beer.

REX

Me? I don't think I want a fake name, as it seems it would only be used against me.

∿

Jack "All Work and No Play" Torrance finally wrote that book—while "settled down" in an arroyo in Mexico, living in the back of a pickup truck, kitesurfing when the wind blew, mountain biking when the wind didn't blow, and considering the possibility of driving all the way to Patagonia . . .

---

60 A final, obscure *Hitchhiker's* reference. As the French say: *jamais deux san trois*. Still, I had a hell of a time setting aside Unko Kanji Doriru as Don's fake name.

He didn't.

He went back to Summit Station instead.

This time during spring.

. . . where he snowkited often, sometimes under fantastic sundogs

Quote Book

Winter Phase 2, 2012-2013

"I don't care what it's shaped like, it tastes great." —Rex

"Everything is poo!" —Don

"Death lasts a long time, unless you go to heaven."
    ... "Oh, f@!#"

"That'll make good poop."

"There's chamomile, if you wanna be gay."

"Why not have Kevlar?"

"Oh, good, I can fart."

"I'm just thinking about killing people."

"You'll just need some lotion for your butt."

"I bring a lot of people home, it's my nature."
    ... "How do you spell *nature?*"

"I've never found the happy light to be very useful."
    ... "Well, that's because you don't believe in Jesus."

"I don't know if I want my piss to smell like this or like that."

"I have no recollection of better recollection."

Acknowledgments

I blame my loving family for accepting and sometimes even encouraging my itinerant lifestyle, thus requiring me to live frugally during extended periods between paychecks.

I blame Neal, Phil, Lance, and Don for being fantastic winter companions, therefore providing no interpersonal tension to enhance the plot of this book.

I must strongly blame the talented Christina Roth for molding a novice manuscript into a professional work, thus eliminating a lot of grammatical humor.

To all the friends who provided a place to crash, or a mailing address, or a storage area, or a ride to the airport, or whatever else I needed between and during adventures, I blame you for making nomadic life that much easier.

As for the wonderful people I've met at McMurdo, Scott, Palmer, and Summit stations, I blame you for providing a reason to return to the ice long after I was over it.

References

p. 173, "If you don't have enough T$_3$ . . . ," Christiane Northrup, "What Is Thyroid Disease?," last updated October 24, 2017, https://www.drnorthrup.com/thyroid-disease/.

p. 173, "In extreme cold . . . ," Emily Stone, "Treating the Antarctic Blues," *Antarctic Sun*, November 7, 2004, https://antarctic-sun.usap.gov/pastIssues/2004-2005/2004_11_07.pdf.

p. 174, "Some of the most . . . ," Jennifer A. Phillips, "Thyroid Hormone Disorders," Cambridge Scientific Abstracts, May 2001.

p. 174, "Hypothyroidism also weakens . . . ," ibid.

p. 182, "Most people will surface . . . ," Andre Fleuette, "The Polar Plungery," *The Siren Song of the Anti-Bears [The Life and Times of an Antarctic Moron]* (blog), June 14, 2008, https://mcpenguin.livejournal.com/226698.html.

p. 191, "I answered all questions . . . ," Nicholas Johnson, *Big Dead Place: Inside the Strange and Menacing World of Antarctica*, Los Angeles: Feral House, 2005.

p. 251, "In the morning there is hours and infinity," Trampled by Turtles, "Whiskey," Banjodad Records, track 3 on *Songs from a Ghost Town*, 2004.

REX NELSON was born in Pennsylvania but calls the Pacific Northwest home. At least, that's where he stores his belongings and occasionally finds time to hang out between adventures. Though an engineer by training, Rex was never comfortable in the salary world, possibly because he never recovered from a period after college when he lived in a van and toured the continental USA.

After six years of contracts in Antarctica and Greenland, with many travels in between, Rex joined the ranks of the "real world" for a few years, returning to his engineering roots. But it wasn't long before the promise of adventure trumped the stability of full-time work. He spent a month in China, then a winter in Mexico. A true testament to his lack of sanity, Rex returned to Greenland for another contract at Summit Station—but *not* for the winter.

Look for Rex on a bike, next to a campfire, under a kite, or in a daze.

Made in the USA
Coppell, TX
22 December 2020